Staying Out
of Court

Staying Out of Court

A Manager's Guide to Employment Law

Cliff Roberson
California State University—Fresno

Lexington Books
D.C. Heath and Company/Lexington, Massachusetts/Toronto

Library of Congress Cataloging in Publication Data

Roberson, Cliff, 1937–
    Staying out of court.

    1. Labor laws and legislation—United States.
I. Title.
KF3319.R63   1985   344.73'01   84–48799
ISBN 0-669-09769-1 (alk. paper)   347.3041

Published simultaneously in Canada
Printed in the United States of America on acid-free paper
International Standard Book Number: 0-669-09769-1
Library of Congress Catalog Card Number: 84-48799

To Clif, Marshall, Kenneth, and Dwayne Roberson,
four young men that I am proud of

Contents

Introduction

Legal issues are ever present in today's business world. No business owner, manager, or supervisor can afford to make a decision or take an action without regard to the possible legal consequences of his or her actions. For example, since more women than men have high school diplomas, there are serious questions of sexual discrimination when high school diplomas are required prior to employment. The rights of employers to hire or fire their employees likewise involve complex legal issues that employers cannot afford to ignore. Courts have recently demonstrated a trend toward restricting the common law rights of employers to terminate employees. These are only two examples of the complex legal problems facing employers today. The purpose of this text is to set forth in plain English the legal issues or concerns which are most likely to cause problems for the business owner, manager, or supervisor.

This book is written not for attorneys, but for the modern businessperson who wants to avoid as many legal problems as possible. It is designed to provide an employer or supervisor with a good working foundation of the legal issues associated with employment. Throughout the book, I use the term "employer" as a shorthand reference to the decision maker in the employment process. The principles are the same whether it is the employer, the supervisor, or the manager who makes the decision or takes the action in question.

Preventive legal aid is the theme of this book. Because even winning a legal case is costly to an employer in both time and money, the best legal cases are those that never develop. Preventive legal aid is the only intelligent avenue open to the employer in today's hectic business world. This book is not intended to replace the advice and guidance of an attorney in specific situations, however. When in doubt, seek the advice and guidance of an attorney. If you do not have an attorney, check with the local bar association for a referral.

The book is divided into six chapters. Each covers a general problem area. The first two chapters, "Selecting New Employees" and "Firing Employees," deal with areas in which the courts have recently been very active. The third chapter, "Terms and Conditions of Employment," concerns the everyday working relationship between employers and employees. The topic of the fourth chapter, "Discrimination," is interrelated with the preceding topics but is presented in a separate chapter in order to provide the reader with a concise summary of the law and rules and regulations in this critical area. The fifth chapter, "Disability and Unemployment Benefits," treats subjects that employers deal with only when illness, injury, or unemployment claims are filed against the employer, but such events occur frequently, so the employer needs a handy reference source. The final chapter contains a general discussion on labor union law, an area of concern to both union and nonunion employers and managers.

At the end of each chapter, I have included a list of resource materials for the reader who wishes to gain a deeper understanding of the problems. A limited legal glossary is included as appendix A to assist the reader in understanding legal terms that are commonly present in any discussion of employment law. Appendix B contains a directory of key government agencies involved in employment regulations. The employer should not hesitate to contact the appropriate agency if assistance is needed on a specific issue. Appendix C is a reprint of the Equal Employment Opportunity Commission's Uniform Guidelines on Employee Selection. Appendixes D through F contain reprints of Title VII of the Civil Rights Act of 1964 (as amended), the Age Discrimination in Employment Act of 1967 (as amended), and EEOC's Guidelines on Discrimination Because of Sex.

1
Hiring New Employees

Establishing Employment Qualifications

After making the decision that new or additional employees are needed, the employer or business manager must decide what preemployment requirements are wanted in the new employees. Until the 1960s, employers could be arbitrary in deciding what they wanted in the new employee. Preemployment qualifications, both written and unwritten, were set to satisfy the personal wishes and prejudices of the employer. Now, however, federal and state statutes, court decisions, and administrative regulations restrict the employer's ability to establish preemployment requirements for job applicants. This section will deal with those restrictions. The basic theory behind the hiring restrictions is equal employment opportunity. Hence, the hiring decision should be based on a comparison of the individual applicant's skill and ability with the skill and ability required for the position. (*Note:* The reader may wish to refer to Equal Employment Opportunity Commission's Guidelines on Employee Selection reprinted in appendix C.)

Common sense and an honest desire to be fair will eliminate most of the legal problems that face employers in establishing preemployment qualifications. Not all small business employers are subject to the fair employment restrictions noted in this chapter; which rules affect an employer depends on the number of employees in a firm and whether the firm is engaged in interstate commerce. Nonetheless, because the courts tend to interpret the commerce clause liberally to extend coverage of the fair opportunity employment restrictions, employers should conduct business affairs as if the rules were applicable to their firms. There are no specific criteria as to when a business is involved in interstate commerce. In one famous case, a restaurant six blocks from an interstate highway was considered to be involved in interstate commerce because travelers frequently detoured from the interstate for Southern fried chicken.

After the employer decides what qualifications are desirable in the new employee, the task of preventive legal action is to determine whether any of the qualifications will unfairly eliminate certain protected classes of prospective employees. If any do, a discrimination problem probably exists.

It is easy to recognize that some requirements openly discriminate against certain minorities, but it is subtler, often unintentionally discriminatory requirements, which often appear neutral, that cause problems to employers.

For example, racial discrimination was considered present in one legal case when an employer refused to hire a woman with sickle cell anemia without first considering her individual situation. In another case, a court stated that it was discriminatory for an employer to refuse to hire persons with poor credit ratings unless the employer could establish a business necessity for a good credit rating, since such a criterion would have an adverse impact on minorities. A railroad could not automatically refuse to hire persons with criminal convictions since this requirement has a disparate impact on minorities and is not justified for all railroad positions.

A classic example of a subtly discriminatory qualification is contained in the U.S. Supreme Court case of *Griggs v. Duke Power Co.* In that case, the employer, Duke Power Company, required a high school diploma as a criterion for employment. Griggs, a member of a minority, applied for a janitorial position with the company but was denied employment because he lacked the necessary high school diploma. The court held that, since in the local employment area more whites than minorities had high school diplomas, requiring a diploma eliminated more minority members than whites from employment; thus the requirement was discriminatory in those employment situations where educational status, as evidenced by the diploma, had little relationship to the ability of the person to perform the duties of the job.

The *Griggs* case stands for the proposition that even seemingly neutral qualifications such as requiring a high school diploma may be illegal if they have an adverse impact on a protected class. There was no evidence in the *Griggs* case on whether or not the discrimination was intentional or unintentional. The court indicated that an intent to discriminate is not required; the fact that an employer has discriminated against a protected class is all that is required to hold the employer liable. The phrase "protected class" is used by the courts to designate a group of persons that are protected under the Civil Rights Act of 1964. The protected classes are those based on race, color, national origin, sex, religion, and age. The concept of a protected class extends not only to minority groups of a protected class, but also to members of the majority group within that class.

The BFOQ Requirement

The Supreme Court stated in the *Griggs* case that the Civil Rights Act of 1964 does not require that "less qualified applicants be preferred over the better qualified simply because of minority origins." The court stated that an employer was free to hire the best qualified person for the position.

Employers are not required to restructure their employment practices to maximize the number of minorities hired—only to provide equal employment opportunity to all. However, if a preemployment qualification has an adverse impact on a protected class, (that is, if it operates to exclude members of a protected class), then the employer has the burden to establish that the qualification is reasonably related to job performance. For example, in the *Griggs* case statistics indicated that only 12 percent of the black males had completed high school in the state compared to 34 percent of the white males. So the high school diploma requirement eliminated 88 percent of the black males compared to only 66 percent of the white males. Accordingly, the requirement had an adverse impact on blacks.

Next, the court determined that the possession of a diploma was not reasonably related to a person's ability to perform in a janitorial position. Had this been a clerical position, the court might have sustained the actions of the employer as reasonable since the skills measured in qualifying for a high school diploma are similar to those needed in a clerical position.

The *Griggs* case established the Bona Fide Occupational Qualification (BFOQ) requirement, which means that a preemployment qualification that has an adverse impact on a protected group must be necessary for the job in order not to be ruled discriminatory. For example, establishing the requirement that prospective employees speak English even though their duties do not require speaking would discriminate against non-English-speakers and thus would be illegal.

The 80 Percent Rule

To determine whether or not a neutral qualification has an adverse impact on a protected class, the "80 percent rule" is used: the qualification will have an adverse impact on a protected class if the percentage of that class qualifying is less than 80 percent of percentage of the class that has the highest percentage qualifying. For example, if 100 blacks apply for a job and only 50 are qualified compared to 75 of the 100 whites who apply, then the qualification rate for blacks would be 50 percent compared to 75 percent for whites. Eighty percent of 75 percent would be 60 percent; therefore, since less than 60 percent of the blacks qualified, the preemployment requirement would be considered to have an adverse impact on blacks as a protected class.

Restrictions and Requirements

The BFOQ allows discrimination in those areas where sex, religion, age, or national origin is a bona fide occupational qualification. It must be reasonably necessary to the normal operation of the business, and the employer has the burden to establish that it is reasonably necessary. For example, a church certainly may require that its minister be of a certain religious faith. But not all situations are so clear-cut. For example, can a basketball coach whose religious beliefs allow him to drink alcohol and smoke be denied employment solely based on his beliefs if he applies for a coaching position at a religious school whose beliefs forbid drinking and smoking? What about the atheist accountant who applies for an accounting position with a church organization?

Fortunately, most employers do not have these problems. The key to staying out of trouble is never to establish qualifications that could be considered discriminatory unless they are absolutely essential. The phrase "degree preferred" sounds less discriminatory, for instance, than the phrase "degree required." However, even use of this phrase should be limited to situations where educational status has a logical relationship to duties of the position. Check all your preemployment qualifications to ensure that they are reasonably related to what will be required of the employee.

Race or color is *never* considered to be a bona fide occupational qualification. The courts have stated on numerous occasions that there are no situations in which race or color can be so considered. In hiring, race and color must be treated as irrelevant. The single exception is in court-approved affirmative action programs (which will be discussed in chapter 4). For example, a black-oriented radio station was liable for racial discrimination against a white disk jockey who was discharged from the station because he did not have a "black voice."

The courts have also used a very narrow interpretation of when sex, national origin, or religion can be a part of the preemployment qualification for the job. The BFOQ rule allows discrimination only in hiring and referral situations, not in discrimination between classes of current employees.

A two-step BFOQ test has been used by most courts: (1) Does the particular job require that the employee be of one sex, national origin, age group, or religion only? (2) If so, is that requirement reasonably necessary to the essence of the employer's business? As you can see, it is almost impossible to justify the restriction.

Gender-Based Requirements

Express sex classifications of employment positions are considered as "suspect" classifications by the courts and are rarely upheld as justified. This is especially true in those situations where the classification is used to exclude female employees. In limited affirmative action programs, the courts have upheld the restriction of employment positions to women only. Normally, however, opening a job for women or men only places a heavy burden on the employer to establish that sex is a BFOQ. Employer must make hiring decisions on some basis other than gender. Not just women, but men, are protected from gender-based discrimination. Note as well that the courts have stated that an employer is not required to rearrange bona fide job requirements just to eliminate duties that women cannot ordinarily do. (See appendix F for EEOC's Guidelines on Discrimination Because of Sex.)

Sex classification plus some other qualification, whether it is marital status or family responsibility, is also an unlawful hiring restriction. For example, refusing to hire women employees with small children would be illegal unless the same requirement were applied to male applicants. As one court stated, the practice of hiring unmarried women only is discriminatory unless there is a similar hiring practice of not hiring married men exists in the firm.

An employer cannot justify the male-only or female-only qualifications on the basis that separate restroom facilities are not available or that it would cost more to provide such facilities. Nor can an employer refuse to consider women applicants based on the possibility that they might get pregnant and either quit or lose time from work. One employer was liable for discrimination for refusing to hire women based on his belief that the turnover rate among women was higher than among men.

Another employer was liable for discrimination when he preferred a male applicant over a better qualified female applicant because the male applicant had a wife and sick child to support. The court noted that most breadwinners are male and thus to give preference to a breadwinner would discriminate against women.

In one case, an employer was held liable for sexual discrimination for refusing to consider female applicants for the position of relief truck driver. It seems that, because of possible objections of the male truck drivers' wives, the employer did not want to hire female drivers to share overnight driving assignments with male drivers. The court did not consider this a sufficient reason to justify the sexual discrimination.

Height and weight requirements for a position must be related to the task to be performed and not a method to restrict the pool of qualified male or female applicants. For example, having a maximum weight requirement of 110 pounds would discriminate against male applicants and would be illegal unless it was reasonably related to the job requirements. As the result of court cases, police departments have removed their minimum height and weight requirements since those requirements were determined to be discriminatory against women applicants, and also against members of certain ethnic minorities.

One major automobile manufacturer established a minimum weight requirement for assembly line workers on the theory that the position involved lifting heavy parts and tools. The federal court, in holding the manufacturer liable for discrimination, stated that this practice discriminated against women and that, since the qualification addressed the weight of the applicant and not the applicant's strength, it had no relationship to actual job requirements. In this case, it is clear that the company would have been in a better position had it specified strength, not weight, as a preemployment requirement.

This case also points out the need to be careful in drafting job qualifications. Recently, the City of New York was liable for unlawful sex discrimination when they used a professionally developed physical abilities test in qualifying applicants for employment as city firefighters. It appears that the test excluded all women applicants. The court denied the city's contention that the test was directly related to the ability to fight fires. The court said that the test measured general human ability, not just firefighting abilities, and therefore was not job related.

Weight requirements for one sex only have also been held illegal. However, a requirement that is applied to both sexes that the applicant have a reasonable weight in relation to height, bone structure, and age was upheld by one court.

In one Supreme Court case, the court stated that it was permissible to hire only males as prison guards in a state's maximum security prison where sex offenders were housed in dormitories with other prisoners. In that case, the court noted that the BFOQ exception to sex bias hiring was "extremely narrow." The same court in another case held the State of Alabama liable for sexual discrimination in its refusal to hire female prison guards for an all-male prison. The only difference in the two cases was apparently the presence in the first case of sex offenders in an open environment. One court held that a male could not be excluded from a cook's job at a female correctional institution.

What about customer preference as to sex of the employees? At a time when most airline business passengers were male, the airlines concluded that the customers preferred female flight attendants over male cabin attendants. However, the courts have uniformly held that the employer may not restrict jobs to one sex just to please customers. In fact, one international oil company was held liable for sex discrimination by refusing to hire female buyers even though most of its Latin American customers would refuse to deal with a woman buyer.

Discrimination against homosexuals is not included in the gender-based protections under Title VII of the Civil Rights Act of 1964. However, many state and local statutes prohibit discrimination against persons because of their sexual preference. Unless prohibited by state or local statutes or regulations, an employer may use the factor of sexual preference in the employment decision, especially if the sex patterns or lifestyles of the applicants would bring discredit to the employer.

At one time, it was not illegal to discriminate on the basis of pregnancy. The courts opined that this was not a discrimination between women and men but between pregnant and nonpregnant persons and thus permissible. The U.S. Marine Corps, which had traditionally discharged pregnant service-women, changed its regulations to require the discharge of pregnant service-members. In 1978, however, the Civil Rights Act was amended by the Pregnancy Discrimination Act. This amendment broadened the definition of impermissible sexual discrimination to include women who are pregnant.

Pregnancy may no longer be used to disqualify a woman from employment unless medical reasons indicate that a danger to the woman or the unborn child would result from the employment. The courts have limited the medical exception to situations that are clearly dangerous to life. One employer who excluded females because the workers were exposed to chemicals could not exclude women on the basis of the need for fetal protection.

An employer may not use a "morality rule" as an excuse for refusing to hire parents of illegitimate children. The rationale for disallowing such a rule is that, since it is the woman who gives birth to the child and traditionally rears offspring, it is easier for a man to hide the fact that he is the parent of an illegitimate child than for a woman. Hence the courts have ruled that so-called morality rules are discriminatory against women.

In one case, an unsuccessful male applicant sued an employer on the theory that he was discriminated against because the employer had hired a female for the job. He contended that the only reason a female was hired was that the employer could pay a woman less than a male would accept. The court stated that, if the allegations were true, there would be a serious question of discrimination, but the discrimination would be against the female employee and not against the male applicant. Accordingly, the man could not sue.

An important point to remember is that sex is not a BFOQ for a job just because that job has traditionally been considered as "women's work" or "men's work."

Religion

Religious bias problems usually concern working conditions and schedules. (These will be discussed in greater detail in chapter 3.) Except for religious institutions, it is unlawful to use religion as a factor in the employment decision. The safest approach in this regard is for the employer not to discuss or ask about the religious beliefs of prospective employees.

The courts have interpreted the definition of religion in its broadest possible sense. Even an atheist is protected from discrimination because of his or her lack of religious beliefs. A member of the Ku Klux Klan, however, was not protected from discrimination based on his membership in that organization. The court stated that the KKK was not a religious organization, but a racist philosophy. In one case, a court upheld an employer's refusal to hire anyone with a beard, even though the applicant contended that it was against his religion to shave. The employer in the latter case had a "no-beard" policy for his family restaurant in order to maintain a clean, wholesome appearance.

Education

The problem with making an educational degree as a requirement for employment, as shown in the *Griggs* case, is that it is a neutral qualification that has a definitely adverse impact on minorities. The percentages of minorities with degrees are substantially less than the percentages of whites with degrees. Accordingly, prior to using an educational degree as an employment qualification, the employer should consider the BFOQ requirement noted earlier. Except for academic positions or professional positions (for which local or state regulations require a degree), it is best for the employer to use the "degree preferred" statement in a want-ad or job posting. However, if the position is one where little or no academic requirements exist, such as a janitorial position, even the "degree preferred" qualification may be considered discriminatory. The requirement for a minimum grade point average or class standing in school is subject to the same restrictions as the diploma qualification.

Residency

State statutes and regulations requiring employers to give preference to state residents are unconstitutional since the U.S. Constitution grants to citizens of each state all the privileges and immunities in the several states. However, local regulations requiring essential public employees such as police officers to live within the local government jurisdiction have been upheld by the courts as legal and serving a public purpose. In addition, the U.S. Supreme Court also upheld a Boston mayoral executive order requiring that construction projects funded by the city be performed by at least 50 percent Boston residents. In the latter case, the court stated that the city was acting as an owner and thus could place the 50 percent limitation on the projects.

What about the private employer who wants to hire only employees from the local community? The real question in this situation is: Does the rule have an adverse impact on a protected group? If there are few minority families living in the local community, the employer may have serious discrimination problems since the rule would limit the employment opportunity of minorities. Except for this question, there is no apparent reason why employers cannot restrict hiring to the local area.

Citizens and Aliens

The Civil Rights Act protection against discrimination based on national origin applies both to citizens and to resident aliens. Aliens who commute daily from Mexico or Canada and who legally work in the United States are also protected against discrimination based on national origin. The rule appears to be that an employer may refuse to hire noncitizens as long as the policy does not amount to discrimination based on national origin. Citizenship may not be used as a basis to refuse employment to certain nationalities. Nor may an employer refuse to hire persons who belong to organizations identified with a national origin or race. National origin discrimination is defined as the denial of equal employment opportunities because of an individual's, or his or her ancestor's, place of origin, or because the individual has the physical, cultural, or linguistic characteristics of a group with a certain national origin.

In regard to hiring illegal aliens, there are no federal sanctions against the employer except the possible embarrassment and inconvenience of having an employee deported. A California statute makes it a crime and a civil liability to knowingly hire illegal aliens. The U.S. Immigration and Nationality Act makes it a felony to knowingly harbor illegal aliens but clearly states that employment does not constitute harboring.

One apparent reason for the lack of federal sanctions for employing illegal aliens is that there are no practical and reliable means of identifying those who are aliens and those who are not. In the last few sessions of the U.S. Congress there have been hearings on this problem and bills proposed, but as yet no laws have been passed that impose sanctions on employers for such actions.

The Migrant and Seasonal Agricultural Workers Protection Act does impose both criminal and civil sanctions against farm labor contractors who knowingly recruit illegal aliens. This statute does not impose sanctions against employers, however.

Language

Having a language qualification in employment situations tends to discriminate against all persons from a different national origin than those to whom the required language is the native language. For example, a rule stating that the employee must speak "good English" even though fluent English is not directly related to the job is discriminatory, as is a rule that the worker speak Spanish when no Spanish is used on the job. Likewise, a requirement that a person be able to write English is illegal if the position requires no writing.

The courts have, however, regularly upheld the requirement that employees must be able to speak both Spanish and English in those parts of the United States where the employees come in contact with persons who speak only one or the other language and employees must communicate with those persons.

Nepotism Restrictions

The courts have uniformly upheld employers' rules against hiring relatives of present or former employees as long as the rule is regularly applied to both sexes. It also appears that the rule may be applied to some categories of employees and not to others as long as it is not being used to discriminate against a protected class. In one case a federal court upheld a "no-spouse" rule even though it was applied to a couple who were living together but not married.

Several states, like Michigan, have statutes prohibiting discrimination based on marital status. In those states it is illegal to refuse to consider an applicant because of the applicant's marriage to a present or former employee.

Handicapped Persons

Removal of employment discrimination against the handicapped has been the emphasis of recent state and federal statutes and regulations. The general theme of these statutes and regulations appears to be that if the handicapped person is qualified to perform the job, he or she should not be excluded from employment consideration because of the handicap. A disability or handicap is considered as any condition, sickness, or physical impairment or characteristic that renders a person unable to perform some normal functions.

The fact that the disability may affect the job is not sufficient to avoid a discrimination charge if the applicant can still perform the job requirements in a reasonable manner. In addition, it is not sufficient to show that the impairment precludes the employee from performing in a perfect manner; the worker is legally required to be only reasonably able to do what the position requires. This does not mean that the employer is required to hire the handicapped, only that the handicapped have an equal employment opportunity in those areas where their handicaps will not substantially restrict their job performance.

The fact that the employer's medical insurance costs will increase because of the disability is not sufficient grounds to refuse employment to an applicant. In one case, an employer refused to hire a person with high blood pressure because of medical insurance problems. He was held liable for discriminating against the handicapped.

Drug addiction may be a medical handicap, but the U.S. Supreme Court has upheld the right of an employer to refuse to hire persons who were drug addicts or participants in methadone maintenance programs. So unless prohibited by state or local regulations, an employer may refuse to hire such applicants.

Age

Persons over the age of forty are protected from employment discrimination. A person over forty may not be excluded from employment consideration unless age is a BFOQ. Discrimination against hiring persons because of their youth is not protected under federal law, however.

There are several states, Maine for example, whose age discrimination statutes protect all age groups. In those states, it would be illegal to discriminate against youths above the age of eighteen years.

Regarding the protected age group, persons age forty or older may be excluded if good and sufficient reason exists. The fact that an employer's medical insurance premiums will be increased by hiring an older applicant is not sufficient grounds for excluding the older applicant from employment. However, a rule limiting employment of new bus drivers to those under thirty-five years was upheld on the basis that new drivers were given the most demanding routes due to the seniority system. Here, the court stated that safety reasons were sufficient to justify the age restriction. This case may be limited to only those situations where the safety reasons are directly related to the aging process.

The Screening Process

The screening process is an additional area in which the employer should use common sense and a concept of fairness. The discrimination concerns and issues noted earlier in this chapter are also present in the screening process. While the formality of the screening process varies with the size of business, type of position involved, and desires of the employer, the theme of fair employment opportunity should remain the same. In those companies where the screening process is very informal, the employer should be on guard for unintentional discrimination based on the subconscious biases of the employer. Note that the *Griggs* case determined that even unintentional discrimination is subject to civil liability.

In the screening process, the employer may consider the relevant experience of the applicants. The requirement of experience, however, may not be used to screen out or eliminate minorities or members of a protected class. This question of the consideration of past experience is one of the many pitfalls present in the screening process. The general rule is that the employer may consider the applicant's experience and may use this factor in the selection process when it is essential or directly relevant to job performance.

One court held that an employer should consider the applicant's complete work record and that a rule considering only recent work experience of an applicant is discriminatory against women because they are more likely than men to have had long periods of work interruption.

Advertising Want-ads

Unless prohibited by state law, newspapers may publish classified advertisements for other employers under "male" and "female" columns since they are advertisers, not employers, in this function. Employers, however, may not legally indicate in job announcements any preference, limitation, or discrimination based on sex, age, race, color, religion, or national origin unless justified under the BFOQ exception. The employer must list the position under both "male" and "female" columns or under a column that does not indicate the preferential sex of applicants or any other prohibited preference. Remember that race or color can never be used as a BFOQ exception.

Use of terms commonly recognized as referring to a certain group or sex is also considered as an indication of a prohibited preference. For example, advertising the position as an "office type position" may be considered as indicating a preference for a female employee. The same problem pertains with indicating a preference for "a recent high school graduate," "sharp recent graduate," or "college-age applicant." This may indicate a preference for a young employee and thus be considered as discriminatory against persons over forty years of age.

The use of a referral system by employees or word-of-mouth advertising are acceptable methods to advertise for new employees, unless it results in discrimination. For example, use of a referral system when the majority of the present employees are from one racial group will probably result in more applicants from that racial group. Thus, a discrimination problem results. An employer with a balanced workforce would not normally have this problem.

Background Checks

The employer may legally conduct background checks of job applicants to determine their fitness for the job. The critical question is what use may the employer make of the information received? Some courts have allowed the employers to rely on letters of recommendation from previous employers which contain negative or unfavorable information even though the information was based on subjective evaluations.

In checking the employment background of an applicant, normally the employer may inquire of former employers as to

1. Skills of the applicant in operating equipment that may be used in the new position
2. The applicant's record of sickness and tardiness
3. Quality and accuracy of the applicant's work
4. Cooperativeness and dependability of the applicant's work
5. Honesty of the applicant
6. Initiative of the applicant
7. Ability of the applicant to work well with fellow employees and supervisors

The courts frown on any general rules that automatically eliminate applicants based on adverse background information. This does not mean that the employer is required to overlook any adverse information discovered in a background check. The general rule appears to be that the employer should evaluate on a case-by-case basis how the adverse information affects the applicant's fitness for the position in question.

If the adverse information is of criminal misconduct, the employer should weigh the seriousness of the past misconduct, lapse of time since misconduct, evidence of rehabilitation, and sensitivity of the job in question. Little if any weight should be given to any arrest record not followed by conviction.

As noted earlier, a railroad company was found liable for discrimination because of its blanket rule automatically disqualifying any applicant who had been convicted of a crime. The court stated that this rule had a disparate impact on minorities and was not job related for every position in the company. If a position is one involving a certain degree of trust, then a prior criminal record may be sufficient to disqualify an applicant.

The courts have also concluded that refusing to hire people with poor credit histories is also discriminatory toward minorities and thus must be job related if it is used as a decision factor. In one case, however, a federal court allowed an employer to refuse to hire any person who had been judged bankrupt. The court stated that there was no evidence of a disparate impact on minorities in using a blanket rule of not hiring persons who have been adjudged bankrupt. The difference in the cases between discriminating against those with poor credit history and those with a record of bankruptcy apparently is based on the fact that the court believed that more minorities have poor credit histories but not more bankruptcies than the majority racial group.

Employment Applications

An employer may consider false material statements on employment applications as a basis to disqualify an applicant. Minor errors or mistakes, however, should not be used to disqualify applicants. Nonetheless, such errors may be considered as an indication of an applicant's ability to complete accurately any required reports or work assignments.

The employment application should not request the religion, race, color, national origin, or political beliefs of the applicant unless absolutely necessary. After the employment decision is made, the employer may request the race, color, or national origin of each applicant to determine if a equal opportunity for employment exists or to rebut a claim of discrimination. This information, however, should not be on the employment application and *may not* be used in the selection process. In fact, the decision makers or those involved in the selection process should not be informed of this type of information on individual applicants.

Since photographs may indicate national origin, race, or color, the applicant should not be requested to attach one to the application. After an applicant has been offered employment, a photograph may be required for identification purposes.

The application form should contain a statement giving the employer the authority to make inquiries regarding any information provided by the applicant when completing the form, including contacting former employers listed on the application. A second statement on the form should advise that if the applicant is hired, the employer has the right to dismiss the employee if false statements or material omissions of fact are discovered on the completed application. An additional condition that would be prudent to include is that any offer of employment is contingent upon the applicant obtaining a favorable health examination. The applicant should also sign the application. As discussed in chapter 3, employers subject to Title VII regulations are required to retain all application forms for six months from the date a decision is made on the position in question.

Preemployment Testing

As most employers are aware, it is sometimes very difficult to choose between two or more applicants for a position, especially since the employer usually knows little about the applicants. To remedy this situation and to establish some objectivity to the selection process, many employers rely on preemployment tests. Generally, employers who use preemployment tests indicate a higher satisfaction with their new employees than the employers who do not.

The key legal questions pertaining to use of preemployment tests are: Do the tests measure the specific qualifications needed for the position? And are the tests nondiscriminatory for protected classes? As noted in the discussion on the *Griggs* case, tests that operate to exclude minorities or other protected groups and that are not job related are illegal. As noted earlier, preemployment tests given in English to persons whose native language is not English and whose language skills have nothing to do with job performance are discriminatory.

After these threshold questions are answered, the employer must next decide on how to evaluate the test scores. One of the big problems is establishing a meaningful cut-off score. If the passing score is determined to be 75, is there much difference in the applicant who makes a 74 compared with the one who makes a 75? The employer would probably be in a better legal position when the employment decisions are being questioned if, instead of using arbitrary scores, the employer were to consider the scores of the applicants along with all other information that is available on the applicants.

To prevent problems with discrimination, many companies conduct validation studies to determine if their tests are valid for minority groups as well as nonminorities. However, the average small business employer has neither the time nor the resources to establish the validity of tests. Employers wishing to use a test will find it safer to use one of the commercially developed tests than to attempt to develop their own tests. There are testing consultants who can assist the employer in finding or developing a valid job-related test. The employer should also consider the possibility of joining with similar companies to conduct one validation study that each can use.

Lie Detector Tests

There is considerable debate among the police departments as to the validity of polygraph tests. One 1984 study by the U.S. Office of Technology Assessment concluded: "There is at present only limited scientific evidence for establishing the validity of polygraph testing." Despite the lack of proof of their validity, polygraph tests are still widely used.

Many companies require as a condition of employment that the applicant pass a polygraph test. The normal procedure in those companies that use the test is to ask the applicant after some preliminary questions, "Is there anything on your employment application which is false?" The employer should not ask any questions that are embarrassing or personal to the applicant unless they are directly related to the position requirements. Some states require the employer to provide the applicant with a list of the questions that will be asked prior to the examination.

Before using the polygraph test, the employer should ascertain if there are any state or local regulations that prohibit or restrict the use of the test. Presently, nineteen states and the District of Columbia prohibit its use as a preemployment screening device.

The employer who uses the test as a preemployment device should obtain written permission from the applicant prior to administering the test and should, after the test, discuss the results with the applicant. The applicant should also be afforded an opportunity to explain any apparent problems with the test results. In addition, the applicant should be afforded the opportunity to decline to answer any specific questions without fear of adverse action by the employer.

Psychological and Stress Tests

Unless prohibited by state law, it is legal to require preemployment psychological or stress tests to determine the fitness of applicants for employment or to screen out some of the applicants. However, if the tests are either discriminatory or have an adverse impact against a protected class, then an illegal discrimination problem is present. (*Note:* The earlier discussion of BFOQ requirements should be considered.) Several states, like Oregon, prohibit employers from using psychological stress tests in the employment screening process.

Educational Testing

The *Griggs* case virtually eliminated the use of educational tests for unskilled and manual labor positions. Unless the job clearly requires a certain level of education, the employer should refrain from using general educational level tests. If the position requires the ability to read or some other skill such as typing, the employer may test applicants as to those requirements. The use of general educational tests that measure no particular employment skills should be avoided.

Using Questionnaires

Each question on the questionnaire must be job related. The personal beliefs of an applicant should never be asked unless the belief is clearly job related. Questions that should not be asked on the employment application or during the employment interview also should be left out of a questionnaire.

Physical Exams

The requirement that an applicant pass a general physical examination and submit a medical history statement prior to employment is not illegal. This judgment by the courts is based on the theory that for insurance purposes the employer needs to know the physical status of the applicant and how that status may affect the person's performance of duty. However, any physical qualifications for a position must be justified on a case-by-case basis consistent with the physical requirements of the employment position. Before an applicant is requested to submit to a physical examination and submit a medical history, most states require that an employment offer be made to the applicant.

How safe is an employer in relying on the statement of a medical doctor regarding the ability or inability of the applicant to work? Courts that have faced this question have allowed the employer to rely on the statement if it was obtained in good faith by the employer.

Strength and agility tests are permissible to screen out applicants if they are job related. If a job involves the lifting of 70-pound garbage cans, then job applicants may be required to demonstrate their ability to lift 70 pounds. The requirement for the applicant to reach with one arm a certain height was upheld in one case where the employer established it as a safety requirement. In another case, however, a court disallowed a strength test where the court found that, with a minor realignment of job duties, the physical strength requirements could be eliminated, thus opening the position to women.

Interviewing Applicants

Many employers tend to rely extensively on the subjective evaluations formed of the applicants during the interview process. The employer should be on guard to prevent unintentional discrimination from influencing subjective evaluations. In addition, the subjective evaluations are hard to justify when defending a discrimination complaint. It is much easier to justify the selection decision based on the applicant's objective qualifications.

The goal of the interviewer should be to analyze the duties, functions, and responsibility of the position and to compare them with the knowledge, skill, and abilities of the applicant.

The Interview Process

Prior to the interview, an employer should have a briefing and conduct a rehearsal with any employees who will be present at the interview. Questions soliciting information that may not be used in the employment decision-making process should not be asked of the applicant. The applicant should be allowed to explain answers given to any of the questions asked. An attitude of fairness should be present during the interview.

Improper Interview Questions

Not all possible forbidden questions can be listed in this book. This section lists some of the most commonly asked improper questions.

The answers to the following questions could result in a disclosure of the national origin of the applicant:

Where did your ancestors come from?

Is _____ your original name?

Where were your parents born?

Do you have grandparents or cousins living in a foreign country?

Answers to the following questions would provide information regarding the personal, religious, or social beliefs of the applicant:

Who is your pastor, priest, or religious leader?

What social clubs or lodges do you belong to?

What religious holidays do you observe?

Do you believe in abortions?

What are your feelings regarding labor unions?

The following questions should not be asked because of sexual bias problems:

Do you expect to have any children?

If you go to work, who will take care of your children?

If your spouse is transferred to a different city, would you also move?

Will your spouse object to your traveling?

What does your spouse do?

Permissible Interview Questions

The following questions have been considered proper and may be asked:

Have you ever been convicted of any crime? (Do not ask the applicant if he or she has ever been questioned regarding a crime.)

What professional organizations do you belong to?

If you are hired, can you provide proof of birthplace?

What foreign languages do you speak? (Ask only if language use is job related.)

How long have you lived at your present address; how long did you live at the previous address?

Why do you want this position?

What can you contribute to our company?

May we check with your previous employers?

Do you know of any reasons or problem that would prevent you from working normal hours? Overtime?

What qualifications do you have for this position?

Do you know of any reasons or problems that would prevent you from traveling? (Ask only if traveling is a part of the duties of the position.)

If possible, all questions should be formulated prior to the interview at a time when the employer can carefully and thoughtfully evaluate for possible problems. Questions regarding the religious beliefs, race, and personal opinions not relevant to the position should not be asked. Questions that would not normally be asked a male applicant should not be asked of a woman applicant.

The Employment Offer

After the decision process is completed, the employer should communicate to the successful applicant a clear and definite offer of employment. The unsuccessful applicants should be informed that the decision was based on many factors and that the selected person better fit the employer's needs and requirements. No derogatory information or specific reasons for their non-selection should be communicated to the unsuccessful applicants.

The determination of the abilities and qualifications of prospective employees is still a function of management. There is an presumption that employment decisions are based on good faith. However, if an objecting party can establish a definite pattern of past discrimination, good faith is no longer presumed. The employer should be on guard for this potential problem.

The selected applicant should carefully be explained the terms of employment and conditions of employment. The applicant should be informed of the length of the probationary period and any standards expected of the applicant. It is important to remember that any statements made by the employer may be considered by the applicant as one of the terms of employment. For example, a statement that the applicant would have a job for as long as he performed his job satisfactorily was later determined to be a contract for employment for as long as the applicant performed satisfactorily. The recommended procedure is to inform the applicant in writing of the conditions and terms of employment and keep a record of it. One employer prefers to inform the selected applicant personally of the terms and conditions of employment. She keeps an audio tape of the briefing for record purposes.

Additional Information

Labor Law Reports. *1984 Guidebook to Fair Employment Practices*. Chicago: Commerce Clearing House, 1984.

Marks, Winifred. *Preparing an Employee Handbood*. New York: International Publications, 1978.

McCulloch, Kenneth J. *Selecting Employees Safely under the Law*. Englewood Cliffs, N.J.: Prentice-Hall, 1981.

Player, Mack A. *Federal Law of Employment Discrimination*. St. Paul, Minn.: West, 1982.

Thomas, Claire Sherman. *Sex Discrimination*. St. Paul. Minn.: West, 1982.

U.S. Presidential Executive Order 11246 (1978).

Court Decisions

Albemarle Paper Co. v. Moody, 422 U.S. 405 (1975).

Allen v. Lovejoy, 534 F.2d 522 (6th Cir. 1977).

Berkman v. City of New York, 30 EPD #33,320 (1983).

Connecticut v. Teal, 457 U.S. 440 (1982).

Dickerson v. U.S. Steel Corp. 439 F.Supp. 55 (E.D. Pa. 1977).

Donnell v. General Motors Corp., 576 F.2d 1292 (8th Cir. 1975).

Dothard v. Rawlinson, 433 U.S. 321 (1977).

Flight Attendants v. Ozark Airlines, 19 FEP Cases 1087 (N.D., Ill. 1979).

Griggs v. Duke Power Co., 401 U.S. 424 (1971).

Harper v. Trans World Airlines, 525 F.2d 409 (8th Cir. 1975).

Meadows v. Ford Motor Co., 510 F.2d 939 (6th Cir. 1975).

Phillips v. Martin Marietta Corp., 400 U.S. 542 (1971).

Tuck v. McGraw-Hill, Inc., 421 F.Supp. 39 (S.D.N.Y. 1976).

Ward v. Westland Plastics, 651 F.2d 1266 (9th Cir. 1980).

2
Firing Employees

An employment of indefinite duration is an employment "at will." Until recently, employment at will referred to those employment relations that could be legally terminated by either the employee or employer at any time. Traditionally, the employer could fire any at-will employee at the employer's pleasure. No cause or justification for the firing was necessary.

This has been changed by court decisions and state and federal statutes. Now there are definite restrictions on an employer's ability to fire an at-will employee. This chapter contains a discussion of the federal limitations on the right to fire employees and a look at the most common restrictions placed on an employer by state law. In this one area, however, there are many varying state laws that further complicate the status of an employer's rights. In over one-half of the states the employee has a right under state law to sue for arbitrary or unfair discharge. The courts in recent years have tended to find theoretical bases when the traditional bases are missing to restrict the previously unrestricted right to fire employees.

The trend toward restricting an employer's right to fire at-will employees started in 1959, when a California court allowed a former employee to recover a substantial sum of money because the sole basis for his discharge was that the employee refused to commit perjury. Since that case, more and more employees are claiming that they are entitled to keep their jobs, absent good reasons for terminations. Clearly, the labor law movement is toward job tenure.

Unjust termination cases have resulted in large monetary awards to former employees who win their cases, because not only do the former employees receive lost wages, but they may also receive punitive damages. Except in California, employers win more than 50 percent of the cases involved in employment discharge situations, but even a loss is expensive in attorneys' fees and other expenses involved. In California, from 1980 to 1984 former employees won 60 percent of the cases involving wrongful terminations.

The two most common limitations on discharging an employee in an at-will status are of contractual and of statutory nature. Recently, a "tort" limitation has been imposed by some courts.

Contractual Limitations

If an employee is employed under a formal written contract, then contract law governs the right of the employer to fire employees. In these cases, only causes that would permit a person to terminate a contract are considered sufficient to justify firing the employee. The usual contractual employee has entered into an agreement with the employer that gives the employee some degree of job security.

Before any formal employment contract is entered into, the employer should provide for the right to terminate the employment if the employee's job performance is unsatisfactory. In addition, the employment contract should have provisions giving the employer the right to cancel the contract should the employer close the business. In formal contract cases, the employer should consult an attorney before firing the employee. Cases involving a union contract will be discussed in chapter 6.

Implied Contracts

Implied contractual limitations have been used by many courts to prevent what the courts consider unjust terminations. By "implied contract" the courts hold that even if no agreed-to written contract exists between employer and employee, an employment contract is implied by the actions or statements of the employer. For example, courts have given contract status to internal employer documents such as employee handbooks, oral statements, memoranda, and other documents that tend to restrict the employer or give employees a sense of job security.

In one case the court held that a company memorandum advising employees that they had a job as long as they satisfactorily performed their jobs was an implied contract to retain the employees and thus was a limitation on the firing ability of the employer. Courts have also given job security to employees based on verbal representations made to employees to induce them to come to work for the employer.

In one case the employee handbook stated that after a normal probationary period, the employee could be discharged for a number of reasons; the handbook then listed the reasons. The court stated that this amounted to a promise to the employees that they would be fired for only those stated reasons and therefore the employer could not justify the firing of a worker except for one of the stated reasons. In a similar case, however, one court stated that the employee was not entitled to rely on the policies set forth in a company handbook that bore a disclaimer at the beginning stating: "THIS BOOKLET IS NOT A CONTRACT."

The best approach to avoid an implied contract limitation appears to be for the employer to inform employees at the onset of employment that the employment is at will and to include a similar statement in any employment handbooks. A written acknowledgment that the employment is at will—even signed by the employee—may, however, be insufficient to prevent this problem if statements and expressions of management indicate otherwise. So not only should the statement be contained in the employment handbook and the employee informed at the onset of the employment, but also statements made by management personnel should not indicate otherwise.

Where the employee has undergone a special detriment to the employee or a special benefit to the employer, many state courts hold that there is an implied promise of continued employment absent just cause to terminate. For example, when an employee quit his old job and moved his family to Hawaii in order to take a new job, the courts found that an implied promise prevented the employer from firing the employee without cause. In one case where an applicant closed his own business, which was in direct competition with the employer, in order to take a position with the employer, the court held that an implied contract of employment existed.

In some states the courts have concluded that the employment relationship itself is contractual in nature and that, as with other contracts, a promise of good faith and fair dealing is implied by law. In these cases, the courts found an implied contract based on the mere fact of employment. Accordingly, these courts have reasoned the employer should not terminate the employment relationship because of malice or bad faith.

One New Hampshire court concluded that the employer's interest in running his business must be balanced against the public interest in keeping employees employed and therefore an employer is not free to terminate employment in at-will situations if the discharge is motivated by bad faith or malice. Fortunately, most courts have required something other than the employment relationship to find an implied contract for continued employment. This does appear, however, to be the trend in recent state statutes and court decisions.

Statutory Limitations

Federal statutes clearly forbid discriminatory discharging of employees. While the major federal statute in this area is Title VII of the Civil Rights Act of 1964, there are several other statutes that prohibit discriminatory discharge of employees. The National Labor Relations Act prohibits firing an employee because the employee is involved in union activities. The Occupational Safety and Health Act of 1970 prohibits discharging employees because they reported violations of that act or unsafe working conditions. The discharge of an employee for service on a federal jury is prohibited by one federal statute. In addition, there are many state statutes that also restrict the employer's right to discharge. The state statutes usually parallel the federal ones and may provide additional limitations on employee discharges.

The key theme in these statutes is public policy. It is not in the best interest of the public to allow an employer to fire an employee for the reasons protected by statute. For example, if the employer could fire a person for serving on a jury, this would discourage employees from serving on juries. The concepts discussed in chapter 1 regarding the equal opportunity in hiring apply also to firing. An employer is thus prohibited from discharging an employee because of the employee's race, color, religion, sex, or age (if in the protected age class).

Tort Limitations

Several states, like California, have used tort limitations to prevent unjust employment discharges. "Tort" is a legal word used to describe a private civil wrong. Being a civil wrong, the employee can sue an employer in civil court for actual damages and in some cases the courts will also award punitive damages to punish the wrongdoer. In these states, rather than find an implied contract because of the employment relationship, the courts find that the unjust firings are violations of public policy and therefore are civil wrongs. Most of the cases in which the courts have used this basis, the firing was clearly unjust (for example, firing an employee for refusing to commit a crime or firing one who reported the commission of a crime by the employer). To sustain an action under this theory, the courts usually require a clear violation of public policy.

Discharge of an employee to prevent the employee from qualifying for a pension or filing for worker's compensation has been determined to be a clear violation of public policy. A similar holding resulted in one case where the employer, to uncover the person responsible for thefts, began to fire employees in alphabetical order.

Recently, an Illinois court established the tort of "retaliatory discharge" and held an employer liable for wrongful discharge of an employee who provided local law enforcement officials with information about a fellow employee's possible criminal conduct. The court stated that it was a clear violation of public policy to punish an employee for cooperating with law enforcement officials.

Preventive Approaches

As the reader will note, it is very difficult to determine the status of at-will employment, because the law is unsettled. The only clear thing appears to be that both the courts and the legislatures are moving in the direction of expanding employees' rights to job security at the expense of employers' rights to run their businesses. It appears that the general rule is than an implied promise of good faith and fair dealing exists in any employment relationship. This is an area that an employer should be especially concerned about since the courts have tended to second guess the employer and, in wrongful discharge cases, have awarded former employees large monetary sums.

In order to limit an employer's liability for wrongful discharge the employer should take the following steps:

1. Rewrite all company handbooks and policy statements to ensure that they contain no statements that could be considered as contractual. Include a statement disclaiming the creation of an employment contract in the handbooks and statements. A similar statement should be included on the employment application.

2. Establish clear standards for layoffs and terminations.

3. Keep accurate employment records of employee performance ratings and avoid too-high appraisals of employees.

4. Maintain a sense of fairness in your decisions. Above all, do not fire an at-will employee for refusing to violate a criminal statute or for refusing to do any act that violates public policy.

5. Provide and retain documentation for your discharge decisions. Record the facts as soon as practicable. The documentation should include statements from both supervisors and co-workers of the discharged employee.

6. Provide instructions to employees who conduct employment interviews to avoid promises of future employment. For example, they should never say, "Do a good job and you will always have a position with the company," or words to that effect.

7. Above all, avoid derogatory remarks when communicating with or about an employee being discharged or who has been discharged.

8. If any doubts exist regarding the legal propriety of your actions, first consult an attorney.

9. Do not give written reasons for discharge, even if the employee requests it, unless required to do so by state or local law.

10. Rather than fire employees, assist them to find new jobs. In this regard many employment experts advise against firing employees on Fridays, since they will have all weekend to brood about it. According to this line of thought, if employees are fired at the first of the week, they are more likely to start looking for new jobs, which they cannot do on a weekend.

Unjust Firings

It is not easy to define either a "just" firing or an "unjust" one. A *just* firing is one made because of economic cutbacks or for valid business reasons. Equitable standards must be used to determine which employees are to be fired or laid off in case of economic cutbacks or other valid business reasons. To help prevent legal problems, this section contains a discussion on how the courts have classified employment discharges as just or unjust in certain cases. The discussion is presented as a guide and not a guarantee as to how a specific court will classify certain situations. Absolute predictability in this area of the law is impossible. This section does not apply to those employment relations covered by formal written contracts. In those cases, the advice of an attorney is essential.

An employer should keep in mind that firing an employee is the most severe employment penalty available to the employer and should be used with caution. Several courts have indicated that if misconduct is by a long-time employee, a duty to warn the employee prior to the discharge exists for most types of misconduct.

Sexual Discrimination

The rules against sexual discrimination in hirings are equally applicable to discharge actions. In addition, the decision as to which employee of several to discharge cannot legally be based on the gender of the employees. In one case a woman attorney was fired because, while on a business trip, she accepted an invitation to dance with a fellow employee who was male. When she returned to her office, she was counseled by her supervisor about dancing with the other employee and criticized for wearing dresses that were too tight and too "flashy." She was then fired. The male employee was not disciplined. She sued and recovered $120,000 for lost pay and future wages on the basis of sexual discrimination.

In another case, a waitress was fired for refusing to serve a male customer who was a friend of the owner. The waitress claimed, and the court believed her, that the customer had been sexually harassing her. The harassment included remarks of a sexual nature, touching, and grabbing. The court stated that, were it not for the fact that the employee was a female, she would not have been harassed. Accordingly, the firing was based on sexual discrimination.

Pregnancy

Firing a woman who is pregnant may be a form of sexual discrimination under the Pregnancy Discrimination Act of 1978. Even requiring a pregnant woman to take a leave of absence in the last two months of her pregnancy may be a form of sexual discrimination, since the physical strain of pregnancy varies from woman to woman and with the type of employment involved. Definite time periods when a pregnant woman must take a leave of absence are frowned on by the courts. The better practice would be to allow the woman and her doctor decide on when in the course of the pregnancy it would be best for her to stop working and when it is safe for her to return to work. The Pregnancy Discrimination Act requires employers to treat pregnancy-related illnesses on an equal basis with all other medical conditions.

In one case a finding of sexual discrimination was found against a hospital that fired an X-ray technician when she revealed that she was pregnant. The court stated that the hospital had failed to rebut the presumption that its fetal protection policy was discriminatory as it applied only to females.

Medical Conditions

An employee's medical condition that substantially prevents the employee from performing his or her duties is adequate grounds to terminate an at-will employee according to most courts. The employer, however, should be concerned with whether or not the employee's medical condition amounts to a physical handicap. If it does, the employer should consider the restrictions against discrimination against the handicapped. If, with minor realignment of position duties, the employee could substantially perform the job requirements, then a handicapped discrimination problem may exist.

In one case, a court determined that the firing of an employee with a heart condition that prevented the employee from working overtime and thus reduced his effectness was a "just" discharge and refused the former employee's claim for damages. In this case, the court found that the heart condition did not amount to a physical handicap. In an Oregon case, a court determined that a risk of future physical incapacitation was not adequate basis to fire a truck driver with a back impairment as long as the driver was presently able to perform his duties.

Recently, an Iowa court allowed the firing of a transsexual despite the claim of discrimination against the handicapped. The court stated that trans-sexuality is not a handicap nor does it qualify for protection from sexual discrimination.

Age

Firing an employee because of the advancing age of the employee is usually an open invitation to a lawsuit. While courts have upheld the firing of certain workers such as airline pilots because of age, in most situations the employer loses these cases. The minimum mandatory retirement age for most positions is seventy.

Criminal Convictions

Most court decisions have supported the right of an employer to fire employees convicted of non-work-related felonies or serious crimes. If the conviction is work related and the employer is not involved in the criminal conduct, it appears that the employer clearly has the right to dismiss the employee. For non-work-related convictions, before making the decision to fire the employee, the employer should consider the impact of the conviction on the ability of the employee to perform his or her job, how the conviction affects the employer's business, and the nature of the criminal conduct.

In cases where the employee has been accused or charged with a serious crime but not yet convicted, the courts have tended to hold against an employer's right to discharge. The best rule to follow in these cases appears to be that if the crime is of such a nature that you would fire the employee, then put the employee on a leave of absence without pay until the court case is decided. If the case ends without a conviction or if the employee is able to plea bargain the charge to a minor offense, the employer should consult an attorney before firing the employee.

If the employee is sent to jail, the employer can consider this time as unexcused absence from work. This absence alone may constitute sufficient grounds to fire the employee.

Political Beliefs

Employers should not fire employees because of employees' political beliefs or statements employees have made away from the company location. Individual political beliefs are protected under the first amendment of the U.S. Constitution. About the only restrictions that a private employer can place on an employee are the requirements that no political campaigning may be conducted on the company premises or on company time and that no actions or statements may be made that involve or imply the involvement of the company in a political issue. Discharge of an employee for membership in a political organization is clearly a violation of the employee's freedom of association under the first amendment and is thus illegal.

If the organization to which the employee belongs, however, is the KKK, Communist party, or similar group and the fact of membership brings discredit on the company, than there may be a right to fire the employee.

Union Activity

Firing an employee for union activity or for attempting to organize a union is prohibited by the National Labor Relations Act (NLRA). Acts or threats of violence during union organizing efforts were considered by one court to be sufficient cause to discharge employees despite their protected status, however. Unannounced strikes or refusals to work or to perform specific duty assignments even though related to union organizing efforts were also considered just grounds to fire employees by the court.

The courts have allowed an employer to discharge employees for insubordination, disobedience, or disloyalty during union organizing efforts. The employer may not, however, use these grounds as an excuse to fire employees where the real reason is the employees' union activities. An employer's mistaken belief that employees were about to sabotage his plant in order to promote their union organizing effort was considered insufficient grounds to fire the employees according to one court. Had the employer been able to establish that an attempt to sabotage was planned, apparently the court would have upheld the firings.

Most courts have allowed employers to fire and replace employees engaged in economic strikes (strikes for increased wages or benefits). The employer, however, may not discriminate in rehiring the discharged employees based on their union activity. For example, in one case the employer rehired all but five union leaders. He was held to have illegally discriminated against the former employees because of their union activity. Most courts have stated that an economic striker has a right to return to his or her job if a permanent replacement has not been secured.

The right to replace strikers may not apply to strikers protesting unfair labor practices of employers. In those cases, the courts usually hold that the employee has a right to return to his or her job if the protest strike was made in good faith. (For more information on labor relations, see chapter 6.)

Business Reasons Exception

If the employer can establish that the firing was in good faith and for legitimate business reasons, then the firing of an employee who is a member of a protected class is not discriminatory. For example in a recent Washington, D.C. case, the court held that there was no discrimination based on age where the employer fired a fifty-eight-year-old security manager when the employer closed his Washington office where the employee was employed. The employer had openings at other offices but did not offer any of them to the employee. Although the other jobs were eventually filled by younger persons, the judge ruled that the man lost his job solely for business reasons and therefore no recovery was warranted against the employer. If the selection of which employee to discharge is based on a protected status (age, sex, race, color, religion, or national origin), then the employee would have a valid claim of discrimination.

Smoking

In San Francisco an office worker has sued her employer because the worker was fired thirty minutes after she complained and asked her boss to stop smoking. This suit is based on the unique San Francisco ordinance that requires employers to ban smoking in the workplace if the employer cannot accommodate both smokers and nonsmokers. While the San Francisco regulation is unique, other cities are considering similar regulations. Firing an employee who complains about smoking or firing an employee for smoking during the employee's nonwork time is not recommended. In these situations the courts would probably hold for the benefit of the employee. If the employer has no-smoking or "smoking in designated places only" rules, the employer may be justified in discharging an employee for violating these rules.

Refusing Work Assignments

There are three common reasons for an employee to refuse a work assignment. First, the employee does not want to do the work assignment. Second, the employee does not feel that the supervisor has the right to make the particular work assignment. Third, the employee does not understand the assignment. The first two reasons are easier to use to justify firing the employee than the third one. It is very difficult to justify the firing of an employee who failed to do the work because the employee did not understand the assignment. Regardless of the reason for the refusal, the employer should consider the employee's past record, the reason for the refusal, and the nature of the work assignment before making a decision to fire the employee.

In one case, a court concluded that the firing was justified for three tree trimmers who refused to work overtime because they were moonlighting by doing cutting work for potential company customers. In another case, the court determined that the firing was just when a truck driver on his own declared that his truck was too dangerous to operate despite the fact that two mechanics opined otherwise. If there had been reasonable doubt about the safety of the truck, the court would probably have considered the firing as unjust.

An absolute refusal to climb a roof to do a welding assignment was not sufficient to fire an employee who was scared of heights. Another employer gave his employee the choice of doing the work or going home. The employee went home. The court stated that this was not sufficient grounds to fire the employee, because he was merely exercising one of the options given to him by the employer.

The courts usually consider the refusal to perform the work assignment as ordered as "just" grounds to terminate the employee if the refusal is accompanied by profanity. In this regard, however, watch for the "mere shop talk" problem. If this is one of those situations where the use of profanity is normal shop talk, then the employer should disregard the profanity in making a decision as to the sanctions to take against the recalcitrant employee. In one case, the use of profanity and refusal to don a safety mask were not sufficient grounds to justify the termination where the manager approached the employee in less than a cordial manner, the use of profanity was common, and enforcement of safety rule was usually lax in the workplace.

Disloyalty

Closely related to the problem of refusing to do work assignments is the problem of disloyalty of the employee. Substantial acts of disloyalty will probably be adequate grounds to terminate an employee. In determining whether or not to discharge the worker for disloyalty, the employer should consider the reason for the disloyalty, the employee's prior record, and the type of disloyalty involved.

A charge of insubordination did not justify termination of an employee who refused to go to the company doctor on his own time, since the employee was injured on the job and through no fault of his own. The court stated that the company had no right to control the off-duty activities of the employee. A different holding may have resulted had the employee been ordered to go to the doctor on company time. The courts usually consider an unreasonable bad attitude of an employee as sufficient grounds to justify firing. Other than where an unreasonable bad attitude is involved, there is probably a need for a record of prior warnings and counseling regarding the employee's attitude.

Insubordination is normally sufficient grounds to terminate the employee if it interferes with work, especially if the insubordination involves the violation of a safety rule. Be sure to distinguish, however, between insubordination and legitimate questioning. Several courts have indicated that if the insubordination involves the violation of a safety rule, there may be a duty on the part of the employer to have previously explained the reason that the rule enhances safety if the reason is not self-evident.

Competition or assisting another business compete with the employer's business is considered adequate grounds to discharge an employee. The mere intent to compete where no trade secrets are involved, however, may not be sufficient. Mere product disloyalty is not grounds to fire an employee, as the Ford Motor Company found out when they attempted to fire an employee for buying a Nash. One court determined that the firing was just when a welder who knew the company's secrets of aluminum fabrication went to work part-time for a competing company owned by the employee's brother. Spying or attempts to sell company trade secrets are normally just reasons to fire an employee. Political disloyalty, as noted earlier, is not normally just grounds to fire an employee.

The firing of a truck driver was considered justified by one court when the driver called the police to report that the company truck was overloaded. In this case there was strong evidence that the overloading was accidental, that the employer did not know that the truck was overloaded, and that the employee was mad at the employer. The firing of a cab driver was considered as unjust where the cab driver reported to the police that the cab company was rigging its meters. In this case the court stated that, since management was involved in the rigging, there was no reasonable expectation that reporting it to the company first would have served any purpose. The court also stated that each citizen has a duty to disclose to the police criminal misconduct. One case held that it was against public policy to fire a bank employee because of his attempts to pressure the employer to comply with state and federal consumer credit laws. Another case found that it was not against public policy to discharge an employee for making unfounded internal complaints about the safety of employer's product.

Sabotage by an employee is grounds for firing. The courts, however, require clear proof that the employee was the one who did the sabotage. Merely suspecting the employee of sabotage is not sufficient justification for discharge.

The disloyalty may be a failure to cooperate in an investigation. In one case involving stolen securities, the firing of an employee in a position of trust who refused to answer questions concerning the securities was ruled justified. In a similar case, the court upheld the firing of the employee when there was a leak of confidential information regarding future business plans and the fired employee refused to cooperate with the investigation. Most courts hold that refusal to take a lie detector test in a company investigation is not proper grounds to fire an employee. There is a lack of unanimity regarding firing an employee for refusing to take a lie detector test in positions involving trust and in those cases where the employee at the beginning of employment agrees as a condition of employment to take the test any time requested. In most such cases, the courts have upheld the firing. In one case, the employee had agreed as a condition of employment to cooperate in any theft investigation. The employee refused to take a lie detector test and was thus fired for failing to cooperate in the active investigation of stolen company property. The court stated that the firing was based on sufficient and adequate grounds. The employer should check local and state statutes in this area before firing an employee for refusing to take the test.

Work Performance

Gross acts of negligence are normally adequate grounds to fire an employee. A similar situation exists when the employee has been involved in numerous accidents and has failed to improve his or her efficiency. A single unrepeated act of negligence is normally not sufficient grounds to fire an employee whose employment record is otherwise satisfactory, since employees are human and they do make mistakes.

Discharges for incompetence are not always considered justified by the courts. This is especially the case where the employee has received prior satisfactory ratings in the same job assignment or where the employee had performed satisfactorily in one position and is promoted to the present position, at which the employee cannot perform. In the latter case, the employer should offer to demote the employee first. The best time to fire an employee for incompetence is during a probationary period. If the employer keeps the employee beyond the probationary period knowing that the employee is unable to perform the job assignment, the employer will have a difficult task justifying a later firing. In those cases where the employee's probationary period is almost over and the employee still cannot perform the duty assignments, the employee should either be terminated at that time or offered continued employment under additional probationary status. The latter course of action should be used only if there is an indication that the employee may eventually perform at satisfactory standards.

Usually sleeping on the job or gross intoxication have been considered by the courts as sufficient grounds to fire an employee. The problem with sleeping on the job is one of proof. The standard defense by an employee is "I wasn't sleeping." In regard to intoxication, the problems deal with the degree of intoxication. Merely having a couple of drinks before work may be insufficient to justify firing the employee unless the safety of the employee or others is threatened. Gross intoxication or drinking on the job, however, are normally adequate grounds to fire an employee.

A record of loafing on the job is normally considered just grounds to dismiss an employee. A history of poor work attendance or tardiness can also be sufficient reason to fire an employee.

Several recent courts have upheld employee firings for "theft of time," where the employee is doing personal tasks during periods when the employee is being paid to work.

False Employment Application

The biggest problem with using a false employment application as grounds for firing is the materiality of the falsification. If the false statement on the application blank would have resulted in denial of employment, then normally the employer is justified in firing the employee. A more difficult question arises when the false statement is a minor or unimportant item. In these cases, the courts normally do not consider the firing justified.

In one case, the employment application blank required a prospective employee to sign a release granting the employer the right to dismiss the employee if any information on the application was false. The employee made a false statement about her age. The court stated that the firing was unjust because age of an applicant should not be a factor in the decision process in this case. The woman had stated that she was thirty-four when she was actually forty-one years old.

Also problematic in this area are those cases where the falsification is not discovered until a long time after the employment has commenced. If an employee has satisfactorily performed a job for six years, for example, is the employer justified in firing the employee when a material falsification is discovered? The courts usually look not at *when* the falsification is discovered but at how much time elapsed after the discovery before action was taken by the employer to determine whether to fire the employee. An employer who discovered that an applicant had made a false statement six years earlier could not wait another two years before he fired the employee for the false statement.

The factors that a court will consider in these cases are the nature and character of falsification, number of matters concealed, the performance of employee, reason for the discovery, the employer's motivation in discharging the employee based on the falsification, the time elapsed between falsification and discovery, and the time that has lapsed between time of discovery and the firing of the employee.

As noted in chapter 1, the employment application form should contain a statement giving the employer the right to discharge the employee for providing false or misleading information on the form.

Employee Financial Problems

Repeated personal financial trouble may be grounds for firing an employee if it affects the employee's work performance or the company's business. At one time it was a common practice for employers to fire employees whose wages were garnished. Now, most states have regulations prohibiting employers from discharging or disciplining employees whose wages have been garnished. The ability of an employee to handle his or her personal financial problems may, however, be considered by the employer as an indication of the judgment of the employee, especially if the employee is in a position of trust or handles company funds.

Employer's Economic Problems

Economic difficulties of the employer are normally a valid reason to terminate employees. In any economic cutback, though, equitable standards must be used to select which employees will be fired. The U.S. Supreme Court has allowed an airline to void a labor contract by declaring bankruptcy.

Termination Benefits

Whether or not the fired employee is entitled to severance pay and pay for unused days of sick leave or vacation is normally decided by the employment contract between the employer and the employee. In cases where the courts determine that a termination is not justified, the courts usually include these items in the award to the employee. A firm's employment policy manual should have definite statements regarding the payment of these benefits, and the employer should ensure that all new employees are aware of the company policy. The payment of termination benefits may lessen the pain of a discharge to the employee and may in many cases prevent a lawsuit. Payment of retirement benefits is normally controlled by the Internal Revenue Service regulations on "qualified" retirement plans.

Whether or not the fired employee qualifies for worker's unemployment compensation depends on the reason for the firing. An employee's misconduct may either disqualify or delay the eligibility of the employee to draw unemployment compensation. As noted in chapter 5, the rules and regulations vary from state to state. A check with the local state employment agency should provide guidance in this area.

Additional Information

Barbash, Joseph, and John D. Feerick. *Unjust Dismissal and At Will Employment.* New York: Practicing Law Institute, 1982.
Coulson, Robert. *The Termination Handbook.* New York: Free Press, 1981.
Hunt, Denis D. *Employment Dismissal Without Fear.* David and Charles, 1979.
Keenan, Denis. *Contract of Employment.* London: Keenan, 1979.
Morin, William J., and Lyle York, *Outplacement Techniques: A Positive Approach to Terminating Employees.* New York: American Management Association, 1982.
Robinson, William C. *The Federal Employment Handbook.* New York: Monarch Press, 1982.

Court Decisions

Fernandez v. Avco Corp., 14 FEP Cases 1004 (D. Conn. 1977)
Lewis v. Ford Motor Co., 17 FEP Cases 933 (E.D. Mich. 1978)
Martinez v. Bethlehem Steel Corp., 17 FEP 113 (E.D. Pa. 1978)
McDonald v. Santa Fe Trail Transportation Co., 515 F.2d 90 (5th Cir. 1975)
Meadows v. Ford Motor Co., 510 F.2d 939 (6th Cir. 1975)
Moore v. Sears, Roebuck & Co., 19 FEP Cases 246 (N.D. Ga. 1979)
Rhoades v. The Book Press, 18 FEP Cases 494 (D.Vt. 1978)
United Air Lines, Inc. v. Evans, 431 U.S. 63 (1977)

3
Terms and Conditions of Employment

I n this chapter, the terms and conditions of the employment relationship will be discussed. Two general guidelines should be used by employers in setting and defining terms and conditions of employment. First, once hired, employees have a right to share in the benefits of employment and not be illegally discriminated against. Second, employees have a right to a safe workplace and an environment free of undue harassment.

Terms of Employment

Under terms of contract, the financial remuneration and fringe benefits of employment are discussed. In determining this aspect of employment, the courts have demonstrated a clear tendency to prefer employees' rights over the ownership rights of companies.

Rest Periods and Lunch Breaks

Except in those occupations subject to federal regulations, required time off for rest periods and lunch breaks is controlled by state statutes and local regulations. The general rule is that the employer must pay the employee during rest breaks but not for lunch time unless the employee is required to be on duty or available for duty during lunch hour. Normally, when an employee is not paid for his or her lunch period, the employee has a certain degree of freedom as to where to eat. The courts have allowed employers to place restrictions on where employees take their lunch breaks only when the employees are being paid during the breaks.

Jury Duty

Time off for jury duty is regulated by state law. All states require that employees be given time off for jury duty. Several states also require that employees be paid the difference in wages between their normal rate of pay and the jury fees. In addition, an employer in most states may not require employees to use vacation time to serve on juries. The rationale is that requiring employees to use vacation time would be against public policy since it would tend to discourage jury service.

Religious Holidays

The term "religious" includes all aspects of religious observance and practice. Even an atheist's lack of religious beliefs is protected. As noted earlier, however, the Ku Klux Klan is not considered a religious belief in view of its racist and anti-Semitic ideology. An employer is required to reasonably accommodate an employee's religious observance and practice. The term "reasonable accommodation" means that the employer may not fire an employee who refuses to work on Saturday for religious reasons unless the employer can establish that an accommodation of the employee's religious belief would work an undue hardship on the company.

The burden of proof is on the employer to demonstrate that any religious accommodation imposes an undue hardship on the business. The U.S. Supreme Court, however, in a case involving an airline, held that the "reasonable accommodation" rule does not require the employer to violate a collective bargaining agreement (labor contract) so that a few employees may observe their religious days. In this case, to make the accommodation would violate an assignment policy based on seniority which protected the rights of all employees. One federal court ruled that a trucking company was not required to allow a driver to take his religious day off (Saturday) when such accommodation would violate the seniority system. In his case, the driver had attempted to establish a special exception to the seniority system used to assign duties. The same court, however, held that a major automobile manufacturer violated an employee's religious rights by refusing to allow him Saturdays off. In the latter case, there were other employees available to fill in at no extra cost to the employer.

One federal court approved a hospital's requirement that an employee who wants a day off for religious purposes must obtain a suitable replacement.

The refusal to grant paid leave to a school teacher for the purposes of observing three religious holidays per year was not discriminatory nor a violation of the right to free exercise of religious beliefs, according to one court. The court held that the employer had only a duty to make reasonable accommodations to an employee's religious beliefs. In this case, the employer gave the teacher two paid days and required that the third day be taken without pay.

An employer may not apply a rule that vacation time has to be taken at a certain time for a worker who requested leave without pay to attend a compulsory religious convention even though other employees would be discontented. Another court held that an employer may not apply a policy of a whole weekend of overtime or none at all to an employee whose religion prohibited work on one of the two weekend days.

An employer may not interfere with the religious beliefs of employees. Accordingly, it is unlawful for an employer to require employees to attend a staff meeting that begins with a prayer. It is also illegal to permit a supervisor to discuss religious beliefs with employees and attempt to "convert" them to his beliefs.

One court upheld the policy of an employer giving all employees a paid holiday on "Good Friday" but not on a Jewish holiday. The court stated that employees were not required to worship on that day and that the relationship between religion and employment as a result of the holiday was remote. In this case, it appears that the court feared that if this practice were not upheld, then companies could not even give their employees a paid holiday on Christmas.

Pay

Employers may set different salary levels for different employment positions as long as the differences are not based on an illegal discriminatory classification. Pay includes not only the base pay but also such fringe benefits as medical, hospital, accident, and life insurance; retirement benefits; profit-sharing plans; bonus plans; vacations; holiday pay; sick leave pay and other fringe benefits. Note that many of these fringe benefits are rewards other than monetary, such as time off. Profit-sharing plans are characterized as a form of wages and are within the equal employment practice laws and regulations.

An employer may not justify the differences in insurance benefits between employees based on the fact that cost of such benefits is greater with respect to one sex or one age group. An employer may not provide greater insurance coverage for the heads of households or principal wage earners than provided other employees, since such coverage tends to be available primarily to male employees and therefore is a form of sex discrimination. An employer may change insurance coverage for new employees or employees starting after a certain date without legal objection unless an employee can establish a previous record of illegal discrimination in hiring.

Health benefits for older workers must be the same as those provided for younger workers. Employer-financed health plans that provide health and disability benefits are required to include coverage for pregnancy, childbirth, or related medical conditions, according to a 1978 amendment to Title VII of the Civil Rights Act (called the Pregnancy Discrimination Act). Abortions, however, may be excluded from coverage except for those necessary for medical reasons. An employer is not required to provide insurance benefits for employees' dependents, but if they are provided for wives of male employees, then they must be provided for husbands of female employees.

Seniority Systems

It is not unlawful for an employer to apply different standards of compensation or different terms, conditions, or privileges of employment pursuant to a bona fide seniority system. The seniority or merit system need not necessarily be in writing. It is highly recommended, however, that the employer have a written and published seniority system plan. This should eliminate many questions regarding the treatment of employees. The plan should be concrete in form, communicated to all employees, and consistently followed by the employer.

The U.S. Supreme Court recently held that a good faith seniority system is not unlawful even though it has some discriminatory consequences. The court held that even approved affirmative action programs should not take priority over good faith seniority plans.

Promotions

As in hiring and firing decisions, an employer may not base promotion decisions on illegal discriminating factors. Most courts have tended to uphold an employer's promotion decision as long as there were adequate business reasons for the decision. To avoid problems, the promotion system should be based on objective criteria and the criteria should be publicized to all employees.

One court held that lack of job-related experience was sufficient grounds to deny promotion to a Hispanic employee. Although he was more qualified than another employee, who was promoted, he lacked the job-related experience. The court stated that it was not necessary for the employer to show that such experience was an absolute requirement for doing the work in question. The court found as well that the employer had acted in good faith and not with a discriminatory intent.

One court held that the failure to promote a black employee based on the fear that racial tension and violence would occur if the black were promoted was an illegal act of discrimination. In this case, the black employee was better qualified and was apparently rejected because he had assumed a leadership role among the black employees.

Equal Pay Act

The Equal Pay Act does not attempt to remedy all forms of pay discrimination, only those based on sex. For the purposes of determining salary under the act, all wages and fringe benefits are included. The basic concept of the act is equal pay for equal work regardless of the sex of the employee. Whether or not the work is equal is an objective question. This means that the motive of the employer is immaterial and good motives do not constitute a defense to a charge of pay discrimination under the Equal Pay Act. The burden is first on the employee to establish the existence of an unequal pay system. Then the duty is on the employer to establish that the difference is based on a factor other than sex.

The Equal Pay Act authorizes pay differentials based on length of employment, merit, incentive system, price rates, and geographic location. The courts use four separate elements to determine if jobs are equal for purposes of this act. The elements are effort, skill, responsibility, and similar working conditions.

The equal skill concept includes the experience, training, education, and abilities of the employees. Equal for the purposes of this statute means roughly equal; identical skills are not required. Also, if two jobs are of substantially different character, then it is not violation of the act because one job pays more than the other.

"Working conditions" is a term of industrial art. It includes all the physical surroundings and hazards of a job. The Supreme Court has, however, held that time of day is not a "working condition" within the meaning of the act. Accordingly, night pay or shift differential pay violates the act unless either sex is permitted to work the premium pay hours. The court stated that shift differential premiums must be uniformly and nondiscriminatorily applied.

If one position requires a different degree of accountability than another position, then the Equal Pay Act does not forbid different pay scales. For example, an employer was allowed legally to pay a male sales clerk more than the female clerks where the male clerk was responsible for approving personal checks. The court held that this additional responsibility warranted the additional pay.

The performance of extra duties is used in many cases to justify higher pay for one employee. To be an adequate justification, the additional duties must be regular and recurring and consume a significant amount of time. Occasional or infrequent assignments even of a significant nature normally will not support higher pay for one employee for the periods when the extra duties are not being performed. The courts have held that minor extra duties such as answering the telephone or turning out the lights are insufficient justification for the higher pay scale. If the employer assigns extra duties of a comparable nature to employees of each sex, then extra duties may not be used to justify the extra pay for one sex.

One court held that prior work experience was justification for paying a male employee more than a female employee. The court stated that the primary consideration in establishing total compensation is the value to the employer measured by the skill, effort, responsibility, and working conditions normally required by the employee position. One court stated that it was unlawful to reclassify a position in order to pay a woman employee less than was paid the prior, male employee with the same duties. This does not prevent an employer, however, from reassigning tasks when an employee leaves and downgrading the position if these changes are accomplished for valid business reasons.

The general rule under the Equal Pay Act is that differences in pay must be based on factors other than sex of employees. The willingness of women to work for less or the fact that prevailing wages for females are less are not considered as factors other than sex. If two jobs are in fact unequal and the employer excludes employees of one sex from performing one of the jobs, then an equal pay problem is present.

One major insurance company was required to pay female sales agents for lost income because the company's compensation policy discriminated against women who received unequal pay for equal work in the form of a lower minimum salary guarantee. In this case, the company had based the minimum guarantee on the salary of the agent prior to joining the company. Here, the court determined that, since historically women employees have been paid less than men employees, basing the minimum salary guarantee on prior wages discriminated against women.

Comparable Worth Doctrine

The theory of comparable worth is being pushed by many as the answer to ensure equal pay for men and women. Under this theory, wage values are assigned to employees' duties according to several factors, including the value of the duties performed by each employee toward the product or service that the business does. In this manner, people in jobs of comparable value to the employer could receive comparable salaries. Critics of the doctrine contend that it fails to consider the going labor market value for the various labor skills in question, a factor that all employers use in determining the pay range for a particular employee position. In the *Spaulding v. University of Washington* case, the Ninth Circuit Court of Appeals rejected the doctrine as an unwarranted extension of Title VII of the Civil Rights Act. Several federal district courts not in the Ninth Circuit have, however, used this doctrine in deciding that employers were discriminating against women employees.

A recent U.S. Labor Department study reported that women who hold full-time jobs receive only about 66 percent as much pay as men who hold jobs requiring the same amount of skill or education.

Overtime Pay

The basic theory behind the requirements that employers pay overtime wages is to encourage employers to hire more employees and thereby assist in obtaining full employment.

Employers subject to the Wage–Hour Law (Fair Labor Standards Act, or FLSA) are required to pay most employees a minimum hourly wage. The law also requires that employers pay employees at least "time and one-half"—that is, their regular hourly wage plus one-half that wage—for all hours worked each week in excess of forty hours. In determining the number of hours worked, an employer may start the work week on any day of the week as long as a uniform work week is used. Outside salespersons and certain management personnel are exempt from the time and one-half requirement.

The Wage–Hour Law applies to many businesses that are engaged in interstate commerce or that make products that are involved in interstate commerce and businesses that directly affect interstate commerce. (The Fair Labor Standards Act is discussed in more detail later in this chapter.) Businesses that are not covered by this statute are usually subject to similar state statutes.

The ability and willingness to work overtime is a factor an employer may consider in hiring or terminating employees.

For an employer to be liable for overtime pay under the FLSA and most state statutes it is not necessary that the employee be requested to work overtime, only that management suffered or permitted the employee to do the work. Thus, if an employee is working additional time and the employer or any person in management knows or should know that the employee is working and does not stop the employee, then the company is liable for overtime pay. The reason that the employee is working the extra time is immaterial. Under most statutes, an employee cannot be required to take compensatory time off in lieu of overtime pay.

Pension and Retirement Plans

Except in certain cases, the involuntary retirement of employees is forbidden until they have reached seventy years of age. Excluded from the federal ban on involuntary retirement are executives who will receive retirement benefits of at least $27,000 annually and certain occupations (such as airline pilot) for occupational safety reasons. Employers cannot legally discriminate in pension plans. The employer should also check the Internal Revenue Service regulations listing the requirements of a "qualified" plan, since only qualified retirement plans may be used as business deductions on tax returns.

Outside Employment

A difficult problem is the extent that an employer may restrict the outside employment of an employee. In most situations, the courts have restricted the rights of employers to control the nonworking hours of employees. Several cases have implied that a public employer may constitutionally restrict its employees to working solely for the government. The converse appears to be the rule in private employment, unless the private employer can establish a reasonable business requirement. For example, an employer in most states may restrict an employee from outside employment with a competitor; this is especially true where trade secrets are involved.

An employee should be advised at the onset of the employment relationship of any restrictions on outside employment and any restrictions on subsequent employment. The terms should be clear. To be legal, any restrictions on employment must be reasonable as to extent of the limitations and length of time they operate.

Fair Labor Standards Act

The Fair Labor Standards Act (FLSA) establishes minimum wage, overtime pay, recordkeeping, and child labor requirements for approximately 40 percent of all employees in the United States.

Covered Employees

All employees of certain businesses engaged in or affecting interstate commerce, producing goods for interstate commerce, or handling, selling, or otherwise working on goods or materials that have moved in or produced for interstate commerce are covered. The businesses include

Laundry or dry cleaning establishments

Building construction companies

Hospitals or sick care institutions

Retail or service establishments whose annual gross volume of sales or business exceeds $362,500

Communication and transportation businesses

Businesses with some employees crossing state lines in the course of their employment

Domestic service employers who work a minimum of days each quarter

Some other businesses are also covered. If the employer is in doubt, it is best to check with the local U.S. Department of Labor office (regional offices are listed in appendix B).

Basic Wage Standards

Covered nonexempt workers are entitled to a minimum wage of not less than $3.35 an hour (as of 1984) and to receive overtime pay at a rate of not less than one and one-half times their regular rates of pay after forty hours of work in a work week. All overtime wages are due at the regular pay day covering that pay period. Thus, an employer may not delay or withhold to a later date any overtime pay due.

Any deductions from an employee's wages for cash shortages, merchandise shortages, and the like are not legal if they reduce the employee's pay below the minimum required rate.

An employer's work week may start on any day of the week as long as the same day is used each week. Hospital and residential care institutions may adopt, with the agreement of the employees, a fourteen-day overtime period in lieu of the usual seven-day work week, if their employees are paid time and one-half for hours worked over eight hours in a day or eighty in a fourteen-day period, whichever is the greater number of overtime hours.

As long as the minimum wages are paid, the FLSA does not regulate or require vacation, holiday, severance, or sick pay; pay raises or fringe benefits; and premium pay for weekend or holiday pay.

Employees Paid by Tips

Employees who customarily and regularly receive more than $30 a month in tips may have the tips considered as part of their wages for the purposes of determining their hourly rate of pay. The employer, however, may not count the tips for more than 40 percent of the minimum wage.

Employer-Furnished Facilities

The reasonable cost or value of any employer-furnished facilities such as room or meals may be considered as part of an employee's wages for purposes of determining the minimum pay requirements if the acceptance of the facilities is voluntary on the part of the employee.

Exemptions

Learners and apprentices may, under certain cicumstances, be paid less than the minimum wage. In addition, casual employees such as baby sitters may likewise be paid less than the minimum wage.

Executives, administrative and professional employees, and outside sales-persons are excluded from the minimum wage or overtime requirements. Farm workers employed by anyone who used no more than 500 man-days of farm labor in any calendar quarter of the preceding calendar year are also excluded.

Announcers, news editors, domestic service workers residing in the employer's residence, employees of motion picture theaters, and taxi-drivers paid on a trip rate plan are exempt from the overtime provisions of the FLSA.

Child Labor Provisions

The FLSA child labor provisions are designed to protect minors' educational opportunities and prohibit their employment under conditions detrimental to their health. The basic restrictions are as follows: Sixteen- and seventeen-year olds may be employed in any nonhazardous job; fourteen- and fifteeen-year-olds for not more than three hours a day during a school day and eight hours on any other day and not during school hours or before 7 A.M. and after 7 P.M. except in the summer. Normally children under fourteen may not be employed outside the home; farm work is excluded. Besides these federal restrictions, most states also have restrictions on child labor that the employer should be familiar with.

Enforcement

The Wage and Hour Division of the U.S. Department of Labor is charged with the responsibility of enforcing the standards. Willful violators may be punished by fines up to $10,000 for a first offense; a second conviction may result in imprisonment.

The FLSA provides for back wages for a period not to exceed two years. The Department of Labor or the aggrieved employee may sue in court to obtain the back wages plus attorneys' fees and costs.

Working Conditions

The employer is under a duty to provide a safe place to work. In this regard, the employer is subject to many state and local regulations that are too lengthy to discuss in this book. Common sense, however, will help employers to protect themselves from liability in this regard.

OSHA

The Occupational Safety and Health Administration (OSHA) was established by the federal government to promote safety and health standards in industry. In addition, most states have their own agencies. One of the duties of OSHA is to establish standards for safe working conditions. Employers may obtain copies of the standards that apply to their type of business by checking with the local branch office of OSHA. Most major cities have a branch office listed under the U.S. Department of Labor.

The Occupational Safety and Health Act applies to all employers who have one or more employees and who are engaged in a business that in any manner affects interstate commerce. This act requires that the employer provide the employees a place to work free from safety hazards. If an OSHA inspector determines that a safety hazard exists, a federal court may close the business until the hazard is corrected or eliminated. Certain employers are subject to scheduled inspection schedules by OSHA. Employers with ten or fewer employees are exempt from these scheduled inspections as long as their occupational injury rate is below the national average.

An employee who thinks that an employer's place of business is unsafe and the employer is subject to OSHA may file a complaint with the local OSHA office. OSHA is required to keep the name of the complaining employee confidential. OSHA can then make an inspection of the business place and, if deemed necessary to correct the problem, obtain a court order directing the employer to correct the condition. It is illegal for an employer to discipline an employee for reporting a possible safety hazard.

If you have any specific questions regarding an OSHA requirement or regulation, call the regional OSHA office listed in the telephone book under U.S. government.

Treatment of Employees

Employees must be treated with dignity and respect appropriate for the circumstances. The use of abusive language is not condoned by the courts. In one case, the employer was held liable for using abusive racial epithets to a half-Indian employee even though the employer was himself half-Indian.

An employer is normally not responsible for the personal conduct of other employees unless the employer has either condoned or encouraged the conduct in question. If management is aware that certain employees are prone to chronic horseplay and takes no action, then the employer could be liable for any injuries resulting therefrom. In regard to fights by employees, a special problem exists in that management is not legally permitted to condone them, but normally is restricted to disciplining only the employee or employees who started the fight—but there is usually a question as to who started the fight. If the employee who starts the fight or horseplay is a managerial level employee, the courts are more likely to hold the employer responsible for any damages.

Sexual Harassment

Sexual harassment has been a constant area of concern for employers. In November 1983 the newspaper columnist Art Buchwald in one of his sarcastic columns advised job applicants to specify whether or not they wanted to be sexually harassed on the job and by whom. This is not a joking matter, since studies indicate that about 50 percent of all female employees have at one time or another been sexually harassed on the job. The courts often hold employers liable for allowing or permitting sexual harassment.

In cases of sexual harassment by management or supervisory personnel, the employer is normally accountable under the theory that the employer has placed the supervisor or manager in the position. The employer should have a standing policy putting employees on notice that sexual harassment will not be tolerated by any employee.

In one case, a female employee failed to get promoted because the employee who *was* promoted was willing to have a sexual affair with the supervisor. A Delaware federal court judge held this to be a form of unlawful sex bias and, indirectly, sexual harassment. This case points out that the sexual harassment guidelines are broadly interpreted.

The employer should establish procedures whereby employees who feel that they are being sexually harassed by managerial employees may report the matter to a manager at a higher level without fear of reprisal.

Smoking or No Smoking

As noted earlier, San Francisco was the first major city to require employers to accommodate the wishes of nonsmokers. With the increased political activity of nonsmokers, the employer should try to accommodate both smokers and nonsmokers. At present five states (Minnesota, Utah, Nebraska, Connecticut, and Montana) limit smoking on the job. Other states, like New York and California, have counties or cities that limit employees' smoking. Accordingly, this is an area that the employer should be alert for possible problems and take active measures to prevent any future problems.

Firing an employee who complains about the smoking of fellow employees may be an open invitation for a lawsuit and is not recommended. Note the discussion in chapter 2 on unjust terminations.

Permitting male workers to smoke during work but restricting female workers to smoking only during breaks is illegal. It would not be illegal, however, if the smoking or no smoking rule depended on the job assignments or work locations of the employees. For example, allowing truck drivers to smoke on the job while not allowing salespersons to smoke on the job would be permissible.

In a recent California Fair Employment and Housing Commission ruling, a nonsmoking employee was allowed $27,397 in back pay plus $10,000 in damages for emotional distress while trying to resolve her conflict with smoking co-workers. The commission ruled that a sensitivity to tobacco smoke was a physical handicap under a state law forbidding job discrimination against handicapped persons. In this case, the employee had requested that her desk be moved away from smokers to alleviate her physical distress. The employer refused to do so, and as a result the employee claimed she missed many days of work because of her allergy to smoke.

Employee Bias Problems

Rules restricting employees' rights must not be based on an illegal bias such as sex, race, color, religion, national origin, or age. The antibias rule must be applied to lockers, restrooms, and so on. For example, providing special facilities in the areas where the women's lockers are but not in the men's area would be illegal sexual bias. Providing preferred parking spaces and other privileges for management or supervisory personnel is permissible since the preference is not based on sex, age, race, color, or national origin. For example, Chrysler at one time assigned preferred parking spaces to employees driving Chrysler products. Assignment of parking spaces in this case was not based on one of the prohibited factors.

An employer for business reasons may prohibit employees from playing a radio during working hours but may not limit an employee's speech except for clear business reasons. For example, requiring employees to speak only English at work was considered by one court as illegal since no clear business reason for the rule was established by the employer.

Crime Prevention

Not only does the employer owe employees a safe place to work, there is also some duty on the employer to ensure that the parking lots and the entrances into the job sites are safe. Several employers have been required to pay damages when their employees were mugged or raped in company parking lots. The courts tend to hold employers responsible for providing adequate lighting and taking other steps to improve the safety of the employees in parking lots and on company premises. Employers may reduce their liability by informing new employees of steps to take to reduce their chances of being victims of crime. For example, the new employee should be advised of the areas to avoid, any lighting problems, and unsafe times to walk alone.

Some companies are sponsoring rape prevention programs. Such a program may prevent a company from being involved in a lawsuit or at least will show the court that the company is concerned with the safety of its employees. In some situations, these programs reduce employers' medical insurance premiums. In addition to helping prevent serious crimes to employees, the programs could keep employees from missing work due to rapes. In a typical rape case, the employee will miss at least two or three days for trauma, one day for police investigation, one day for pretrial court hearings, one day for grand jury appearances, and at least two days for criminal court trials. Moreover, even if the employee returns to work without any substantial loss of time, the employee is not going to be very efficient for a significant period of time.

Employee Dress and Grooming

The Supreme Court has stated on many occasions that the manner in which people dress is a form of expression and is protected to some extent by the first amendment of the Constitution. In spite of this, the courts have normally upheld employers' dress codes as long as they were reasonable and not discriminatory toward a protected class. The test that is most commonly used by the courts regarding grooming or dress requirements is the "minimal rationality requirements" test. This means that if the grooming or dress code does not illegally discriminate and has some rational business requirement for the code, then it is permissible. For example, the employer may require that "conservative dress" be worn by employees who deal with the public if the company is trying to maintain a conservative image.

An employer, however, may not restrict women from wearing slacks or pant-suits, since this would discriminate against women unless men were also restricted from wearing slacks. I have attempted to discover a case in which men were exempt from wearing a "coat and tie" as a sex-based classification, but could not find any. Thus, it appears that an employer may require male employees to wear coats and ties and female employees appropriate attire. An employer should not require female employees to wear bras or hose, since these are gender-based requirements. However, there is nothing wrong in requesting female employees to wear bras or hose on a voluntary basis.

The courts have allowed employers to regulate the hair length of employees for sufficiently valid business reasons and providing that there was no discrimination based on sex or race. Recall the employer mentioned earlier who was allowed to enforce a "no beard" rule in his family restaurant. A bus company, however, could not prohibit its drivers from wearing facial hair since the rule had the effect of discriminating against black males who suffered from a skin disease that made shaving extremely uncomfortable.

Employee Discipline

The courts have assumed that employers have the right, when justified, to suspend, demote, or fire employees. The key thing to remember in these situations is to maintain a sense of fairness and to avoid illegal discrimination. If you have grounds to terminate an employee, normally a lesser penalty of suspension or demotion is permissible. (The discussion in chapter 2 on employee terminations should be considered.)

The employer should make a habit of requiring accurate records on which to base any possible future employee discipline. The employer should also publicize company policies so that employees are aware of the expectations placed on them. A counseling program may assist in preventing some of the most common discipline problems.

Promotion and Performance Ratings

A review of the employee rating system and education of managerial personnel in completing performance rating is highly recommended. Classic problems in this area are too high performance ratings, lack of adequate guidelines to managerial level employees who complete the ratings, and failure to have a review system for ratings.

Appraisals should be strictly job related and any negative comment should have a factual basis included in the rating. Courts have held that, if a company has a system of performance ratings, then it should be used when making decisions regarding promotions, raises, and length of employment.

Regarding promotions, the courts have consistently ruled that a person cannot legally object or claim discrimination in employment decisions unless the person has applied for the position. Informal inquiries to first-line supervisors, however, have been ruled as applications when the employee was discouraged from applying for the promotion. Accordingly, the employer should educate line managers and first-line supervisors regarding questions on promotion opportunities.

It is recommended that employee career advancements not be promised as work incentives. When the promises cannot be kept, then breach of contract may be charged. Not only are such promises legally inadvisable, but behavioral scientists contend that promising employees promotions will distract the employees from their present positions since they are looking ahead to the new job.

Personnel Records

Restrictions on what information may be requested on employment applications also apply to personnel records. Certain records, however, are required to be kept on each employee by Title VII of the Civil Rights Act and by the Wage–Hour Law. The Equal Employment Opportunity Commission (EEOC) requires that applications for employment be retained for a period of six months from the date that a decision is made on the application. One court found that the failure of an employer to retain the applications for the required six-month period could be considered as evidence of illegal discrimination by the employer.

Employers subject to the Wage–Hour Law (see discussion on overtime pay) are required to maintain certain records on employees and retain the records for a period of three years. The data required to be maintained under this law are the names and home addresses of each employee, sex, occupation, date of birth if the employee is under nineteen, hour and day of week that the work week begins, hours worked each day and total hours each work week, record of overtime pay, all deductions and additions to wages, normal salary or hourly pay, wages paid each pay period and date of payment. Similar requirements are placed on employers by state disability and unemployment compensation programs (see chapter 5).

Employees should be informed of the types of information the employer keeps on them, of their right to inspect their individual records for accuracy, and of how the records will be used in regard to promotions, retention, etc. Employees have a right to confidentiality in their records. An employer should not disclose personal information on an employee or former employee unless the employee has consented in writing to the disclosure of the information. This is especially critical in the case of social security numbers, because credit bureaus and other agencies often file personal information by social security number.

Employers should establish uniform recordkeeping procedures. Varying procedures based on sex or other characteristics of the employees is unwarranted and could subject the employer to allegations of discrimination. Requiring female employees to use their husband's last name is also illegal.

Employees in nine states have the right to inspect any personnel records that an employer keeps on them. A recent study determined that the right-of-access statutes cost little to comply with, precipitated few problems, and did not provoke strong reactions from employers in those states either negatively or positively.

Steps should be taken by the employer to ensure that certain information, such as age and race, not be used in a discriminatory manner. To prevent problems in this regard, the decision makers in hiring, retention, and promotion decisions should not have available to them this type of information.

Additional Information

Backhouse, Constance, and Leak Cohen. *Sexual Harassment on the Job*. Englewood Cliffs, N.J.: Prentice-Hall, 1981.

Deboard, Robert. *Counseling People at Work*. New York: Gower, 1983.

Dobbins, Richard, and Barrie Pettman. *Disclosing Financial Information to Employees*. Des Moines, Iowa MCB Publications, 1978.

Miramontes, David J. *How to Deal With Sexual Harassment*. San Diego, Calif.: Network Communications, 1980.

Women, Work, and Wages: Equal Pay for Jobs of Equal Value. Washington, D.C., National Academy Press, 1981.

Court Decisions

American Tobacco Co. v. Patterson, 452 U.S. 553 (1977).

County of Washington v. Gunther, 721 U.S. 161 (1981).

Franks v. Bowman, 424 U.S. 747 (1976).

Hein v. Oregon College of Education, 32 EPD #33,895 (9th Cir. 1983).

Hoppe v. McDonald, 30 EPD #33,317 (Ida SCt. 1983).

Houston v. Inland Marine Industries, 30 EPD #33,296 (D.C. Cal. 1983).

Kyriazi v. Western Electric.Co., 461 F.Supp. 894 (1978).

NLRB v. Weingarten, Inc., 420 U.S. 251 (1975).

Pullman Standard v. Swint, 451 U.S. 902 (1982).

Spaulding v. University of Washington, 740 F2d. 686 (1984).

United Air Lines v. Evans, 431 U.S. 553 (1977).

Walton v. Avant Development Corp. dba CBS, 32 EPD #33,748 (D.C., Ga. 1983).

4
Discrimination

This chapter contains a brief survey on the law of employment discrimination. When considering a possible discrimination problem in a particular employment situation, the reader should also refer to the discussion in this book of that particular employment situation. For example, if you are examining the equal employment opportunity requirements in hiring situations, not only should you look at this chapter, but you should also refer to the discussion on hiring employees contained in the first chapter of this book. Also see appendixes C–F, which contain selected federal statutes and guidelines on equal employment.

The majority of discrimination problems that employers get involved in are not the result of deliberate discrimination but are unintentional violations. Accordingly, the employer should be on guard for any possible unintended discriminatory practices. Regardless of an employer's personal feelings about discrimination based on age, sex, race, national origin, color, or religion, the employer cannot afford to violate the law in this regard. Some of the largest court awards are the result of unintentional discriminatory practices.

The primary basis of present-day legislation on employment discrimination is Title VII of the Civil Rights Act of 1964. The federal courts had as early as the 1940s interpreted national labor relations statutes in a manner to prohibit the most blatant forms of discrimination in labor unions. Presidential executive orders in the 1950s and early 1960s prohibited racial discrimination by government employers and employers under government contracts. In addition, a number of states enacted equal employment statutes in the 1950s. Civil rights legislation was introduced in the U.S. Congress from 1943 to 1963 without success. Finally, the first employment discrimination statute passed by the U.S. Congress and enacted into law was the Equal Pay Act of 1963. A year later, the Civil Rights Act of 1964 was passed.

Because of constitutional restrictions, all federal laws must have a basis in the U.S. Constitution. Most federal discrimination statutes, like the Civil Rights Act of 1964, are based on the right of the federal government to regulate interstate commerce under the commerce clause of the Constitution. Thus, not all small businesses are covered under Title VII or other federal equal employment statutes. Most states, however, have their own equal employment opportunity laws to protect those employees not covered by the federal law.

Title VII

Title VII of the Civil Rights Act of 1964, which became effective in July 1965, is the backbone of most employment discrimination regulations and court decisions. The other titles of the act deal with discrimination in housing and education. Basically, Title VII prohibits discrimination because of an individual's race, color, sex, religion, or national origin. From the time Title VII became effective until the summer of 1976, the U.S. Supreme Court decided only seven cases involving discrimination issues under it. Since 1976, however, the court has been very active in defining and setting forth the requirements under Title VII. (See appendix C for a reprint of the EEOC's Uniform Guidelines on Employment Selection.)

Under Title VII, it is unlawful for employers to refuse to hire, to fire, or otherwise to discriminate against any person with respect to pay or terms or conditions of employment because of the individual's race, color, sex, or national origin. It is also illegal under the act to limit, segregate, or classify applicants or employees in a manner that limits the employment opportunities of any person because of race, color, religion, sex, or national origin.

The Supreme Court has interpreted the act to include all aspects of the employment relationship from establishing the job requirements to providing postemployment references.

As noted in chapter 1, the U.S. Supreme Court has interpreted Title VII to prohibit not only direct discrimination but also indirect discrimination. For example, allowing employees with Spanish surnames to wait only on minority customers was considered illegal by one court. Neutral employment practices that have a disproportionate impact on a protected class are also prohibited unless justified by business necessity.

An employer is defined under the act as any person engaged in an industry affecting commerce who has fifteen or more employees for each working day in each of twenty or more calendar weeks in the current or preceding calendar year. An employer may be an individual, partnership, corporation, trust, union, or an association. Employers specifically excluded from coverage are the U.S. government, corporations wholly owned by the federal government, Indian tribes, agencies of the District of Columbia, and bona fide private membership clubs that are tax exempt.

Foreign employers operating within the United States are included within the provisions of Title VII for those activities which take place within the United States. Employees of the federal government and the District of Columbia are covered under a separate act. A 1972 amendment resulted in state and local governments and private educational institutions being included as employers under Title VII.

Equal Employment Opportunity Commission

The Equal Employment Opportunity Commission (EEOC) was established by section 705(a) of the Civil Rights Act of 1964. Its basic purpose is to administer and enforce Title VII. As the result of a 1979 Presidential Reorganization Order, the EEOC also has responsibility for enforcement of the Age Discrimination in Employment Act and the Equal Pay Act.

The commission is composed of five members, not more than three of whom may be members of the same political party. Members of EEOC are appointed by the president by and with the consent of the Senate for a period of five years. One of the members is designated by the president as the chairperson of the commission. Three members constitute a quorum. There is also a general counsel, an attorney who is appointed by the president with the consent of the Senate for a term of four years. The general counsel is responsible for the conduct of all litigation under Title VII, the Equal Pay Act, and the Age Discrimination in Employment Act of 1967. The counsel also provides legal opinions to the public and reviews EEOC regulations, guidelines, and contracts.

The EEOC is further organized into an administrative headquarters and district and area offices. The EEOC has delegated much of its authority to act in individual cases to its district directors and other designated representatives. The district directors may receive or consent to withdrawal of charges, issue subpoenas and notices, issue right-to-sue letters, and enter into and sign conciliation agreements. Only commission members may issue subpoenas on charges under the Equal Pay Act.

Most of the enforcement by EEOC is through suits filed in federal district courts and through intervention in actions commenced by private individuals. The EEOC has jurisdiction to act on any complaint filed with it by an aggrieved individual or on request of any commission member. An additional role of the EEOC is that of conciliation.

Processing Complaints With the EEOC

Before an individual may file a court action on an employment practice complaint under Title VII, the person must first file the charge with the EEOC or with a state or local equal opportunity employment agency.

Discrimination complaints under Title VII are required under the act to be filed within 180 days after the alleged unlawful employment practice occurred. Notification of filing of the charge, including the date, place, and circumstances of the alleged unlawful employment practice, will be made by the EEOC to the person against whom the charge is made within ten days after the charge is filed with the EEOC.

If the alleged unlawful practice occurs in a state that has a state or local law prohibiting the act alleged and also has established a state or local authority to administer or grant relief in employment discrimination cases, then the complaining individual should first file the charge with the state or local authority. The state or local agencies are commonly referred to as "706 agencies" because section 706 of Title VII sets forth the required qualifications for designation as a local or state agency. In most areas, the complaint should first be filed with the local or state commission before it is filed with the EEOC. In fact, the statute states that an individual must wait sixty days after filing with the local or state employment discrimination commission before the charge may be filed with the EEOC. The sixty-day delay is to provide the local authority time to settle the issue without referral to the EEOC.

An aggrieved person may circumvent this requirement to file with the state or local agency first, by filing the charge with the EEOC in the first instance. In this event, the EEOC will transmit a copy of the charge to the local commission and consider that the charge is automatically filed with both agencies. The EEOC will, however, wait sixty days before taking any action on the charge.

A charge may be made in person or by mail at the offices of the EEOC or any of its district or area offices or with any designated representative of the commission. The charge must be in writing, signed and verified (sworn and signed before a notary). Each charge should contain the full name, address, and telephone number of the person making the charge; the full name and address of the person against whom the charge is made (if those details are known), and a clear and concise statement of the facts, including pertinent dates, constituting the alleged unlawful employment practice.

The written charge need not identify by name the person on whose behalf it is made. A person may request that the commission keep his or her name secret. The person, however, is required to disclose his or her name, address, and telephone number to the commission.

The commission has held that a charge is sufficient when the commission receives from the person making the charge a written statement sufficiently precise to identify the parties and to describe generally the action or practices complained of. The charge may be amended later to cure defects or omissions and the amendments will relate back to the date the charge was first received.

If the local agency has not resolved the complaint within sixty days or if the local agency waives its jurisdiction, then the EEOC asserts its own jurisdiction. Normally, the first step the EEOC takes is to schedule an informal conference between the charging party and the party charged against. At this conference, the EEOC tries to settle the matter without any admission of liability by anyone. If the EEOC is unable to resolve the charge and determines that there may be some merit to the charge, then the next step by the EEOC is to investigate the charge formally to determine whether or not there is reasonable cause to believe that a violation of Title VII or other federal equal employment statute under the commission's jurisdiction has occurred. If the EEOC determines that no reasonable cause exists to believe that a violation has occurred, then the EEOC notifies the complaining party and takes no further action.

The complaining party may, within ninety days of receiving notice that the EEOC is going to take no further action, file a suit in federal court in his or her own name. This notice from the EEOC is commonly referred to as the "right-to-sue letter," since included in the notice is permission for the aggrieved person to pursue the remedy in federal court should he or she desire to.

The commission has the duty to make a reasonable cause determination as soon as practicable and within 120 days from the filing of the charge or from the date that the commission was authorized to take action with respect to the charge.

Under the act, nothing said or done during and as a part of the informal endeavors to settle the matter by the EEOC may be made public by the commission, its officers or employees, or used in evidence in a subsequent proceeding without the written permission of the party concerned. The purpose of this provision is to encourage a full and free discussion by both parties in an attempt to settle the problem without fear that any statements made can later be used against the party making the statement.

Should the EEOC determine that reasonable cause exists that an unlawful employment practice has occurred, the commission must first try to settle the issue by conference, conciliation, or persuasion.

Because most charges are filed by individuals in their own behalf, if the EEOC after its investigation determines that additional persons or groups should be included or that additional parties should be named as violating parties, then the EEOC may on its own initiative add other parties. For example, if a person complains that he was discriminated against because of his race and the EEOC determines that all persons of that race are being discriminated against by the employer, it may amend the charge to include the entire class of discriminated applicants. Also, if the applicant charged only the employer with a complaint, the EEOC may charge additional parties, such as labor unions or other employers, with involvement in the discriminatory practices.

If the EEOC determines that there is reasonable cause to believe that a Title VII violation has occurred and is unable to settle the matter without court action, then the EEOC can file in federal court against a private party. If the charged party is a state or local governmental body, then the EEOC refers the matter to the Office of the U.S. Attorney General.

If the EEOC decides not to file a suit or to refer the matter to the attorney general, then the complaining party is notified and receives a right-to-sue letter. At this point, the complaining party may institute court action in federal court within ninety days of receiving the letter. Any time after the EEOC has had a charge for at least 180 days, the complaining party may request the right-to-sue letter. In such an event, the private party may file suit in court even though the EEOC has not completed its investigation. In the latter situation, there may be two suits eventually filed against the charged party, one by the individual and one by the EEOC. For the first 180 days after the EEOC acquires jurisdiction, only the EEOC or the attorney general may file suit.

If the case is tried in court, the suit can include any unlawful practice reasonably related to the original charge. The charging party (the plaintiff) has the duty to prove a discriminatory practice by the defendant. Then the defendant has the duty to establish any legal justification for the practice or else judgment will be against the defendant. If the court determines that a violation has occurred, the court has broad powers to correct the problem.

The EEOC has established procedural regulations for the processing of complaints. The EEOC has also published detailed guidelines regarding lawful and unlawful conduct under Title VII. The courts have held that these EEOC guidelines are not binding on employers but constitute only the EEOC's opinion on permissible conduct under Title VII. The Supreme Court has, however, stated that the guidelines are entitled to "great deference" and that, if followed by an employer, may establish that the employer acted in good faith by following the guidelines.

If there is an employment contract or collective bargaining agreement that allows for arbitration in such cases, the U.S. Supreme Court has allowed the employee to seek concurrent remedies under the arbitration process and with the EEOC.

Remedies

If a court determines that the defendant has an unlawful employment practice, then the court may order the defendant to stop the practice and order such affirmative action as the court deems appropriate. The affirmative action may include ordering the defendant to reinstate, hire, or promote certain individuals with or without back pay. The maximum back pay that a court may order is no more than two years prior to the date the charge was originally filed. The courts have very broad powers in correcting continuing discriminatory practices.

The court can also award attorney's fees to the winning party. The courts are, however, hesitant to award attorney's fees to the defendants under the theory that such practice would discourage injured parties from seeking court relief. In most cases, the court will award attorney's fees to the defendant (the employer) only when the court considers that the suit in question was clearly frivolous and without merit. The courts have not hesitated, however, to award attorney's fees against defendants when the charging party (applicant or employee) has established a violation of a fair employment practice.

Requests for EEOC Opinions

An employer may request a written interpretation or opinion from the EEOC regarding an employment practice under the authority of the EEOC. The request for an "opinion letter" should be in writing, signed by the person making the request, and addressed to the Chairperson, Equal Employment Opportunity Commission, 2401 E Street, N.W., Washington, D.C. 20506. The request should contain (1) the name and address of the person making the request and of other interested persons, (2) a statement of all known relevant facts, and (3) a statement of reasons why the interpretation or opinion should be issued. The issuance of such an opinion letter or an interpretation by the EEOC is discretionary.

Employer Information Report

On or before March 1 of each year, employers subject to Title VII who have 100 or more employees are required to file an Employer Information Report (Standard Form 100) with the EEOC.

On or before September 30 of each year, joint labor and management committees who have five or more apprentices enrolled in the program at any time during August or September and represent at least one employer and at least one labor organization which are subject to Title VII are required to file an Apprenticeship Information Report (EEO-2 form). Some state equal employment opportunity agencies also require periodic reports.

Petitions

Any person may petition to the EEOC, in writing, requesting the amendment or repeal of an EEOC rule or regulation. The petition should be filed with the commission at the address set forth under "Requests for EEOC Opinions" earlier in this chapter. The petition should identify the rule or regulation in question and should contain a statement of reasons or grounds in support of the petition.

Retaliation

It is an unlawful employment practice for an employer to retaliate or discriminate in any manner against any person or labor organization because the person or organization has complained or filed a charge of an unlawful employment practice or has testified, assisted, or participated in any manner in an investigation, proceeding, or hearing under Title VII, the Equal Pay Act, or the Age Discrimination in Employment Act.

State Laws

Under specific provisions of Title VII, state laws prohibiting employment discrimination are not cancelled by this statute. However, any employment practice that is permitted by state law which is a violation of federal law on employment discrimination is prohibited. This prohibition has invalidated many state laws designed for the protection of female employees, because such laws discriminated in favor of women. If the state has stronger antidiscrimination statutes than the federal statutes, then those statutes are permissible and the employer is bound by the higher standard.

Suspect Classifications

The Supreme Court has used the term "suspect classification" to describe those classifications that are made on the basis of a person's race, color, sex, age, religion, or national origin. This means that the classifications are considered illegal discrimination unless the employer can clearly establish a bona fide occupational qualification (BFOQ). Note, however, that classifications based on race or color can never be justified as a BFOQ.

Protected Classifications

Protected classifications are those groupings which are protected under the equal employment statutes. (The primary discussion on each classification in this book is contained under the name of the employment situation where the particular issue normally occurs. For example, most questions involving discriminatory hiring practices are discussed in chapter 1. Listed below are some of the unique requirements or situations under each classification.)

Sex

The first six chapters of the Civil Rights Act of 1964 did not include any protections against sexual discrimination. Title VII as originally drafted also did not include any protection against sexual bias; it was amended prior to passage, however, to include sex as one of the protected classes. The protection against sexual discrimination includes men as well as women. (The EEOC's Guidelines on Discrimination Because of Sex are reprinted in appendix F.)

Equal Pay Act

As noted in chapter 3, the Equal Pay Act deals only with inequalities in pay between males and females. An employee may file an equal pay claim under the

EEOC procedures as set forth in Title VII or the employee may file an action directly in federal court. (See the discussion in chapter 3 regarding the Equal Pay Act.)

Maternity

The Supreme Court in *General Electric Co. v. Gilbert* (1976) decided that discrimination based on the fact of pregnancy was not included under the protection against sexual bias. Congress two years later amended Title VII with the Pregnancy Discrimination Act of 1978. Under the provisions of this amendment, an employer must treat pregnancy in the same manner as any other temporary disability and any discrimination because of pregnancy is considered sex discrimination.

Age

The 1967 Age Discrimination Act is the basic protection that employees over the age of forty years have against discrimination based on their age. This act also protects workers against mandatory retirement. An employer may not force an employee to retire before the employee reaches seventy years of age except in cases based on safety considerations and in the case of executives who receive more than $27,000 annual retirement pay. This $27,000 annual retirement pay exception is subject to upward revision by Congress. Except for the fact that they may be involuntarily retired, employees seventy years of age or older are still protected against employment discrimination because of their age.

Religion

A 1972 amendment to Title VII defined "religion" to include all aspects of religious observance, practice, and belief. The commission has defined religious practices to include moral or ethical beliefs as to what is right and wrong which are sincerely held with the strength of traditional religious views. The fact that no other religious group holds such beliefs or the fact that the religious group to which the individual belongs may not accept such a belief will not determine whether the belief qualifies as a religious belief under Title VII.

The 1972 amendment also placed a duty on employers to reasonably accommodate employees or prospective employees in their observance or practice of religion unless the accommodation would create an undue hardship of the employer. Employers have the burden under the act of establishing that they are unable to accommodate the employee's religious observances. (See the discussion in chapter 3 on the employer's duty to accommodate an employee's religious beliefs.)

National Origin

The EEOC defines national origin discrimination broadly as including, but not being limited to, the denial of equal employment opportunity because of an individual's, or his or her ancestor's place of origin; or because an individual has the physical, cultural, or linguistic characteristics of a national origin group. Also prohibited under Title VII is discrimination against a person because the person is married to or otherwise associated with persons of a certain national origin group or because the person belongs to an organization identified with or promoting a certain national origin group.

In those circumstances where the requirement of U.S. citizenship has the effect of discriminating against an individual on the basis of national origin, the requirement is considered an illegal discriminatory practice.

The BFOQ exception discussed in chapter 1 applies to discrimination based on national origin, but the courts strictly construe this exception.

The harassment of a person because of his or her national origin is also an illegal employment practice under Title VII of the Civil Rights Act. If an employer permits other employees to harass a person because of his or her national origin, this also constitutes an illegal employment practice. Even ethnic slurs and other verbal or physical conduct relating to an individual's national origin are prohibited by the act.

Color

As noted earlier, an individual's skin color may not be used as a basis for an employment decision. For example, hiring the applicant with the lightest skin color or the darkest complexion solely because of the skin color is illegal even when all the applicants are members of the same minority.

Race

One of the difficulties in avoiding racial discrimination is that it is not always easy to determine to which racial grouping an individual belongs. For purposes of determining the minority employment experience, the EEOC allows the classification of employees by the minority group in which they appear to belong or to which they are regarded as belonging in the community.

Handicap

A handicapped status is defined by federal law to embrace any physical or mental impairment that substantially limits one or more major life activities. Business firms performing federal contracts or subcontracts of $2,500 or more are under a duty to take affirmative action to facilitate the employment of handicapped persons. Private employers who are receiving federal financial assistance are also prohibited from discriminating against handicapped persons.

There are also state laws providing employment protection for handicapped persons. These laws provide equal employment opportunity for the handicapped in those situations not covered by federal law.

Veterans

Private employers who perform under federal contracts or subcontracts in excess of $10,000 are required to take affirmative action to hire qualified veterans. There are also state statutes giving veterans preferential employment rights. The employment protection applies to reservists and National Guardsmen who need time off to attend summer camps or other training periods.

A problem with veterans' preference statutes is the fact that such statutes usually discriminate against women, since women are less likely to be veterans than men. For example, several state courts have held that state veterans' preference statutes are illegal because they are a form of sex discrimination and a violation of state law. The U.S. Supreme Court has, however, stated that even though more men than women are veterans, the preference accorded to veterans is not in violation of Title VII or federal regulations on sex discrimination.

Reverse Discrimination

Title VII protects not only minority groups, but all groups in the protected categories from illegal employment discrimination. The leading case in this regard is the *McDonald v. Santa Fe Trail Transportation* case. In this case, the U.S. Supreme Court stated that Title VII also prohibited reverse discrimination against white employees. In the case, three employees—one black and two white—were accused of stealing merchandise from a shipment. The employer fired the two white employees and retained the black employee. The court found that, since all three were equally involved, firing the white employees and not the black employee was discriminatory toward the discharged white employees.

Affirmative Action

Affirmative action programs are programs designed to give minorities a preference based on the concept of affirmative action to make up for past discrimination against them. The *McDonald v. Santa Fe Trail Transportation* case raised serious questions as to the illegality of affirmative action programs that discriminate in favor of minorities. The Supreme Court, however, upheld the legality of these programs in the *Kaiser Aluminum Corporation v. Weber* case. In that case, the employer entered an agreement with the union to reserve at least 50 percent of its craft training program for black employees. Weber, a white employee, was denied admission to the training program even though some of the black employees admitted to the program had less seniority with the company than he. The Supreme Court ruled that an employer and a union may voluntarily adopt affirmative action programs designed to end traditional patterns of segregation even though the program may grant preference to members of one protected group over members of another group.

Despite the *Kaiser Aluminum* case, employers are taking a chance any time one group of a protected class is granted preference over another group. Unless an affirmative action program is approved by a federal court, an employer would normally be in a safer position treating all groups equally and not granting preference to any group.

Remedies

Most remedies under the discrimination statutes are designed to allow persons who are subject to illegal discrimination to regain any losses that were caused by the discriminatory action. Typical damages allowed by the courts are back pay for up to two years from the date the claim was filed, reinstatement, promotion, seniority, and attorneys' fees. Punitive damages are sometimes awarded to punish the employer for the illegal conduct. Injunctions ordering employers to stop certain employment practices may also be issued by the courts.

Additional Information

Labor Law Reports. *1984 Guidebook to Fair Employment Practices.* Chicago: Commerce Clearing House, 1984.
McCulloch, Kenneth J. *Selecting Employees Safely under the Law.* Englewood Cliffs, N.J.: Prentice-Hall, 1981.
Player, Mack A. *Federal Law of Employment.* St. Paul, Minn.: West, 1982.
Thomas, Claire. *Sex Discrimination.* St. Paul, Minn.: West, 1982.

Court Decisions

Contreras v. City of Los Angeles, 656 F.2d 1267 (9th Cir. 1981).
Kaiser Aluminum & Chemicals Corp. v. Weber, 99 S.Ct. 2721 (1979).
Laffey v. Northwest Airlines, 366 F.Supp. 763 (D. D.C. 1973).

New York City Transit Authority v. Beazer, 440 U.S. 568 (1979).

Osborne v. Cleland, 620 F.2d 195 (8th Cir. 1980).

Phillips v. Martin Marietta Corp., 400 U.S. 582 (1971).

Saxbe v. Bustos, 419 U.S. 65 (1974).

U.S. v. Local 189, 416 F.2d 980 (1975).

Yartzoff v. State of Oregon, No. 83-3885 (9th Cir. Oct 18, 1984).

5
Disability and Unemployment Benefits

I n this chapter, both worker's disability compensation and unemployment benefits programs will be discussed. Care should be taken in dealing with either program to check out any specific differences that may exist in your state. Since both are federally approved programs and depend to some extent on federal funds to operate, there is a degree of uniformity among the various programs in each state.

Both programs are normally financed by taxes on the employer's payroll. Therefore, this is an area where the employer can reduce expenses by establishing a claims management program to ensure that only meritorious claims are paid. For example, one company was able to reduce its unemployment taxes by $62,000 a year with an active claims management program.

Worker's Disability Compensation

Generally, a state's worker's disability program applies to all employers who employ workers for a certain number of weeks per quarter. The worker's disability compensation benefits are usually in the form of a disability insurance. Employers are required either to purchase a state-approved insurance program or to establish their financial ability to insure themselves. The insurance rates are based on the hazards of the industry and the employer's history of accidents and on-the-job safety records. Thus, employers that can keep their employees' injury rates low will obtain lower insurance rates.

The disability may be either temporary or permanent. An employee qualifying under a disability compensation program is eligible to receive medical expenses and wage-substitution payments. In those cases where the injury prevents the employee from returning to the same type of work, the employee may receive retraining expenses and wage-substitution payments while undergoing a retraining program. If the employee is killed or dies from a work-related accident, the surviving spouse or children may be paid survivors' benefits.

The courts have indicated a tendency to construe broadly the work-related concept to include workers in borderline cases. For example in one recent Nevada Supreme Court case, a casino was required to pay disability benefits to two women blackjack dealers because of sore hands. The occupational injury was labeled as "carpal tunnel syndrome," which is an irritation of the tendons in the hands that occurs when the same motions are performed continually.

There are two basic requirements for employee coverage: (1) the injury must occur in the course of employment, and (2) the employee must be engaged in the general type of work that he or she was hired to perform.

Court review of a disability commission decision is normally by a writ of review to the state supreme court or courts of appeal. The court review is usually limited to legal issues only.

Defenses

The disability program is a form of insurance to protect employees; therefore, negligence on the part of the injured worker is seldom a defense to a claim for disability benefits. Willful misconduct is a defense in most cases. In a recent odd case, a widow was denied survivor's benefits when her husband was killed as the result of his horseplay on the job. Apparently he placed his head in a molding machine. He then waved his arms to attract other workers and accidentally hit the machine's operating lever. He died of head and neck injuries.

If an employee deliberately violates instructions regarding the time, place, or manner of performing his or her work, the employee may not be protected by worker's compensation if the violation is willful and the direct cause of the employee's injury.

If an employee is faking an injury, is receiving compensation benefits from another state, or is drawing unemployment benefits without informing the benefits commission, the employee is committing fraud and if discovered will be ordered to repay previously paid benefits.

Another defense that may prevent a claim from being charged against the employer is that an injury or disability occurred either prior to employment or is not a work-related injury. In either case, if the injury or disability is aggravated by employment, then it is usually classified as a work-related injury or disability.

As noted earlier, for the employee to be covered by worker's compensation insurance, the injury must be considered as within the scope of the employee's duties. If the activity is personal and not related to the employment, the employee is not protected. The fact that the accident was sustained after normal working hours is not grounds to exclude the employee from insurance coverage if the employee is performing acts for the benefit of the employer.

Going and Coming Rule

In most cases, the employee is not covered by worker's disability insurance while going and coming to work. There are several exceptions to this general rule. One is where enroute to home or work, the employee runs an errand for the employer; then, there is a strong implication that the worker is still on the job. In several cases, where an employee has come to employer's premises while off duty and was injured performing some voluntary task for the business, the employee has been determined to be injured in the course of employment and therefore covered by disability benefits. For example, one off-duty employee went to his workplace to buy a package of cigarettes and there discovered a robbery in progress, which he attempted to thwart. It was determined by the court that the employee was covered by disability insurance for injuries he sustained in the robbery.

Unemployment Benefits

The purpose of unemployment insurance is to provide unemployed persons with a minimum level of financial support while they are without work. In most states the benefit period lasts approximately twenty-six weeks. In a few states the maximum period is thirty-two weeks. Nationwide, approximately 30 percent of workers who do draw unemployment benefits, draw them for the maximum period. Most states allow a partially unemployed person to draw reduced benefits.

Employers pay for unemployment insurance benefits, either by paying a tax on their payrolls or by reimbursing the unemployment insurance fund for the benefits paid to their former employees. In 1983 the *Wall Street Journal* estimated that employers pay approximately $240 per year in unemployment compensation taxes for each full-time employee. The unemployment taxes paid by an employer vary from about 1 percent to 4.7 percent depending on the claims chargeable against the employer. Thus, while an employer with a favorable history regarding unemployment claims may pay an unemployment tax of 1 percent of the payroll, an employer with an unfavorable history may pay four times as much.

Any time a new claim is filed, a copy of the claim is forwarded to the applicant's last employer for comment. The employer is, in this manner, afforded an opportunity to provide any factual data that may bear on the applicant's eligibility for the benefits. The employer should include the reasons that the applicant is no longer employed. The claimant is usually required to file a continued-claim form each week to continue to receive benefits.

Basic Requirements

The basic requirements for eligibility for unemployment benefits are as follows: a claimant must be unemployed through no fault of his or her own, be registered for work with the local state employment office in an effort to find employment, be able and available to work, have recently worked a minimum period of time in a job covered by unemployment protection (usually all jobs except farm work), and have filed for the benefits. There is a waiting period of at least one week before the person may draw unemployment benefits.

Methods of Reducing Unemployment Costs

The most obvious way of reducing unemployment costs is to reduce employee turnover by careful screening of applicants for employment and reducing discharges of present employees. In lieu of firing employees, an employer can assist employees in finding new employment or retrain employees to handle different duties.

A good claims management program will help prevent unjust claims. The program should include the documentation of all employees separations by use of exit interviews, recording all acts of misconduct, and taking an active part in the unemployment claim processing.

Defenses to Unemployment Claims

Accurate factual records should be retained regarding all employee separations; the records should be in a form that may be provided to the decision maker in the unemployment benefits office. The employer should ensure that any possible grounds for disqualification of benefits are made known to the benefits office.

The three most common defenses are that the worker was fired for misconduct, that the worker voluntarily quit, and that the unemployment was the result of a labor dispute. In cases where the employer alleges that the applicant was fired for misconduct, the burden is on the employer to establish that the former employee committed willful misconduct and that the firing was justified.

If the former employee voluntarily quits work without just cause, then the worker is not eligible for the benefits. If, however, the claimant can establish that just cause existed for quitting, then the claimant can normally draw unemployment. Good cause could be that the former employee was being unjustly harassed by managerial personnel or that the spouse of the former employee has been transferred and the former employee moves with the spouse to a new location. Good cause was found by one employment commission in a case where the former employee, a public school teacher, quit because she had been hit by one of her students.

The general test in these cases involving voluntary quitting is the question, Would a person of reasonable prudent judgment quit under these circumstances? The burden of proof to establish eligibility for unemployment benefits in voluntary termination cases is on the former employee. The employer should conduct exit interviews in any situation where employees voluntarily quit, in order to document any possible defenses to future unemployment benefit claims. A skillful interviewer may be able to uncover the employee's real motivation for leaving and obtain statements from the employee that may be used later in any benefit hearing. Ensure that the interviewer takes notes and that the notes are retained for record purposes.

In the majority of states, unemployment as the result of a labor strike where the former employee is out of work because of being one of the strikers or supporting the strike will disqualify the claimant. Employees out of work because of a labor dispute in which they are not participants, normally will not be disqualified from receiving benefits. In these situations, there may be factual disputes as to whether the employee is involved in the labor dispute. Thus, the employer may need to provide the unemployment decision maker with additional information regarding the claimant's involvement in the labor dispute.

Other possible defenses to unemployment benefits are that the claimant is not available for employment, that claimant has refused suitable employment, or that the ex-employee is receiving other government benefits, such as disability benefits, G.I. Bill benefits, or veterans' pensions that may disqualify the claimant. False statements or misstatements of information in the claim can also act to disqualify the claimant.

In some cases, the possible defenses noted above may not completely disqualify the claimant, but only for a stated period, usually two to sixteen weeks.

Claim Procedures

After a claim is filed by the claimant, a copy of the claim is forwarded to the last employer. The employer has a certain number of days to return the form, usually about seven working days. It is important that the employer return the form within the allotted time period with documentation of any information thatbears on the eligibility of the claimant. This is the first opportunity that an employer is given to prevent the company from being charged with an unwarranted unemployment benefit claim. The employer should not include any statements in the report that cannot be substantiated.

If the eligibility of the claimant is undisputed, then usually the former employee is notified of the award based on a published schedule of benefits. If, however, there is a dispute as to the eligibility of the claimant, then the claim is referred to an administrative law judge (ALJ), who acts in a function similar to the trial judge in a court case. The ALJ conducts a hearing at which the claimant has a right to be present with a representative, who may or may not be an attorney.

In most states, the hearing is informal and the rules of evidence do not apply. On conclusion of the hearing, the ALJ issues findings on the facts of the claim and determines whether the claimant is eligible for the claimed benefits. The decisions of the ALJ may be appealed to the state unemployment commission. The procedures vary slightly in different jurisdictions.

The hearing is important to an employer because it offers the employer the last opportunity to create a record regarding the ineligibility of the claimant. After this hearing, any appeals are decided only on the basis of the record created at the hearing. Although the rules of evidence do not apply, the courts have tended to require an employer to present the evidence in a more technical form than required of a claimant (former employee). To be safe, the employer should present the evidence unfavorable to the claimant with the same formalities required in civil courts, using live witnesses rather than written statements.

Requests for reconsideration of previous awards may be submitted to the state benefits administrator or commission if new evidence or fraud is discovered. In the cases of newly discovered evidence, the employer must establish that the earlier failure to discover the evidence prior to the original award was not caused by a lack of reasonable diligence on the employer's part. There are usually standard forms for an employer to use to submit a request for reconsideration. Included in any such request should be a specific and detailed offer of proof, including the names of any witnesses with a summary of their expected testimony and a description of any new documentary evidence. The petition should also include the reasons that the newly discovered evidence was not discovered prior to the original determination.

Required Records

State unemployment and disability statutes and regulations require that employers keep certain records on each party. Generally the requirements are twofold: (1) a list of all workers and former employees and their status (that is, employed, on leave of absence, on vacation, or laid-off) and (2) the record of wages paid to each employee. (See the discussion in chapter 3 regarding recordkeeping requirements for employers.)

Additional Information

Eastman, Crystal. *Work Accidents and Laws*. Salem, N.H.: Ayer, 1969.

Griffes, Ernest J., ed. *Employee Benefits Programs*. New York: Dow Jones-Irwin, 1983.

Personnel Policies Forum, *Layoff and Unemployment Compensation Policies*. Washington, D.C.: Bureau of National Affairs, 1980.

Margaronis, Stan. *Stand Up: A Guide to Worker's Rights*. San Francisco: Public Media Center, 1982.

Court Decisions

Edwards v. Chico, 28 C.A. 3d 148 (1972).
Harrington v. Department of Public Welfare, 434 A.2d 221 (Pa. Commw. 1981).
Le Gase v. Board of Review, 444 A.2d 1151 (Pa. Commw. 1982).
Thomas v. Review Board, 101 SCt. 1425 (1981).

6
Dealing with Labor Unions

Introduction to Labor Law

Federal labor law policy is based on four major statutes: the Norris–LaGuardia Act (1932), the National Labor Relations Act (1935), the Labor–Management Relations Act (1947), and the Labor–Management Reporting and Disclosure Act (1959). The recognized objectives of these acts are to promote collective bargaining as a means of keeping industrial peace and the self-organization of employees as a method of obtaining equal bargaining power with employers.

Norris–LaGuardia Act

Congress enacted the Norris–LaGuardia Act in 1932 to restrict the power of federal courts in dealing with labor strikes. Prior to that act, federal courts by use of injunctions uniformly prevented labor unions from engaging in strikes against employers. In addition to limiting the power of federal courts to stop peaceful labor strikes, the act provides that employees have the right to organize themselves and to select representatives of their own choosing to negotiate with employers regarding the terms and conditions of employment. While the act strengthened the right of labor unions to act on behalf of employees, it placed no affirmative obligation on an employer to bargain with labor unions.

The courts have interpreted the provisions of this act to exempt legitimate labor union activities from the antitrust provisions of the Clayton Antitrust Act or the Sherman Antitrust Act. As long as the union is acting in the interest of its own members and uses only lawful means, the federal courts will not intervene in a labor strike on antitrust grounds.

The act also prohibited "yellow-dog" contracts. These are contracts that many employers, prior to the act's passage, required applicants for employment to sign in which the applicant agrees, if hired, not to join a labor union on penalty of losing the job. The act also limited the civil liability of labor unions for violence resulting from a strike called by the union. Under the provisions of this law, if the violence is not caused by any members of the union and the union has taken reasonable steps to prevent violence, then the union is not responsible for any violence that results.

National Labor Relations Act

At the time that the National Labor Relations Act (NLRA), also known as the Wagner Act, was passed in 1935, the nation was in the depths of the Great Depression and the political power of the labor unions had reached new heights. The passage of this act marked the start of affirmative support of unionism and collective bargaining by the federal government.

The basic provisions of the NLRA guarantee employees the freedom to form, join, or assist labor unions, to bargain collectively with employers, and the right to engage in peaceful concerted activities for purposes of collective bargaining and for self-protection. The act established the concept of "unfair labor practices" to cover employer tactics that are prohibited under the statute. The act also placed a duty on employers for the first time to bargain collectively and in good faith with labor unions. Employers are now obligated to bargain with designated labor unions who act as representatives for employees. The collective bargaining process and requirements are discussed in more detail under "Collective Bargaining" later in this chapter.

The major limitation of the NLRA is that the act is concerned primarily with the right of labor unions to organize and deals only with the tactics of employers and not with the tactics of labor unions. The act, moreover, fails to address the substantive terms of employment, but leaves this to the private negotiations between unions and employers.

Labor–Management Relations Act

The Labor–Management Relations Act (LMRA) of 1947, better known as the Taft–Hartley Act, was passed at a time when the public was concerned about the increasing power of labor unions. Whereas the first two laws discussed in this chapter were prolabor, this law was an attempt by Congress to limit some of the labor unions' powers.

The LMRA, which amended the NLRA, placed constraints on labor unions similar to those previously placed on employers by the NLRA. For the first time the concept of unfair labor practices was also applied to labor union tactics. While stating that collective bargaining was the preferred method of settling labor disputes between labor unions and employers, the LMRA provided two alternative procedures for settling labor disputes between labor and management. One of the alternative methods is by use of the Federal Mediation and Conciliation Service, which was established under the statute. The act also gave the president the authority to intervene when a labor dispute imperils the nation's health or safety. Under this provision, the president has the authority to call for a "cooling-off" period of not more than eighty days and can obtain an injunction requiring the workers to return to their jobs for the duration of this period.

The act also prohibits labor unions from setting up closed shops. A "closed shop" is one where only union members may be hired by an employer. Now, union membership can not be a preemployment requirement. The LMRA also provides employers with legal remedies for the enforcement of labor agreements with labor unions. Accordingly, an employer now may bring a lawsuit to enforce a labor agreement with employees by suing their labor union.

Labor–Management Reporting and Disclosure Act

The Labor–Management Reporting and Disclosure Act, also known as the Landrum–Griffin Act, was passed by the U.S. Congress in 1959 as the direct result of the Senate investigations into labor union corruption during the 1950s. The Senate was also unhappy with the lack of democratic procedures in many of the larger labor unions. The act imposed regulations of the internal affairs of labor union to make them more democratic and established for the first time a "bill of rights" for union members. Regulations regarding the trusteeships over local unions by international unions were established. The act also defines additional unfair labor practices against labor unions.

National Labor Policy

A review of the four major labor relations acts previously discussed establishes a definite national labor policy. The policy's main aims are as follows:

To promote industrial peace between employers and labor unions by use of the collective bargaining process

To promote the self-organization of employees

To place restraints on certain labor practices such as featherbedding, secondary strikes or boycotts, and jurisdictional disputes

To encourage the use of conciliation and mediation services in labor disputes affecting interstate commerce

To provide for cooling-off periods in labor disputes that threaten the health and welfare of the nation

To allow federal intervention in those limited cases where all else fails and in extreme national emergencies, when the federal government may intervene by seizure of the industry or by use of the National Guard or military

As can be noted by a review of the four major labor relations acts, the federal government has shifted from a very prolabor stance in the 1940 and

1950s to a more neutral stance in any conflict between labor and management. Several states, however, have retained their pro-labor approach to labor relations.

Role of State Laws

There are numerous state labor laws covering a wide range of subjects. Where state and federal law overlap, except for certain specified areas, the federal law prevails. Since the federal courts have interpreted the provisions of NLRA very broadly, if an activity is even arguably covered by federal law, the courts will normally hold that states lack jurisdiction because of the federal preemption doctrine. Under this doctrine, if the federal statutes are designed to regulate the subject matter, then state laws are preempted by the federal statutes. The theory behind the federal preemption doctrine is that a uniform national policy is needed and that effective implementation of federal processes must be ensured.

State Statutes

There are three general types of state labor relations statutes. One type is under state antitrust statutes and it bans or limits union activities in those areas not covered by the federal statutes. Another type sets up comprehensive labor relations framework similar to the NLRA for those employment cases where the NLRA has no jurisdiction. The third type of state statute bans picketing and boycotting entirely in those areas not preempted by federal statutes.

Overriding Local Concern

Despite the broad jurisdiction of the federal statutes, there are several areas where the courts have allowed state laws to apply. One of the permitted areas is when the subject matter is of "overriding local concern." Under this exception, the courts have allowed the states to take action to prevent acts of violence or threats in labor disputes. Thus, a state court may, pursuant to a state statute, issue the necessary orders to restrain violence and may award damages against those involved in acts of violence even though the acts in question may also be considered as unfair labor practices under the NLRA.

The federal courts under the overriding-local-concern exception have recognized the interest of states in preventing malicious defamations by any party involved in labor disputes and have thus allowed state courts to award damages in cases involving such defamations. Included also are the interests of states in preventing the intentional infliction of mental distress on persons engaged in labor disputes. State statutes and regulations determining the eligibility of employees for unemployment benefits during strikes have also been upheld by federal courts as a matter of local concern.

Limited Federal Concern

The U.S. Supreme Court has ruled that federal law does not take priority over state laws in those labor areas where the matter is of only peripheral concern to the federal labor policy. Included in this exception are those matters that involve purely internal union matters. For example, where a union member sues the union for breach of contract, normally the suit would be brought in state court and would be controlled by state law.

State Laws That Promote Federal Labor Policy

When state regulations promote the federal labor policy, then the federal courts have likewise permitted the state regulations to apply. An additional area where the federal courts have allowed state intervention is in those cases involving the failure of a union to represent all of its members fairly. Even though this is also an unfair labor practice and thus covered by the NLRA, the Supreme Court has stated that the duty of a union to represent all of its members fairly is so fundamental the state courts can also enforce this duty.

Statutory Exceptions

The exceptions just noted have been created by the federal courts in their decisions. In addition, there are several statutory exceptions that permit states to act in federal labor relations areas. First, the LMRA (the Taft–Hartley Act) permits suits involving breach of collective bargaining agreements to be instituted in either state or federal courts. Also, under this act the employer may sue in state or federal court for certain unlawful strikes or boycotts. A third area where state action is permitted are cases where the National Labor Relations Board (NLRB) has declined jurisdiction because of an insubstantial effect on interstate commerce.

Right-to-Work Laws

The NLRA provides that states may prohibit union security agreements that are otherwise valid under federal law. Union security agreements, also known as union or agency shop agreements, either require that the employee join the union (under the union shop) or, if the employee chooses not to join, that he or she must still pay union dues (in agency shop). The federal labor statutes permit states under "right-to-work" laws to prohibit union or agency shop agreements. Closed shops, where the employee must be a union member prior to employment, are prohibited by both state and federal laws.

National Labor Relations Board

The National Labor Relations Act (NLRA) established the National Labor Relations Board (NLRB) in 1935 as an independent federal agency to enforce the rights guaranteed to workers under the NLRA. The board's principal responsibilities now are to oversee federal laws relating to labor relations. Some of the specific responsibilities include determining whether or not employees want union representation, ensuring the right of employees to organize as collective bargaining units (unions), and preventing and remedying unfair labor practices.

The NLRB has jurisdiction over nongovernmental employers whose businesses affect interstate commerce, nonretail businesses with a gross annual business volume of $50,000, and retail businesses with a gross annual business volume of $500,000. Nursing homes with $100,000 annual business and newspapers with gross dollar volumes in excess of $200,000 are also subject to the jurisdiction of the NLRB if they affect interstate commerce.

NLRB Membership

The NLRB consists of five members appointed by the president and approved by the Senate. Their terms of membership are five years. One of the five is named by the president with the consent of the Senate as the chairperson of the board. Normally the board decides cases in three-person panels. In major cases, the board will decide cases *en banc* (with all five members sitting together in one panel).

The LMRA also established a separate, independent general counsel who is appointed by the president and confirmed by the Senate for a four-year term. The general counsel acts like a prosecutor for the NLRB in those cases involving unfair labor practices.

The NLRB also has over thirty regional offices located throughout the country. Each regional office is headed by a director appointed by the NLRB. The regional director has the authority to make decisions in cases involving union representation problems. In addition, the director serves as a local representative of the general counsel. The regional offices have career civil service attorneys who serve as field examiners. The primary function of the field examiners is to act as investigators in those NLRB cases involving unfair labor practices or union representation problems.

Filing Procedures

Any employee or job applicant whose employer is subject to the jurisdiction of the NLRB may file a charge of an unfair labor practice by completing an NLRB form 501 with the local regional NLRB office. The form may be obtained from the regional office. A charge must be filed within six months of the date of the alleged unlawful conduct or unfair labor practice. The charge should contain the name, address, and telephone number of the person filing the charge; the name and address of the employer against whom the charge is brought; and a specific statement as to the facts, dates, places, and so on that constitute the basics of the charge. Approximately 40,000 unfair labor practice charges are filed each year in the various regional offices.

The individual who files the charge must declare that the statements contained in the charge are true to the best of his or her belief and knowledge. Willfully filing a charge containing known false statements is a criminal offense and the individual involved can be punished by fine, imprisonment, or both.

Once a charge is filed in the regional office, a copy of it is required to be served on the charged party (the employer). In most cases, copies are served on the charged party by mail. The charge is then referred to a field examiner within the regional office for investigation. The field examiner examines the fact, reviews the law on the matter, takes statements from witnesses, and requests from the charged party a statement as to its position on the charge and if it has any new evidence it wishes to submit.

The case is then submitted to the regional director. In a few limited areas, all cases involving certain issues are required by NLRB regulations to be submitted directly to the General Counsel's Office for resolution. If the question is unique or the law is unclear, the regional director may refer the charge to the Office of General Counsel (Advice Section) for recommendations and advice. If the charge is referred to the General Counsel's Office, it is said to be "on advice."

If the regional director after examining the case file determines that the charge lacks merit, then the director will request the charging party withdraw the charge. If the charging party refuses to withdraw the charges and the director still believes that it lacks merit, then the director may dismiss the charges by notifying both the charging and charged parties. There are two prescribed formats that a director may use in dismissing a charge. A "short form" may be used when the director merely wishes to inform the parties that the charge has been dismissed and to advise them of their rights of appeal. If the charging party requests a detailed written reason for the dismissal, then the director will use the "long form." In either situation, the charging party has the right to appeal the dismissal to the Office of the General Counsel (Appeals Division). Such appeals are almost always denied.

If the regional director believes that the charge is true, in cases involving unlawful picketing, secondary boycotts, or unlawful hot cargo agreements, the director is required by the LMRA to seek an injunction in federal court to stop the practice. In other cases, if the regional director decides that there is some substance to the charge, the director will attempt to settle the matter. The director will try to reach an agreement with both the charging party and the charged party to end the unfair practice and take corrective action as may be necessary, to include (if appropriate) back pay or damages. The settlement may either be informal or formal. A formal settlement must be approved by the NLRB and are normally used only in cases involving extensive unfair labor practices.

If the regional director believes that the charge has merit and the charged party is unwilling to agree to a settlement, then the director drafts a formal complaint. A complaint is a formal legal document that sets forth in the required format the charge against the charged party. It contains sufficient information to establish the board's jurisdiction, a summary of the facts regarding the charge and a list of the sections of the law that the charged party is alleged to have violated. The complaint may also include new charges that were discovered during the investigation. The complaint is then forwarded to the Office of the General Counsel. The NLRB will only hear those cases in which a complaint is issued.

While a charging party must file a charge within six months from the date of the alleged violation, there is no time limit for issuing a complaint by the director after he or she receives the charge. In fact, in some cases many months elapse between the filing of a charge and the issuance of a complaint.

Procedures before the NLRB

The complaint is then referred to an administrative law judge (ALJ), a civil service appointeee. The ALJ is independent of the NLRB. The ALJs are assigned to NLRB offices in New York, Washington, D.C., and San Francisco and they travel to the regional office locations for the hearings.

The hearing on an unfair labor practice is similar to a civil trial by judge alone. The ALJ functions as the judge. The hearing is a formal proceeding. The federal rules of evidence govern the admissibility of evidence. An attorney from the Office of the General Counsel is assigned as trial counsel with the burden of proving that an unfair labor practice occurred. Both the charging and charged parties have the right to have their own attorneys present at their expense during the hearing.

After the hearing is concluded, the ALJ makes a report to the NLRB containing recommended findings, exhibits, and proposed board order. Either party may file a statement of exceptions to the report for consideration by the NLRB. The statement of exceptions is a formal document similar to an appellate brief in a civil case. It normally contains a listing of alleged errors by the ALJ and proposed remedies.

The board makes a decision in the case and issues an order based on the transcripts of the hearing before the ALJ and the ALJ's report, exhibits, and statements of exceptions (if any). There are no new hearings before the NLRB. The NLRB then issues a cease-and-desist order that is binding and enforceable on the parties. If the respondent voluntarily complies with the order, then the case is closed. If the respondent does not comply with the NLRB order, then the NLRB may apply to a U.S. Court of Appeals for an order of enforcement.

If the respondent or any other interested party is aggrieved by the board's order, he or she can appeal to a U.S. Court of Appeals in the state in which the alleged unlawful practice occurred or in the U.S. Court of Appeals for the District of Columbia. On appeal, it is the duty of the court of appeals to determine from examining the complete record that was before the NLRB and briefs and counterbriefs filed by the parties to the appeal, if there is sufficient evidence to sustain (support) the decision of the NLRB. The appellate court does not decide whether the board reached the same conclusions that the court would have; rather it decides only whether the NLRB's decision is correct in law and is supported by the facts.

Any aggrieved party may petition the decision of a court of appeals to the U.S. Supreme Court. The Supreme Court may affirm, reverse, or modify the court of appeals' decision on questions of law. Few petitions are, however, accepted by the Supreme Court. Accordingly in most cases, the decision by a court of appeals is final.

After the unfair labor practice charge is decided, the appropriate regional director has the responsibility to ensure that the settlement, order, or court decision is complied with. To perform this function, there is a compliance officer in each regional office who has the duty to monitor each case after the board's decision. If the charging party was awarded back pay, the compliance officer will issue a statement of the amount due to the respondent (employer).

If there is a dispute as to the amount of back pay due, the director may refer the question to an ALJ to hold a limited hearing to determine the amount due. The same procedures that were followed in the original complaint are followed in disputes over back pay, including a right to appeal.

Normally, the compliance officer simply checks with the necessary parties about two months after a decision to determine if the decision has been complied with. If it has been, the case is closed. If not, the officer reports the matter to the director, who forwards it to the NLRB for court enforcement. A decision is made by the NLRB as to whether or not the respondent is complying with the order, and if the respondent is not complying, the NLRB decides the appropriate action to take.

The majority of all charges originally filed are settled by agreement with the parties involved. Only about 10 percent of the charges are decided by the NLRB and less than 1 percent are eventually appealed to a court of appeals. In those cases that end up in an appellate court, it is not unusual for the entire process to take three years from the date that charges are filed by the charging party to the date of a decision by the court of appeals.

Union Representation Selection

Section 8 of the NLRA requires that the employer bargain with the designated representative of the employees (union). Accordingly, the first step is the selection by the employees of a bargaining representative. One of the major responsibilities of the NLRB is to determine whether or not employees wish to be represented by a labor union and, if so, which one. In this process, the NLRB must balance the interest of the employees in the free choice of a representative (union) against the interest of the employer in the proper functioning of the employer's business.

A petition for an NLRB representation election can be filed by labor unions, employees, or employers. The purpose of a representation election is for the employees to select a bargaining agent (union) to act on their behalf.

Consent Elections

If the employer and the employees all agree on which employees are eligible to vote, when and where the election will be held, and the appropriate bargaining units, the parties may enter into a "consent election" agreement, which is subject to approval by the NLRB.

Contested Elections

When the employer and the employees cannot agree to the terms and conditions of the election or when the employees cannot agree among themselves, then the NLRB or the regional director may order a representation hearing by a hearing officer from the district director's office.

At that hearing, the appropriateness of holding an election, the identification of bargaining units and the determination of eligible employees to vote will be made. Normally, the hearing will be informal and without formal rules of evidence. At times, the hearings become highly adversarial in nature. The recommendations of the hearing officer are then forwarded to the regional director, who may then order an election.

If an election is ordered by the regional director, it is by secret written ballot and is supervised by a representative of the director's office. The losing party in the election may file a list of objections to the director. The director may hold a hearing to determine if the objections have substance. Next, the director will certify the results of the election; that is, the director will either approve the election or set aside the election and order a new one. After the director certifies the election, a losing party may appeal to the NLRB. The NLRB accepts appeals only on a discretionary basis. In most cases, the regional director's decision on the election is final and binding.

Certification Elections

As noted earlier, a labor union may file a petition for an election. Before the union can file a petition, however, it must acquire signed and dated authorization cards by at least 30 percent of the employees in the bargaining unit that the union wishes to represent. The authorization cards necessary to establish the showing of interest are forwarded to the regional director, who administratively determines their authenticity. An employer is not permitted to see the cards nor to challenge the decision of the director regarding the authenticity of the cards. Instead of cards, the union may establish the required showing of employee support by use of membership applications from employees, a dues record book, or individual petitions from the employees.

Decertification Elections

A decertification election is requested by the employees when they no longer wish to be represented by the recognized union. A petition for a decertification election requires a showing that 30 percent or more employees support the request. If 50 percent or more of the employees vote for decertification, then the union is decertified. Note the additional requirement that the election cannot legally be held until at least one year has passed since the last election.

Employees Eligible to Vote

Normally all employees who are on the payroll during the pay period just prior to the election are eligible to vote. Temporary absence from work does not disqualify an employee from voting. In exceptional cases when the work is of a seasonal nature, the district director may establish a different period of eligibility.

Bargaining Units

Before a labor union may be designated as the bargaining representative of a group of employees, the employees must constitute an appropriate bargaining unit. A unit can be all of the nonmanagement employees at a business or it can be a section or part of the business, like the retail clerks or the shipping clerks. The determination of the appropriate unit is determined by the duties, skills, wages, and working conditions of the employees; the type of business involved; and industry traditions. The question as to whether a group of employees constitutes an appropriate bargaining group, if disputed, is usually decided by the district director.

Professional employees may nót be included in a bargaining unit with nonprofessional employees unless the majority of the professional employees vote to be included. Security guards who are responsible for the security of the business cannot be included in the same bargaining unit with other employees.

Discouraging Union Activities

The NLRA makes it an unfair labor practice for employers to interfere with, restrain, or coerce employees in their efforts to form labor unions. The NLRA does not, however, prevent all efforts by employers to discourage labor unions. The courts have held that an employer has the freedom of speech on matters involving the operation of the employer's business. The employer, however, should be careful in this area. When in doubt, it may be better not to act than to be in a position of defending an unfair labor practice.

An employer is not permitted to show favoritism in cases involving competing unions. In addition, any actions by a management level or supervisor will be attributed to the employer.

Interrogation of Employees. In the *NLRB v. Dale Industries* case, the Sixth Circuit Court of Appeals stated that interrogation of employees about union membership or activities is subject to close scrutiny and in some situations may constitute an unfair labor practice.

Polling of Employees. The NLRB has determined that the polling of employees by the employer in union representation contests is illegal in most cases.

Surveillance of Employees. An employer cannot cause or authorize the use of spies or informers without being guilty of an unfair labor practice. The courts have prohibited this type of activity, either covert or overt, in any phase of the union organization process. An employer may listen to an employee volunteer information about confidential union activities; however, the employer may not ask the employee for additional information regarding the activities.

Free Speech by an Employer. Coercive statements by an employer are not protected under the right of free speech. Promising additional benefits to the workers who do not join a union is illegal. Threatening adverse consequences of union membership may also be illegal. For example, an employer's statement that the union was controlled by "strike-happy hoodlums" and would make impossible demands on the company and force the company out of business was considered by one court as illegal.

The NLRB determined that it was within an employer's permissible free speech to publicize a history of store closings for economic reasons after unionization of the stores. In addition, the courts have recognized that an employer has the right to go out of business for any reason, including antiunion feelings. Employers may not, however, threaten employees that they will go out of business if their businesses are unionized.

In determining if the employer's statements are coercive or a legitimate exercise of free speech, the courts and the NLRB will look at the context in which the speech is made. There is a twenty-four-hour ban on speeches by both the employer and the union prior to an election, as a cooling-off period. This ban however does not apply to employer speeches if the attendance is voluntary and on the employees' own time. Excluded also from the cooling-off period ban is legitimate campaign literature. (Note: Scheduling elections on Mondays favors unions since they will have the weekend to get out the vote.)

The employer is also prohibited from changing employee benefits in an attempt to prevent or influence a union election. In this regard, providing extra benefits shortly before an election has been considered as an unfair labor practice. An employer's best course of action during a union organizing effort may be business as usual.

Other prohibited activities include making threats through third persons, stating that management will not deal with the union, encouraging employees to persuade other employees not to support the union and asking job applicants about past union activities. Also prohibited is circulating a letter encouraging employees to petition for a union decertification election.

Permissible Employer Activities

The employer can publish information to the employees regarding the recent past history of the union. However, the employer should be accurate in the facts published. When in doubt, consult an attorney regarding the precise language to use.

One employer was permitted to pass out a letter stating in a fair manner the history of the union for labor troubles. To encourage employees to read the letter, the employer offered prizes for correct answers to questions at the end of letter that referred to information in the letter.

An employer has been permitted to inform employees that the union dues may be deducted from their take-home pay, thereby reducing it. The employer may reveal how much the union leaders are paid in most states. The employer may not threaten to withdraw benefits or reduce pay, nor may the employer promise pay raises or increases in benefits if the union loses the election. The employer may, however, compare the existing company salary structure and benefits with those of comparable companies in the local area who have unions. In addition, the employer may stress that salaries and benefits will not necessarily increase with union involvement.

The employer is legally permitted to point out that unionization of the company may reduce the company's flexibility in the management of employees and operation of the company.

Restricting Activities on Company Property. Employers may nondiscriminatorily restrict the solicitation and distribution of union literature on company property during working hours. An employer normally may not restrict this activity, however, during an employee's lunch period, rest break, or other free time for which the employee is not being paid.

The courts have permitted an employer to restrict union solicitation during the employee's free time in those areas where the employees come in contact with the public, such as in the sales area of retail stores. A hospital was permitted by one court to restrict union solicitation in the halls and waiting rooms under the theory that such activity would inhibit patients' treatment and recovery.

One court upheld the right of an employer in a nondiscriminatory manner to bar off-duty employees from soliciting on company property. The employer has also been permitted to limit the distribution of union material to nonworking areas. Normally, the employer may prevent nonemployees from soliciting or distributing union literature if the union has other means available to communicate with employees.

Collective Bargaining

The LMRA (the Taft–Hartley Act) does not require that the employer and the labor union agree on a labor contract, only that both sides bargain in good faith. The U.S. Supreme Court has stated that the duty to bargain does not mean that the LMRA was designed to force employers to enter into collective bargaining agreements. Absent a "no strike" clause, the union may strike during the bargaining process except in those cases where a required cooling-off period is required.

Bargaining Subjects

The LMRA requires that an employer bargain over wages, hours, terms, and conditions of employment. The employer is not required to bargain, however, over every aspect of the labor relationship. Management decisions that deal with policy and long-range planning are not normally subject to mandatory bargaining by an employer.

Bargaining Agent

The determination of the proper bargaining agent in collective bargaining cases is often the subject of litigation or disagreements under the NLRB rules noted earlier in this chapter. If there is no disagreement, the employer may in good faith voluntarily agree to recognize and bargain with a union. In other cases, the bargaining agent is selected pursuant to a "representation election" supervised by the NLRB or the director of the NLRB regional office. In the latter cases, the NLRB or the director will certify a union as the appropriate bargaining agent.

Arbitration

Most labor contracts provide for arbitration as the primary method of solving disputes between the parties under the contract. Recently, a common practice has been to require arbitration in all disputes if requested by either the labor union or the employer.

An arbitrator may be selected each time there is a dispute or the contract may provide for a permanent arbitrator for all disputes under it. The arbitration is usually by a one person or by a panel consisting of three members. In the latter case, one member is normally selected by each party and the third member selected by the two parties' selected arbitrators. In some cases, provisions will be made in the contract to use a neutral agency, such as either the Federal Mediation and Conciliation Service or the American Arbitration Association.

The time and place of the arbitration hearing will usually be decided by the parties, whereas the rules of procedure for the hearing are decided by the arbitrator. The labor contract may apply different requirements, however. Unless otherwise stated in the labor contract, the hearing is usually informal in nature.

The NLRB or a regional director has the jurisdiction to refer an issue to arbitration if the board or the director decides that the dispute is covered by the arbitration clause of the labor contract. When the dispute concerns a refusal to bargain on the behalf of the parties, the NLRB or regional director may in certain cases defer to arbitration.

Authority of the Arbitrator

An arbitrator has no inherent authority to act, only that authority provided for in the labor contract or agreed to by the parties. The U.S. Supreme Court has, however, broadly interpreted any powers given to an arbitrator. For example, a provision in one labor contract that required the parties to arbitrate "any dispute" was held to give the arbitrator the authority to hear all disputes under the contract, including the question as to whether the union was negligent in failing to institute grievance procedures on the behalf of a union member.

A recent federal court of appeals decision held that any ambiguities in a disputed clause of a collective bargaining agreement should be decided by a trial court. In this case, one part of the agreement provided that either party could seek legal relief in the event of a strike or walkout without first invoking the arbitration clause. Another part of the contract provided that neither party would seek legal relief without first resorting to grievance or arbitration procedures set forth in the contract. The court stated that any ambiguities regarding the arbitrability of a dispute should be resolved by a trial court, not an arbitrator.

Precedence of Arbitration Decisions

Arbitrators are not required to follow prior arbitration decisions, even when the same question is involved under the same or a similar labor contract. Arbitrators, however, will consider and generally follow previous decisions when the facts are similar. If either party agrees to arbitration of a certain issue, in subsequent disputes involving the same issue, neither party is bound to submit to arbitration again unless the labor contract so requires.

Rights of Union Members

The Labor–Management Reporting and Disclosure Act (LMRDA) of 1959 established basic rights for union members. All labor organizations (unions) engaged in an industry affecting commerce are under the provisions of this law. Federal employee labor unions are, however, regulated under a different law with similar regulations. The basic rights as set forth under LMRDA are as follows:

1. Union members have a right to elect most union officials by secret written ballot elections.
2. A labor union must disclose its financial statements to any members who request to view them.
3. All members have an equal right to be nominated as candidates for elected union offices, attend union meetings, and participate in union activities.
4. A union member has a right to freedom of speech at any union function without fear of intimidation, subject only to reasonable rules and union regulations.
5. Any increase in dues or any assessments by the union must be by majority vote of the members in a secret ballot. An international union may, however, increase its per capita dues at its convention without a secret ballot.
6. All union members have a right to examine the collective bargaining agreement between the labor union and the members' employer.
7. All union members have the right to inspect the union books and records that relate to the financial disclosure reports the union makes to the U.S. Department of Labor.
8. Any union member has the right to file a civil court action in the local federal court to seek enforcement of this law.

The LMRDA provides for the right of an international union to take over a local union in order to correct corruption or financial malpractice in the local union. First, the international union must file notice with the U.S. Department of Labor that it is putting the local union in "trusteeship." It must also file regular progress reports with the Department of Labor regarding the status of the trusteeship. If the trusteeship extends beyond eighteen months, the Department of Labor can require the international union to go to court for approval.

It is a criminal offense for any union official or member to use force or threats of force to interfere with the rights of any union member.

Union Membership and Union Security Devices

The NLRA prohibits employer discrimination on the basis of union membership. There are, however, certain measures that a union may take to encourage or require employees to join the union. These measures are more commonly referred to as "union security devices." The rationale behind these measures is that they permit the union to retain a strong bargaining posture.

Union Shops

The Taft–Hartley Act (the LMRA) of 1947 provides that except where prohibited by state law, if the union is the exclusive bargaining agent for the employees the union may, under the terms of the labor contract, require union membership of all employees within thirty days after they have been hired (a union shop). In addition, the labor contract can require that a dues check-off system be used (unless it is prohibited by state law). The theory behind this section of the act is that employees who benefit from the union's activity should not be allowed a free ride.

In 1980 the NLRA was amended to provide that employees who for religious reasons object to union membership are not required to join or pay union dues, but must donate an amount equal to their union dues to a charity instead.

If a new employee applies for membership and offers to pay the required initial membership fee and regular dues but is rejected by the union for membership, then the employee is not required to be fired by the employer. Moreover, the rejected employee is not required to pay any union dues.

A union may not negotiate with an employer for a union security agreement without the explicit authority of the employees. This authority must be by secret written vote and may be rescinded by majority vote of employees.

Closed Shops

"Closed shops," those that require union membership before employment, are illegal. A system of job referrals by the union (where the union operates a hiring hall) is not illegal if the union does not discriminate in referrals based on union membership.

Agency Shops

Unless prohibited by state right-to-work laws, an agency shop is legal. In this type of security agreement, all employees are required either to join the union or to agree to pay union dues within thirty days after being employed. The religious objection exception applies to these types of agreement.

Union Dues

The NLRB and the regional directors have the authority under the NLRA to determine that the union dues are excessive under the circumstances, since section 8 of the NLRA makes it an unfair labor practice for a union to require employees to pay excessive or discriminatory dues. Initial membership fees are also included in this restriction.

The NLRB defines union dues as payments by union members used to meet a union's general and current obligations. Any special payments for specific purposes or for a limited period of time are considered as assessments, not dues. A union member may be required to pay any special assessments that are duly passed before the member may enjoy full membership rights such as voting. A member may also be sued for failure to pay any special assessments. In an agency or union shop, the employer may fire an employee who does not pay the initial union membership fee or union dues, but not for failure to pay any special assessments.

Normally, if the employee is expelled from union membership for any reason other than the failure to pay the initial union membership fee and regular dues, the union may demand that the employer fire the employee.

Membership Maintenance

Unions may have reasonable rules that assist in the maintenance of members. For example, the union can limit the right of a union member to resign within fifteen days of a strike or require a thirty-day delay period prior to a resignation taking effect. An agreement that prohibits a union member from resigning from the union is rarely enforceable in the courts. The resigned member may still be required to pay union dues under the union security agreement.

Enforcement of Union Security Agreements

The responsibilty to enforce any union security agreement is with the union. Unless the union notifies the new employee of his or her requirements to join the union, then there is no cause to fire an employee for failure to join. Notification by an employer is not sufficient to relieve the union of this duty.

The union's notification to the new employee must tell the employee when he or she is required to join the union or pay union dues, the amount of the dues, due date for payment, who and where to pay, any installment payment procedures, and any grace periods for late payments. The employee must be advised of the availability of any dues check-off methods of payments and where to obtain the necessary forms if a system exists. In addition, the union, not the employer, has the obligation to notify the employee when the employee is delinquent in the payment of union dues.

Discipline of Union Members

A labor union has certain rights to discipline union members who fail to pay their dues or assessments or otherwise violate certain internal rules of the labor union. The union may not, however, discriminate in applying sanctions against the members. There are also state and federal laws regulating union activity in this area. These statutes try to strike a balance between the rights of individual members and the right of a union to maintain a strong bargaining position.

Union rules apply only to union members and a union may not take action against a nonunion employee who violates a union rule. For example, a union member who resigns from the union may not be disciplined for working during a strike.

Before a member can be disciplined for violation of a union rule, the rule must be in the "legitimate interests" of the union and not violate any federal labor policies. Even if the union rule is valid, the attempt to enforce it by inappropriate means may constitute an unfair labor practice.

Unions have been allowed to discipline members for failing to pay dues or assessments, for working when the union has called a duly authorized strike, for participating in an illegal work stoppage (a "wildcat strike"), spying for the employer, and for joining a rival union. Unions may not discipline its members for doing their civic duty by testifying in court or before investigative bodies, for refusing to take part in an illegal work stoppage, for lawful advocacy of political beliefs and for reporting violations of law to an employer or to law enforcement agencies.

Individual Grievance Actions

If an individual union member has a grievance against the employer, he or she normally presents the grievance via the union representative under the labor contract. The employee may, however, bypass the union and present the grievance directly to the employer. The employer is not required to hear the complaint.

In most cases, when the employee presents the complaint directly to the employer, the union representative has a right to be present at any hearing held by the employer.

If the member files the grievance with the union, the union has a duty to press the member's complaint if it is made in good faith. Failure of the union to process a member's complaint, when the refusal is arbitrary or in bad faith, is considered an unfair labor practice. In the latter situation, the union member may charge the union with an unfair labor practice under the NLRB procedures, institute an action against the union and/or the employer in court under the LMRA, or charge the union with a violation of Title VII of the Civil Rights Act under the provisions of that act.

Strikes and Boycotts

A strike is a concerted stoppage of work by the employees. Closely associated with a strike is the picketing of the place of business by the union members. The courts have held that to a certain degree picketing is a form of free speech and thus protected by the U.S. Constitution. States have, however, been permitted to regulate some aspects of picketing, especially to prevent any violence or other illegal activity. The primary rules regarding the right to strike and picket are contained in the LMRA as amended. The LMRA expressly grants employees the right to strike and picket in certain situations.

The statutory right to strike may be waived by the labor contract entered into by the union and the employer. "No-strike" clauses in labor contracts will be enforced by the courts and the NLRB. The courts will broadly construe any waiver of the right to strike.

"Primary" strikes are direct strikes against the employer with whom the union has a dispute. A "secondary" strike or boycott is a strike against another employer or business to pressure the business from dealing with the employer or business that the union has a disagreement with. A secondary strike or boycott is unlawful and an unfair labor practice.

Economic Strikes

An economic strike is a strike for better hours, better working conditions, higher wages, and/or more benefits. The employer has a right to continue business during an economic strike and can replace any workers who are on strike for economic reasons. If the employer permanently replaces a striking employee, the employer has no obligation to rehire the striker after the strike is ended. The employer must, however, place the replaced worker on a waiting list and rehire the employee with full seniority rights when a vacancy exists.

Unfair Labor Practice Strikes

An unfair labor practice strike is a strike protesting an alleged unfair labor practice by the employer. If the strike concerns both economic grievances and unfair labor practice charges, the NLRB and the courts will normally consider it an unfair labor practice strike unless it is determined that the unfair labor practice charge is not made in good faith.

Normally, a striker is not entitled to be paid by the employer during an unfair labor practice strike or any other strike. The worker's eligibility to draw unemployment compensation is determined by state law.

An employer may temporarily hire replacements and continue business during an unfair labor practice strike. If this strike is in good faith by the workers, the employer is, however, under a duty to rehire the workers when the strike is over. Normally, the NLRB allows employers a five-day delay period to reemploy the striking workers.

If an employer wrongly refuses to rehire a striker involved in an unfair labor practice strike, the NLRB has held that the striker is entitled to back pay from the date the employee should have been rehired.

Sympathy Strikes

"Sympathy strikes" occur when union workers refuse to cross picket lines of another union. For example, a truck driver may refuse to deliver products to a business being picketed by its employee union. Another form of a sympathy strike occurs when one bargaining unit of a business goes on strike and employees in other bargaining units of the same business refuse to cross the picket lines. For example, clerical employees may, under a sympathy strike, refuse to cross the picket lines established by the loading-dock workers.

Sympathy strikers have the same rights as the employees whose strikes they are supporting. Thus, if the strike concerns an unfair labor practice, then the sympathy strikers have the same rights as employees striking for unfair labor practices.

No-Strike Clauses

The labor agreement between the employer and the union may contain a no-strike clause and require that disputes be settled through arbitration. If the union violates the no-strike clause, it is subject to a breach of contract suit in court or an unfair labor practice charge.

Exceptions to no-strike clauses are concerning safety issue disputes and unfair labor practice strikes. The union may waive their right to engage in sympathy strikes. If the union has waived this right, then a sympathy strike is a violation of the contract.

Organizational Picketing

Organizational strikes are strikes by a union to encourage employees to join or select the striking union as their bargaining agent. The organizational strikes are illegal if the employer has lawfully recognized another union and the question of representation is not legally raised or if there has been a valid representation election less than twelve months prior to the picketing. Also, to be legal, there must be an election petition filed within thirty days of the start of the picketing.

Recognitional Picketing

Recognitional picketing is picketing to induce or persuade an employer to recognize the union as the bargaining agent of its employees. The restrictions noted regarding organizational picketing also apply to recognitional picketing.

Misconduct by Strikers

Serious misconduct by a striking employee against the employer or the employer's business during a strike may be grounds to discharge the employee or it may relieve the employer of the obligation to rehire the worker. The mere use of vulgar language or minor misconduct is not sufficient to justify firing or not reemploying the employee in most cases. In addition, the courts have not allowed an employer to use this justification where the real purpose of the sanction is to punish the employee for union activity.

Additional Information

Feldacker, Bruce S. *Labor Guide to Labor Law*. Reston, Va.: Reston, 1980.

Goldman, Alvin L. *The Supreme Court and Labor–Management Relations Law*. Lexington, Mass.: Lexington Books, 1976.

Gould, William B. *A Primer on American Labor Law*. Cambridge, Mass.: MIT Press, 1982.

Leslie, Donald L. *QUX (Labor Law)*. St. Paul, Minn.: West, 1981.

Margaronis, Stan. *Stand Up: A Guide to Workers' Rights*. San Francisco: Public Media Center, 1982.

Player, Mack A. *Employment Discrimination Law*. St. Paul, Minn.: West, 1979.

Taylor, Benjamin J. and Fred Witney. *Labor Relations Law*. 4th ed. Englewood Cliff, N.J.: Prentice-Hall, 1983.

U.S. Government, *Code of Federal Regulations*, Title 29, chapter XIV. Washington, D.C., 1983.

Court Decisions

Grand Lodge of International Association of Machinists v. King, 335 F.2d 340 (9th Cir. 1964).

NLRB v. Bell Aerospace, 416 U.S. 267 (1974).

NLRB v. Dale Industries, Inc., 335 F.2d 851 (6th Cir. 1966).

NLRB v. Weingarten, 420 U.S. 251 (1975).

Salzhandler v. Caputo, 316 F.2d 445 (2d. Cir. 1963).

Appendix A
Legal Glossary

Note: For legal terms not listed in this glossary, the reader may refer to *Black's Law Dictionary* or *Cochran's Law Dictionary* in the reference section of most libraries.

adverse impact Disadvantage to members of the protected class due to a substantially different rate of selection in hiring, firing, promotion, or other employment decisions.

affidavit A written statement of facts, signed and sworn to before an official with the authority to administer oaths.

affirm To ratify or approve the judgment of a lower court or an administrative decision.

agent A person with the authority to do an act for another.

appeal A request or application to a higher court to set aside or modify the decision or ruling of a lower court.

appellant The party who initiates the appeal.

appellee The party to a lawsuit against whom an appeal is taken.

arbitration The submission of a dispute to the nonjudicial judgment of one or more disinterested persons, called arbitrators.

assign To transfer rights to another party, called the "assignee." The party who assigns the rights is called the "assignor."

bona fide In good faith, honestly, and without fraud.

bona fide occupational qualification (BFOQ) A good faith, honest, and without fraud preemployment qualification that is essential to establish the ability of the applicant to perform the necessary and required duties of the position in question. (For a discussion of this requirement, see chapter 1.)

book value The net worth of a business's assets, minus liabilities without considering any value for goodwill.

brief A prepared statement of a party's position in a legal proceeding.

burden of proof The duty of a party to present the evidence to establish that party's contentions or version of the facts. Failure to meet the burden of proof will result in a decision for the opposing party.

case law Judicial precedent set forth in prior court opinions that will bind parties in future lawsuits.

caveat A warning.

circumstantial evidence Evidence not directly proving the existence of a fact in question but tending to imply its existence.

Civil Rights Act of 1964 The civil rights act that forms the basis of most equal opportunity requirements. Title 42, U.S. Code, section 1447 et seq. (See chapter 4.)

civil service commissions Various groups of local, state, or federal officials which supervise public employees.

claimant A person who makes a claim for benefits.

Clayton Act The act that amended the Sherman Antitrust Act and that prohibits unlawful restraints on trade.

collective bargaining The bargaining between management and labor unions regarding the terms and conditions of employment.

commerce clause Article I, section VIII of the U.S. Constitution, which gives the U.S. Congress the authority to regulate trade between the states.

common law An ambiguous term used to describe the concept of law that relies on precedent (previous court opinions) and traditions.

compensatory damages The measure of actual damages or losses.

concurrent jurisdiction The authority of two or more courts to entertain a particular lawsuit.

consequential damages A measure of damages referring to the indirect injuries or losses that a party suffers.

defendant The party against whom a lawsuit is initiated.

de novo a new, fresh start.

deposition Oral questions and answers reduced to writing for possible use in a legal proceeding.

dictum Statement in a judicial opinion which is not necessary to support the decision in that case and therefore not considered as precedence.

Equal Employment Opportunity Commission (EEOC) A commission established under the Civil Rights Act of 1964 to administer the act. (See chapter 4.)

et seq Latin term meaning "and following parts."

Fair Labor Standards Act of 1938 An act designed to establish fair labor standards in employment involved in interstate commerce. (See chapter 4 and Title 29 U.S. Code, section 201 et seq.)

good faith An honest and fair purpose without the intent to commit an unjust act.

hearsay evidence Statements made by witnesses in legal proceedings regarding information obtained from a third person.

injunction A court order directing a party to refrain from certain activity.

interstate commerce Any trade, transportation, or communication among the several states or with the District of Columbia. Affecting interstate commerce means involved in, having an impact on, burdening, or obstructing it.

job analysis A detailed statement of work behaviors and other information relevant to a job.

job description A general statement of the duties and responsibilities entailed in a job.

jurisdiction The authority for a court or administrative body to hear and decide a dispute.

labor arbitration A nonjudicial settlement of disputes between labor and management. (See chapter 6.)

labor dispute Any dispute under a labor contract between the employer and the labor union concerning the terms, conditions, or tenure of employment or concerning the representation of persons in negotiating, maintaining, or changing the terms or conditions of employment.

Labor–Mangement Relations Act of 1947 (LMRA)   The Taft–Hartley Act, which amended the National Labor Relations Act, to provide additional facilities for mediation of labor disputes and place obligations on labor organizations similar to those earlier placed on management. (See chapter 6 and Title 29, U.S. Code, section 141 et seq.)

Labor–Management Reporting and Disclosure Act of 1959 (LMRDA)   An act designed to ensure democratic procedures in labor unions and establish a bill of rights for union members. (See chapter 6.)

labor organization   Any labor organization, committee, or group that is organized for the benefit of employees and subject to the provisions of the Civil Rights Act of 1964 or the federal labor management acts.

National Labor Relations Act of 1935 (NLRA)   The Wagner Act, which established the NLRB and designed to support unionism and collective bargaining. (See chapter 6.)

National Labor Relations Board (NLRB)   A commission established by the NLRA to enforce the rights of employees under the act. (See chapter 6.)

nationality   The status acquired by belonging or associated with a nation or state. It arises by birth or nationalization.

Norris–LaGuardia Act   An act passed by U.S. Congress in 1932 designed to stop federal courts from issuing injunctions in labor strikes. (See chapter 6 and Title 29, U.S. Code, sections 101–115.)

original jurisdiction   The court with the authority to first hear the case. The trial court.

plaintiff   The party who initiates a lawsuit.

pleadings   The formal written statements of parties to a lawsuit which establish the basis of each party's contentions before the court.

prejudice   A bias that interferes with a person's impartiality and sense of fairness.

right-to-work laws   State antiunion laws that prohibit labor contracts requiring all employees to join a union. (See chapter 6.)

Sherman Antitrust Act   An act, passed in 1890, designed to protect trade and commerce by prohibiting certain restraints of trade and monopolies. (See Title 15, U.S. Code, section 1 et seq.)

strike   An organized refusal to work by the employees that is designed to place economic pressure on the employer.

Taft–Hartley Act   See **Labor–Management Relations Act** and chapter 6.

total disability   A physical disability that prevents a person from performing all of the substantial acts necessary for the person's job or occupation.

Wagner Act   See **National Labor Relations Act** and chapter 6.

Appendix B
Directory of Government Offices

U.S. Department of Labor

200 Constitution Avenue, N.W., Washington, DC 20210
(202) 523–8165.

Regional Offices—U.S. Department of Labor

Region 1 (Connecticut, Maine, Massachusetts New Hampshire, Rhode Island, and Vermont)
JFK Federal Building
Boston, MA 02203
(617) 223–6767

Region 2 (New Jersey, New York, Puerto Rico, and Virgin Islands)
1515 Broadway
New York, NY 10036
(212) 944–3435

Region 3 (Delaware, District of Columbia, Maryland, Pennsylvania, Virginia, and West Virginia)
3535 Market Street
Philadelphia, PA 19101
(215) 596–1139

Region 4 (Alabama, Florida, Georgia, Kentucky, Mississippi, North Carolina, South Carolina, and Tennessee)
1371 Peachtree Street, N.E.
Atlanta, GA 30309
(404) 881–4495

Region 5 (Illinois, Indiana, Michigan, Minnesota, Ohio, and Wisconsin)
230 South Dearborn Avenue
Chicago, IL 60604
(312) 353–6976

Region 6 (Arkansas, Louisiana, New Mexico, Oklahoma, and Texas)
555 Griffin Square Building
Dallas, TX 75202
(214) 767–4776

Region 7 (Iowa, Kansas, Missouri, and Nebraska)
Federal Office Building
911 Walnut Street
Kansas City, MO 64106
(816) 374–5481

Region 8 (Colorado, Montana, North Dakota, South Dakota, Utah, and Wyoming)
Federal Office Building
1961 Stout Street
Denver, CO 80294
(303) 837–4234

Region 9 (Arizona, California, Hawaii, Nevada, and Guam)
Federal Office Building
450 Golden Gate Avenue
San Francisco, CA 94102
(415) 556–3423

Region 10 (Alaska, Idaho, Oregon, and Washington)
Federal Office Building
909 First Avenue
Seattle, WA 98174
(206) 442–7620

Regional Offices—Occupational Safety and Health Administration

Region 1: (Boston) 16–18 North Street, Boston MA 02109

Region 2: (New York) 1515 Broadway, New York, NY 10036

Region 3: (Philadelphia) 3535 Market Street, Philadelphia, PA 19104

Region 4: (Atlanta) 1375 Peachtree Street, N.E., Atlanta, GA 30309

Region 5: (Chicago) 230 South Dearborn, Chicago, IL 60604

Region 6: (Dallas) 555 Griffin Square Building, Dallas, TX 75202

Region 7: (Kansas City) 911 Walnut, Kansas City, MO 64106

Region 8: (Denver) 1961 Stout Street, Denver, CO 80294

Region 9: (San Francisco) 450 Golden Gate Avenue, San Francisco, CA 94102

Region 10: (Seattle) 909 First Avenue, Seattle, WA 98174

Equal Employment Opportunity Commission

2401 E Street, N.W., Washington, DC 20506
(202) 634–6930

National Labor Relations Board

1717 Pennsylvania Avenue, N.W., Washington, DC 20570
(202) 655–4000

Small Business Administration

1441 L Street, N.W., Washington, DC 20416
(202) 653–6365

Appendix C
Equal Employment Opportunity Commission's *Uniform Guidelines on Employee Selection*

(3) Relationship to the Job
(4) Use of Construct Validity Study Without New Criterion-Related Evidence
  (a) Standards for Use
  (b) Determination of Common Work Behaviors

DOCUMENTATION OF IMPACT AND VALIDITY EVIDENCE

1607.15. Documentation of Impact and Validity Evidence
A. Required Information
  (1) Simplified Recordkeeping for Users With Less Than 100 Employees
  (2) Information on Impact
    (a) Collection of Information on Impact
    (b) When Adverse Impact Has Been Eliminated in The Total Selection Process
    (c) When Data Insufficient to Determine Impact
  (3) Documentation of Validity Evidence
    (a) Type of Evidence
    (b) Form of Report
    (c) Completeness
B. Criterion-Related Validity Studies
  (1) User(s), Location(s), and Date(s) of Study
  (2) Problem and Setting
  (3) Job Analysis or Review of Job Information
  (4) Job Titles and Codes
  (5) Criterion Measures
  (6) Sample Description
  (7) Description of Selection Procedure
  (8) Techniques and Results
  (9) Alternative Procedures Investigated
  (10) Uses and Applications
  (11) Source Data
  (12) Contact Person
  (13) Accuracy and Completeness
C. Content Validity Studies
  (1) User(s), Location(s), and Date(s) of Study
  (2) Problem and Setting
  (3) Job Analysis—Content of the Job
  (4) Selection Procedure and Its Content
  (5) Relationship Between Selection Procedure and the Job
  (6) Alternative Procedures Investigated
  (7) Uses and Applications
  (8) Contact Person
  (9) Accuracy and Completeness
D. Construct Validity Studies
  (1) User(s), Location(s), and Date(s) of Study
  (2) Problem and Setting
  (3) Construct Definition
  (4) Job Analysis
  (5) Job Titles and Codes
  (6) Selection Procedure
  (7) Relationship to Job Performance
  (8) Alternative Procedures Investigated
  (9) Uses and Applications
  (10) Accuracy and Completeness
  (11) Source Data

  (12) Contact Person
E. Evidence of Validity from Other Studies
  (1) Evidence from Criterion-Related Validity Studies
    (a) Job Information
    (b) Relevance of Criteria
    (c) Other Variables
    (d) Use of the Selection Procedure
    (e) Bibliography
  (2) Evidence from Content Validity Studies
  (3) Evidence from Construct Validity Studies
F. Evidence of Validity from Cooperative Studies
G. Selection for Higher Level Jobs
H. Interim Use of Selection Procedures

DEFINITIONS

1607.16. Definitions

APPENDIX

1607.17. Policy Statement on Affirmative Action (see Section 13B)
1607.18. Citations

AUTHORITY: Secs. 709 and 713, Civil Rights Act of 1964 (78 Stat. 265) as amended by the Equal Employment Opportunity Act of 1972 (Pub. L. 92-261); 42 U.S.C. 2000e-8, 2000e-12.

SOURCE: 43 FR 38295 and 43 FR 38312, Aug. 25, 1978, unless otherwise noted.

GENERAL PRINCIPLES

§ 1607.1 Statement of purpose.

A. *Need for uniformity—Issuing agencies.* The Federal government's need for a uniform set of principles on the question of the use of tests and other selection procedures has long been recognized. The Equal Employment Opportunity Commission, the Civil Service Commission, the Department of Labor, and the Department of Justice jointly have adopted these uniform guidelines to meet that need, and to apply the same principles to the Federal Government as are applied to other employers.

B. *Purpose of guidelines.* These guidelines incorporate a single set of principles which are designed to assist employers, labor organizations, employment agencies, and licensing and certification boards to comply with requirements of Federal law prohibiting employment practices which discriminate on grounds of race, color, religion, sex, and national origin. They are designed to provide a framework for determining the proper use of tests and other selection procedures. These guidelines do not require a user to conduct validity studies of selection procedures where no adverse impact results. However, all users are encouraged to use selection procedures which are valid, especially users operating under merit principles.

C. *Relation to prior guidelines.* These guidelines are based upon and supersede previously issued guidelines on employee selection procedures. These guidelines have been built upon court decisions, the previously issued guidelines of the agencies, and the practical experience of the agencies, as well as the standards of the psychological profession. These guidelines are intended to be consistent with existing law.

§ 1607.2 Scope.

A. *Application of guidelines.* These guidelines will be applied by the Equal Employment Opportunity Commission in the enforcement of title VII of the Civil Rights Act of 1964, as amended by the Equal Employment Opportunity Act of 1972 (hereinafter "Title VII"); by the Department of Labor, and the contract compliance agencies until the transfer of authority contemplated by the President's Reorganization Plan No. 1 of 1978, in the administration and enforcement of Executive Order 11246, as amended by Executive Order 11375 (hereinafter "Executive Order 11246"); by the Civil Service Commission and other Federal agencies subject to section 717 of Title VII; by the Civil Service Commission in exercising its responsibilities toward State and local governments under section 208(b)(1) of the Intergovernmental-Personnel Act; by the Department of Justice in exercising its responsibilities under Federal law; by the Office of Revenue Sharing of the Department of the Treasury under the State and Local Fiscal Assistance Act of 1972, as amended; and by any other Federal agency which adopts them.

B. *Employment decisions.* These guidelines apply to tests and other selection procedures which are used as a basis for any employment decision.

Employment decisions include but are not limited to hiring, promotion, demotion, membership (for example, in a labor organization), referral, retention, and licensing and certification, to the extent that licensing and certification may be covered by Federal equal employment opportunity law. Other selection decisions, such as selection for training or transfer, may also be considered employment decisions if they lead to any of the decisions listed above.

C. *Selection procedures.* These guidelines apply only to selection procedures which are used as a basis for making employment decisions. For example, the use of recruiting procedures designed to attract members of a particular race, sex, or ethnic group, which were previously denied employment opportunities or which are currently underutilized, may be necessary to bring an employer into compliance with Federal law, and is frequently an essential element of any effective affirmative action program; but recruitment practices are not considered by these guidelines to be selection procedures. Similarly, these guidelines do not pertain to the question of the lawfulness of a seniority system within the meaning of section 703(h), Executive Order 11246 or other provisions of Federal law or regulation, except to the extent that such systems utilize selection procedures to determine qualifications or abilities to perform the job. Nothing in these guidelines is intended or should be interpreted as discouraging the use of a selection procedure for the purpose of determining qualifications or for the purpose of selection on the basis of relative qualifications, if the selection procedure had been validated in accord with these guidelines for each such purpose for which it is to be used.

D. *Limitations.* These guidelines apply only to persons subject to Title VII, Executive Order 11246, or other equal employment opportunity requirements of Federal law. These guidelines do not apply to responsibilities under the Age Discrimination in Employment Act of 1967, as amended, not to discriminate on the basis of age, or under sections 501, 503, and 504 of the Rehabilitation Act of 1973, not to discriminate on the basis of handicap.

E. *Indian preference not affected.* These guidelines do not restrict any obligation imposed or right granted by Federal law to users to extend a preference in employment to Indians living on or near an Indian reservation in connection with employment opportunities on or near an Indian reservation.

§ 1607.3 Discrimination defined: Relationship between use of selection procedures and discrimination.

A. *Procedure having adverse impact constitutes discrimination unless justified.* The use of any selection procedure which has an adverse impact on the hiring, promotion, or other employment or membership opportunities of members of any race, sex, or ethnic group will be considered to be discriminatory and inconsistent with these guidelines, unless the procedure has been validated in accordance with these guidelines, or the provisions of section 6 below are satisfied.

B. *Consideration of suitable alternative selection procedures.* Where two or more selection procedures are available which serve the user's legitimate interest in efficient and trustworthy workmanship, and which are substantially equally valid for a given purpose, the user should use the procedure which has been demonstrated to have the lesser adverse impact. Accordingly, whenever a validity study is called for by these guidelines, the user should include, as a part of the validity study, an investigation of suitable alternative selection procedures and suitable alternative methods of using the selection procedure which have as little adverse impact as possible, to determine the appropriateness of using or validating them in accord with these guidelines. If a user has made a reasonable effort to become aware of such alternative procedures and validity has been demonstrated in accord with these guidelines, the use of the test or other selection procedure may continue until such time as it should reasonably be reviewed for currency. Whenever the user is shown an alternative selection procedure with evidence of less adverse impact and sub-

stantial evidence of validity for the same job in similar circumstances, the user should investigate it to determine the appropriateness of using or validating it in accord with these guidelines. This subsection is not intended to preclude the combination of procedures into a significantly more valid procedure, if the use of such a combination has been shown to be in compliance with the guidelines.

§ 1607.4 Information on impact.

A. *Records concerning impact.* Each user should maintain and have available for inspection records or other information which will disclose the impact which its tests and other selection procedures have upon employment opportunities of persons by identifiable race, sex, or ethnic group as set forth in subparagraph B below in order to determine compliance with these guidelines. Where there are large numbers of applicants and procedures are administered frequently, such information may be retained on a sample basis, provided that the sample is appropriate in terms of the applicant population and adequate in size.

B. *Applicable race, sex, and ethnic groups for recordkeeping.* The records called for by this section are to be maintained by sex, and the following races and ethnic groups: Blacks (Negroes), American Indians (including Alaskan Natives), Asians (including Pacific Islanders), Hispanic (including persons of Mexican, Puerto Rican, Cuban, Central or South American, or other Spanish origin or culture regardless of race), whites (Caucasians) other than Hispanic, and totals. The race, sex, and ethnic classifications called for by this section are consistent with the Equal Employment Opportunity Standard Form 100, Employer Information Report EEO-1 series of reports. The user should adopt safeguards to insure that the records required by this paragraph are used for appropriate purposes such as determining adverse impact, or (where required) for developing and monitoring affirmative action programs, and that such records are not used improperly. See sections 4E and 17(4), below.

C. *Evaluation of selection rates. The "bottom line."* If the information called for by sections 4A and B above shows that the total selection process for a job has an adverse impact, the individual components of the selection process should be evaluated for adverse impact. If this information shows that the total selection process does not have an adverse impact, the Federal enforcement agencies, in the exercise of their administrative and prosecutorial discretion, in usual circumstances, will not expect a user to evaluate the individual components for adverse impact, or to validate such individual components, and will not take enforcement action based upon adverse impact of any component of that process, including the separate parts of a multipart selection procedure or any separate procedure that is used as an alternative method of selection. However, in the following circumstances the Federal enforcement agencies will expect a user to evaluate the individual components for adverse impact and may, where appropriate, take enforcement action with respect to the individual components: (1) Where the selection procedure is a significant factor in the continuation of patterns of assignments of incumbent employees caused by prior discriminatory employment practices, (2) where the weight of court decisions or administrative interpretations hold that a specific procedure (such as height or weight requirements or no-arrest records) is not job related in the same or similar circumstances. In unusual circumstances, other than those listed in (1) and (2) above, the Federal enforcement agencies may request a user to evaluate the individual components for adverse impact and may, where appropriate, take enforcement action with respect to the individual component.

D. *Adverse impact and the "four-fifths rule."* A selection rate for any race, sex, or ethnic group which is less than four-fifths (⅘) (or eighty percent) of the rate for the group with the highest rate will generally be regarded by the Federal enforcement agencies as evidence of adverse impact, while a greater than four-fifths rate will generally not be regarded by Fed- eral enforcement agencies as evidence of adverse impact. Smaller differences in selection rate may nevertheless constitute adverse impact, where they are significant in both statistical and practical terms or where a user's actions have discouraged applicants disproportionately on grounds of race, sex, or ethnic group. Greater differences in selection rate may not constitute adverse impact where the differences are based on small numbers and are not statistically significant, or where special recruiting or other programs cause the pool of minority or female candidates to be atypical of the normal pool of applicants from that group. Where the user's evidence concerning the impact of a selection procedure indicates adverse impact but is based upon numbers which are too small to be reliable, evidence concerning the impact of the procedure over a longer period of time and/or evidence concerning the impact which the selection procedure had when used in the same manner in similar circumstances elsewhere may be considered in determining adverse impact. Where the user has not maintained data on adverse impact as required by the documentation section of applicable guidelines, the Federal enforcement agencies may draw an inference of adverse impact of the selection process from the failure of the user to maintain such data, if the user has an underutilization of a group in the job category, as compared to the group's representation in the relevant labor market or, in the case of jobs filled from within, the applicable work force.

E. *Consideration of user's equal employment opportunity posture.* In carrying out their obligations, the Federal enforcement agencies will consider the general posture of the user with respect to equal employment opportunity for the job or group of jobs in question. Where a user has adopted an affirmative action program, the Federal enforcement agencies will consider the provisions of that program, including the goals and timetables which the user has adopted and the progress which the user has made in carrying out that program and in meeting the goals and timetables. While such affirmative action programs may in design and execution be race, color, sex, or ethnic conscious, selection procedures under such programs should be based upon the ability or relative ability to do the work.

(Approved by the Office of Management and Budget under control number 3046-0017)

(Pub. L. No. 96-511, 94 Stat. 2812 (44 U.S.C. 3501 et seq.))

[43 FR 38295, 38312, Aug. 25, 1978, as amended at 46 FR 63268, Dec. 31, 1981]

§ 1607.5 General standards for validity studies.

A. *Acceptable types of validity studies.* For the purposes of satisfying these guidelines, users may rely upon criterion-related validity studies, content validity studies or construct validity studies, in accordance with the standards set forth in the technical standards of these guidelines, section 14 below. New strategies for showing the validity of selection procedures will be evaluated as they become accepted by the psychological profession.

B. *Criterion-related, content, and construct validity.* Evidence of the validity of a test or other selection procedure by a criterion-related validity study should consist of empirical data demonstrating that the selection procedure is predictive of or significantly correlated with important elements of job performance. See section 14B below. Evidence of the validity of a test or other selection procedure by a content validity study should consist of data showing that the content of the selection procedure is representative of important aspects of performance on the job for which the candidates are to be evaluated. See 14C below. Evidence of the validity of a test or other selection procedure through a construct validity study should consist of data showing that the procedure measures the degree to which candidates have identifiable characteristics which have been determined to be important in successful performance in the job for which the candidates are to be evaluated. See section 14D below.

C. *Guidelines are consistent with professional standards.* The provisions of these guidelines relating to valida-

tion of selection procedures are intended to be consistent with generally accepted professional standards for evaluating standardized tests and other selection procedures, such as those described in the Standards for Educational and Psychological Tests prepared by a joint committee of the American Psychological Association, the American Educational Research Association, and the National Council on Measurement in Education (American Psychological Association, Washington, D.C., 1974) (hereinafter "A.P.A. Standards") and standard textbooks and journals in the field of personnel selection.

D. *Need for documentation of validity.* For any selection procedure which is part of a selection process which has an adverse impact and which selection procedure has an adverse impact, each user should maintain and have available such documentation as is described in section 15 below.

E. *Accuracy and standardization.* Validity studies should be carried out under conditions which assure insofar as possible the adequacy and accuracy of the research and the report. Selection procedures should be administered and scored under standardized conditions.

F. *Caution against selection on basis of knowledges, skills, or ability learned in brief orientation period.* In general, users should avoid making employment decisions on the basis of measures of knowledges, skills, or abilities which are normally learned in a brief orientation period, and which have an adverse impact.

G. *Method of use of selection procedures.* The evidence of both the validity and utility of a selection procedure should support the method the user chooses for operational use of the procedure, if that method of use has a greater adverse impact than another method of use. Evidence which may be sufficient to support the use of a selection procedure on a pass/fail (screening) basis may be insufficient to support the use of the same procedure on a ranking basis under these guidelines. Thus, if a user decides to use a selection procedure on a ranking basis, and that method of use has a greater adverse impact than use on an appropriate pass/fail basis (see section 5H below), the user should have sufficient evidence of validity and utility to support the use on a ranking basis. See sections 3B, 14B (5) and (6), and 14C (8) and (9).

H. *Cutoff scores.* Where cutoff scores are used, they should normally be set so as to be reasonable and consistent with normal expectations of acceptable proficiency within the work force. Where applicants are ranked on the basis of properly validated selection procedures and those applicants scoring below a higher cutoff score than appropriate in light of such expectations have little or no chance of being selected for employment, the higher cutoff score may be appropriate, but the degree of adverse impact should be considered.

I. *Use of selection procedures for higher level jobs.* If job progression structures are so established that employees will probably, within a reasonable period of time and in a majority of cases, progress to a higher level, it may be considered that the applicants are being evaluated for a job or jobs at the higher level. However, where job progression is not so nearly automatic, or the time span is such that higher level jobs or employees' potential may be expected to change in significant ways, it should be considered that applicants are being evaluated for a job at or near the entry level. A "reasonable period of time" will vary for different jobs and employment situations but will seldom be more than 5 years. Use of selection procedures to evaluate applicants for a higher level job would not be appropriate:

(1) If the majority of those remaining employed do not progress to the higher level job;

(2) If there is a reason to doubt that the higher level job will continue to require essentially similar skills during the progression period; or

(3) If the selection procedures measure knowledges, skills, or abilities required for advancement which would be expected to develop principally from the training or experience on the job.

J. *Interim use of selection procedures.* Users may continue the use of a selection procedure which is not at the moment fully supported by the required evidence of validity, provided: (1) The user has available substantial evidence of validity, and (2) the user has in progress, when technically feasible, a study which is designed to produce the additional evidence required by these guidelines within a reasonable time. If such a study is not technically feasible, see section 6B. If the study does not demonstrate validity, this provision of these guidelines for interim use shall not constitute a defense in any action, nor shall it relieve the user of any obligations arising under Federal law.

K. *Review of validity studies for currency.* Whenever validity has been shown in accord with these guidelines for the use of a particular selection procedure for a job or group of jobs, additional studies need not be performed until such time as the validity study is subject to review as provided in section 3B above. There are no absolutes in the area of determining the currency of a validity study. All circumstances concerning the study, including the validation strategy used, and changes in the relevant labor market and the job should be considered in the determination of when a validity study is outdated.

§ 1607.6 Use of selection procedures which have not been validated.

A. *Use of alternate selection procedures to eliminate adverse impact.* A user may choose to utilize alternative selection procedures in order to eliminate adverse impact or as part of an affirmative action program. See section 13 below. Such alternative procedures should eliminate the adverse impact in the total selection process, should be lawful and should be as job related as possible.

B. *Where validity studies cannot or need not be performed.* There are circumstances in which a user cannot or need not utilize the validation techniques contemplated by these guidelines. In such circumstances, the user should utilize selection procedures which are as job related as possible and which will minimize or eliminate adverse impact, as set forth below.

(1) *Where informal or unscored procedures are used.* When an informal or unscored selection procedure which has an adverse impact is utilized, the user should eliminate the adverse impact, or modify the procedure to one which is a formal, scored or quantified measure or combination of measures and then validate the procedure in accord with these guidelines, or otherwise justify continued use of the procedure in accord with Federal law.

(2) *Where formal and scored procedures are used.* When a formal and scored selection procedure is used which has an adverse impact, the validation techniques contemplated by these guidelines usually should be followed if technically feasible. Where the user cannot or need not follow the validation techniques anticipated by these guidelines, the user should either modify the procedure to eliminate adverse impact or otherwise justify continued use of the procedure in accord with Federal law.

§ 1607.7 Use of other validity studies.

A. *Validity studies not conducted by the user.* Users may, under certain circumstances, support the use of selection procedures by validity studies conducted by other users or conducted by test publishers or distributors and described in test manuals. While publishers of selection procedures have a professional obligation to provide evidence of validity which meets generally accepted professional standards (see section 5C above), users are cautioned that they are responsible for compliance with these guidelines. Accordingly, users seeking to obtain selection procedures from publishers and distributors should be careful to determine that, in the event the user becomes subject to the validity requirements of these guidelines, the necessary information to support validity has been determined and will be made available to the user.

B. *Use of criterion-related validity evidence from other sources.* Criterion-related validity studies conducted by one test user, or described in test manuals and the professional literature, will be considered acceptable for use by another user when the following requirements are met:

(1) *Validity evidence.* Evidence from the available studies meeting the standards of section 14B below clearly demonstrates that the selection procedure is valid;

(2) *Job similarity.* The incumbents in the user's job and the incumbents in the job or group of jobs on which the validity study was conducted perform substantially the same major work behaviors, as shown by appropriate job analyses both on the job or group of jobs on which the validity study was performed and on the job for which the selection procedure is to be used; and

(3) *Fairness evidence.* The studies include a study of test fairness for each race, sex, and ethnic group which constitutes a significant factor in the borrowing user's relevant labor market for the job or jobs in question. If the studies under consideration satisfy (1) and (2) above but do not contain an investigation of test fairness, and it is not technically feasible for the borrowing user to conduct an internal study of test fairness, the borrowing user may utilize the study until studies conducted elsewhere meeting the requirements of these guidelines show test unfairness, or until such time as it becomes technically feasible to conduct an internal study of test fairness and the results of that study can be acted upon. Users obtaining selection procedures from publishers should consider, as one factor in the decision to purchase a particular selection procedure, the availability of evidence concerning test fairness.

C. *Validity evidence from multiunit study.* If validity evidence from a study covering more than one unit within an organization statisfies the requirements of section 14B below, evidence of validity specific to each unit will not be required unless there are variables which are likely to affect validity significantly.

D. *Other significant variables.* If there are variables in the other studies which are likely to affect validity significantly, the user may not rely upon such studies, but will be expected either to conduct an internal validity study or to comply with section 6 above.

§ 1607.8 Cooperative studies.

A. *Encouragement of cooperative studies.* The agencies issuing these guidelines encourage employers, labor organizations, and employment agencies to cooperate in research, development, search for lawful alternatives, and validity studies in order to achieve procedures which are consistent with these guidelines.

B. *Standards for use of cooperative studies.* If validity evidence from a cooperative study satisfies the requirements of section 14 below, evidence of validity specific to each user will not be required unless there are variables in the user's situation which are likely to affect validity significantly.

§ 1607.9 No assumption of validity.

A. *Unacceptable substitutes for evidence of validity.* Under no circumstances will the general reputation of a test or other selection procedures, its author or its publisher, or casual reports of it's validity be accepted in lieu of evidence of validity. Specifically ruled out are: assumptions of validity based on a procedure's name or descriptive labels; all forms of promotional literature; data bearing on the frequency of a procedure's usage; testimonial statements and credentials of sellers, users, or consultants; and other nonempirical or anecdotal accounts of selection practices or selection outcomes.

B. *Encouragement of professional supervision.* Professional supervision of selection activities is encouraged but is not a substitute for documented evidence of validity. The enforcement agencies will take into account the fact that a thorough job analysis was conducted and that careful development and use of a selection procedure in accordance with professional standards enhance the probability that the selection procedure is valid for the job.

§ 1607.10 Employment agencies and employment services.

A. *Where selection procedures are devised by agency.* An employment agency, including private employment agencies and State employment agencies, which agrees to a request by an employer or labor organization to device and utilize a selection procedure should follow the standards in these guidelines for determining adverse impact. If adverse impact exists the agency should comply with these guidelines. An employment agency is not relieved of its obligation herein because the user did not request such validation or has requested the use of some lesser standard of validation than is provided in these guidelines. The use of an employment agency does not relieve an employer or labor organization or other user of its responsibilities under Federal law to provide equal employment opportunity or its obligations as a user under these guidelines.

B. *Where selection procedures are devised elsewhere.* Where an employment agency or service is requested to administer a selection procedure which has been devised elsewhere and to make referrals pursuant to the results, the employment agency or service should maintain and have available evidence of the impact of the selection and referral procedures which it administers. If adverse impact results the agency or service should comply with these guidelines. If the agency or service seeks to comply with these guidelines by reliance upon validity studies or other data in the possession of the employer, it should obtain and have available such information.

§ 1607.11 Disparate treatment.

The principles of disparate or unequal treatment must be distinguished from the concepts of validation. A selection procedure—even though validated against job performance in accordance with these guidelines—cannot be imposed upon members of a race, sex, or ethnic group where other employees, applicants, or members have not been subjected to that standard. Disparate treatment occurs where members of a race, sex, or ethnic group have been denied the same employment, promotion, membership, or other employment opportunities as have been available to other employees or applicants. Those employees or applicants who have been denied equal treatment, because of prior discriminatory practices or policies, must at least be afforded the same opportunities as had existed for other employees or applicants during the period of discrimination. Thus, the persons who were in the class of persons discriminated against during the period the user followed the discriminatory practices should be allowed the opportunity to qualify under less stringent selection procedures previously followed, unless the user demonstrates that the increased standards are required by business necessity. This section does not prohibit a user who has not previously followed merit standards from adopting merit standards which are in compliance with these guidelines; nor does it preclude a user who has previously used invalid or unvalidated selection procedures from developing and using procedures which are in accord with these guidelines.

§ 1607.12 Retesting of applicants.

Users should provide a reasonable opportunity for retesting and reconsideration. Where examinations are administered periodically with public notice, such reasonable opportunity exists, unless persons who have previously been tested are precluded from retesting. The user may however take reasonable steps to preserve the security of its procedures.

§ 1607.13 Affirmative action.

A. Affirmative action obligations. The use of selection procedures which have been validated pursuant to these guidelines does not relieve users of any obligations they may have to undertake affirmative action to assure equal employment opportunity. Nothing in these guidelines is intended to preclude the use of lawful selection procedures which assist in remedying the effects of prior discriminatory practices, or the achievement of affirmative action objectives.

B. *Encouragement of voluntary affirmative action programs.* These guidelines are also intended to encourage the adoption and implementation of voluntary affirmative action programs by users who have no obligation under Federal law to adopt them; but are not intended to impose any new

obligations in that regard. The agencies issuing and endorsing these guidelines endorse for all private employers and reaffirm for all governmental employers the Equal Employment Opportunity Coordinating Council's "Policy Statement on Affirmative Action Programs for State and Local Government Agencies" (41 FR 38814, September 13, 1976). That policy statement is attached hereto as appendix, section 17.

TECHNICAL STANDARDS

§ 1607.14 Technical standards for validity studies.

The following minimum standards, as applicable, should be met in conducting a validity study. Nothing in these guidelines is intended to preclude the development and use of other professionally acceptable techniques with respect to validation of selection procedures. Where it is not technically feasible for a user to conduct a validity study, the user has the obligation otherwise to comply with these guidelines. See sections 6 and 7 above.

A. *Validity studies should be based on review of information about the job.* Any validity study should be based upon a review of information about the job for which the selection procedure is to be used. The review should include a job analysis except as provided in section 14B(3) below with respect to criterion-related validity. Any method of job analysis may be used if it provides the information required for the specific validation strategy used.

B. *Technical standards for criterion-related validity studies.* (1) *Technical feasibility.* Users choosing to validate a selection procedure by a criterion-related validity strategy should determine whether it is technically feasible (as defined in section 16) to conduct such a study in the particular employment context. The determination of the number of persons necessary to permit the conduct of a meaningful criterion-related study should be made by the user on the basis of all relevant information concerning the selection procedure, the potential sample and the employment situation. Where ap-

Chapter XIV—Equal Employment Opportunity Comm. § 1607.14

propriate, jobs with substantially the same major work behaviors may be grouped together for validity studies, in order to obtain an adequate sample. These guidelines do not require a user to hire or promote persons for the purpose of making it possible to conduct a criterion-related study.

(2) *Analysis of the job.* There should be a review of job information to determine measures of work behavior(s) or performance that are relevant to the job or group of jobs in question. These measures or criteria are relevant to the extent that they represent critical or important job duties, work behaviors or work outcomes as developed from the review of job information. The possibility of bias should be considered both in selection of the criterion measures and their application. In view of the possibility of bias in subjective evaluations, supervisory rating techniques and instructions to raters should be carefully developed. All criterion measures and the methods for gathering data need to be examined for freedom from factors which would unfairly alter scores of members of any group. The relevance of criteria and their freedom from bias are of particular concern when there are significant differences in measures of job performance for different groups.

(3) *Criterion measures.* Proper safeguards should be taken to insure that scores on selection procedures do not enter into any judgments of employee adequacy that are to be used as criterion measures. Whatever criteria are used should represent important or critical work behavior(s) or work outcomes. Certain criteria may be used without a full job analysis if the user can show the importance of the criteria to the particular employment context. These criteria include but are not limited to production rate, error rate, tardiness, absenteeism, and length of service. A standardized rating of overall work performance may be used where a study of the job shows that it is an appropriate criterion. Where performance in training is used as a criterion, success in training should be properly measured and the relevance of the training should be shown either through a comparsion of the content

of the training program with the critical or important work behavior(s) of the job(s), or through a demonstration of the relationship between measures of performance in training and measures of job performance. Measures of relative success in training include but are not limited to instructor evaluations, performance samples, or tests. Criterion measures consisting of paper and pencil tests will be closely reviewed for job relevance.

(4) *Representativeness of the sample.* Whether the study is predictive or concurrent, the sample subjects should insofar as feasible be representative of the candidates normally available in the relevant labor market for the job or group of jobs in question, and should insofar as feasible include the races, sexes, and ethnic groups normally available in the relevant job market. In determining the representativeness of the sample in a concurrent validity study, the user should take into account the extent to which the specific knowledges or skills which are the primary focus of the test are those which employees learn on the job.

Where samples are combined or compared, attention should be given to see that such samples are comparable in terms of the actual job they perform, the length of time on the job where time on the job is likely to affect performance, and other relevant factors likely to affect validity differences; or that these factors are included in the design of the study and their effects identified.

(5) *Statistical relationships.* The degree of relationship between selection procedure scores and criterion measures should be examined and computed, using professionally acceptable statistical procedures. Generally, a selection procedure is considered related to the criterion, for the purposes of these guidelines, when the relationship between performance on the procedure and performance on the criterion measure is statistically significant at the 0.05 level of significance, which means that it is sufficiently high as to have a probability of no more than one (1) in twenty (20) to have occurred by chance. Absence of a statistically significant relationship between a se-

lection procedure and job performance should not necessarily discourage other investigations of the validity of that selection procedure.

(6) *Operational use of selection procedures.* Users should evaluate each selection procedure to assure that it is appropriate for operational use, including establishment of cutoff scores or rank ordering. Generally, if other factors reman the same, the greater the magnitude of the relationship (e.g., correlation coefficent) between performance on a selection procedure and one or more criteria of performance on the job, and the greater the importance and number of aspects of job performance covered by the criteria, the more likely it is that the procedure will be appropriate for use. Reliance upon a selection procedure which is significantly related to a criterion measure, but which is based upon a study involving a large number of subjects and has a low correlation coefficient will be subject to close review if it has a large adverse impact. Sole reliance upon a single selection instrument which is related to only one of many job duties or aspects of job performance will also be subject to close review. The appropriateness of a selection procedure is best evaluated in each particular situation and there are no minimum correlation coefficients applicable to all employment situations. In determining whether a selection procedure is appropriate for operational use the following considerations should also be taken into account: The degree of adverse impact of the procedure, the availability of other selection procedures of greater or substantially equal validity.

(7) *Overstatement of validity findings.* Users should avoid reliance upon techniques which tend to overestimate validity findings as a result of capitalization on chance unless an appropriate safeguard is taken. Reliance upon a few selection procedures or criteria of successful job performance when many selection procedures or criteria of performance have been studied, or the use of optimal statistical weights for selection procedures computed in one sample, are techniques which tend to inflate validity estimates as a result

of chance. Use of a large sample is one safeguard: cross-validation is another.

(8) *Fairness.* This section generally calls for studies of unfairness where technically feasible. The concept of fairness or unfairness of selection procedures is a developing concept. In addition, fairness studies generally require substantial numbers of employees in the job or group of jobs being studied. For these reasons, the Federal enforcement agencies recognize that the obligation to conduct studies of fairness imposed by the guidelines generally will be upon users or groups of users with a large number of persons in a a job class, or test developers; and that small users utilizing their own selection procedures will generally not be obligated to conduct such studies because it will be technically infeasible for them to do so.

(a) *Unfairness defined.* When members of one race, sex, or ethnic group characteristically obtain lower scores on a selection procedure than members of another group, and the differences in scores are not reflected in differences in a measure of job performance, use of the selection procedure may unfairly deny opportunities to members of the group that obtains the lower scores.

(b) *Investigation of fairness.* Where a selection procedure results in an adverse impact on a race, sex, or ethnic group identified in accordance with the classifications set forth in section 4 above and that group is a significant factor in the relevant labor market, the user generally should investigate the possible existence of unfairness for that group if it is technically feasible to do so. The greater the severity of the adverse impact on a group, the greater the need to investigate the possible existence of unfairness. Where the weight of evidence from other studies shows that the selection procedure predicts fairly for the group in question and for the same or similar jobs, such evidence may be relied on in connection with the selection procedure at issue.

(c) *General considerations in fairness investigations.* Users conducting a study of fairness should review the A.P.A. Standards regarding investigation of possible bias in testing. An investigation of fairness of a selection procedure depends on both evidence of validity and the manner in which the selection procedure is to be used in a particular employment context. Fairness of a selection procedure cannot necessarily be specified in advance without investigating these factors. Investigation of fairness of a selection procedure in samples where the range of scores on selection procedures or criterion measures is severely restricted for any subgroup sample (as compared to other subgroup samples) may produce misleading evidence of unfairness. That factor should accordingly be taken into account in conducting such studies and before reliance is placed on the results.

(d) *When unfairness is shown.* If unfairness is demonstrated through a showing that members of a particular group perform better or poorer on the job than their scores on the selection procedure would indicate through comparison with how members of other groups perform, the user may either revise or replace the selection instrument in accordance with these guidelines, or may continue to use the selection instrument operationally with appropriate revisions in its use to assure compatibility between the probability of successful job performance and the probability of being selected.

(e) *Technical feasibility of fairness studies.* In addition to the general conditions needed for technical feasibility for the conduct of a criterion-related study (see section 16, below) an investigation of fairness requires the following:

(i) An adequate sample of persons in each group available for the study to achieve findings of statistical significance. Guidelines do not require a user to hire or promote persons on the basis of group classifications for the purpose of making it possible to conduct a study of fairness; but the user has the obligation otherwise to comply with these guidelines.

(ii) The samples for each group should be comparable in terms of the actual job they perform, length of time on the job where time on the job is likely to affect performance, and other relevant factors likely to affect validity differences; or such factors

should be included in the design of the study and their effects identified.

(f) *Continued use of selection procedures when fairness studies not feasible.* If a study of fairness should otherwise be performed, but is not technically feasible, a selection procedure may be used which has otherwise met the validity standards of these guidelines, unless the technical infeasibility resulted from discriminatory employment practices which are demonstrated by facts other than past failure to conform with requirements for validation of selection procedures. However, when it becomes technically feasible for the user to perform a study of fairness and such a study is otherwise called for, the user should conduct the study of fairness.

C. *Technical standards for content validity studies—(1) Appropriateness of content validity studies.* Users choosing to validate a selection procedure by a content validity strategy should determine whether it is appropriate to conduct such a study in the particular employment context. A selection procedure can be supported by a content validity strategy to the extent that it is a representative sample of the content of the job. Selection procedures which purport to measure knowledges, skills, or abilities may in certain circumstances be justified by content validity, although they may not be representative samples, if the knowledge, skill, or ability measured by the selection procedure can be operationally defined as provided in section 14C(4) below, and if that knowledge, skill, or ability is a necessary prerequisite to successful job performance.

A selection procedure based upon inferences about mental processes cannot be supported solely or primarily on the basis of content validity. Thus, a content strategy is not appropriate for demonstrating the validity of selection procedures which purport to measure traits or constructs, such as intelligence, aptitude, personality, commonsense, judgment, leadership, and spatial ability. Content validity is also not an appropriate strategy when the selection procedure involves knowledges, skills, or abilities which an employee will be expected to learn on the job.

(2) *Job analysis for content validity.* There should be a job analysis which includes an analysis of the important work behavior(s) required for successful performance and their relative importance and, if the behavior results in work product(s), an analysis of the work product(s). Any job analysis should focus on the work behavior(s) and the tasks associated with them. If work behavior(s) are not observable, the job analysis should identify and analyze those aspects of the behavior(s) that can be observed and the observed work products. The work behavior(s) selected for measurement should be critical work behavior(s) and/or important work behavior(s) constituting most of the job.

(3) *Development of selection procedures.* A selection procedure designed to measure the work behavior may be developed specifically from the job and job analysis in question, or may have been previously developed by the user, or by other users or by a test publisher.

(4) *Standards for demonstrating content validity.* To demonstrate the content validity of a selection procedure, a user should show that the behavior(s) demonstrated in the selection procedure are a representative sample of the behavior(s) of the job in question or that the selection procedure provides a representative sample of the work product of the job. In the case of a selection procedure measuring a knowledge, skill, or ability, the knowledge, skill, or ability being measured should be operationally defined. In the case of a selection procedure measuring a knowledge, the knowledge being measured should be operationally defined as that body of learned information which is used in and is a necessary prerequisite for observable aspects of work behavior of the job. In the case of skills or abilities, the skill or ability being measured should be operationally defined in terms of observable aspects of work behavior of the job. For any selection procedure measuring a knowledge, skill, or ability the user should show that (a) the selection procedure measures and is a representative sample of that knowl-

edge, skill, or ability; and (b) that knowledge, skill, or ability is used in and is a necessary prerequisite to performance of critical or important work behavior(s). In addition, to be content valid, a selection procedure measuring a skill or ability should either closely approximate an observable work behavior, or its product should closely approximate an observable work product. If a test purports to sample a work behavior or to provide a sample of a work product, the manner and setting of the selection procedure and its level and complexity should closely approximate the work situation. The closer the content and the context of the selection procedure are to work samples or work behaviors, the stronger is the basis for showing content validity. As the content of the selection procedure less resembles a work behavior, or the setting and manner of the administration of the selection procedure less resemble the work situation, or the result less resembles a work product, the less likely the selection procedure is to be content valid, and the greater the need for other evidence of validity.

(5) *Reliability.* The reliability of selection procedures justified on the basis of content validity should be a matter of concern to the user. Whenever it is feasible, appropriate statistical estimates should be made of the reliability of the selection procedure.

(6) *Prior training or experience.* A requirement for or evaluation of specific prior training or experience based on content validity, including a specification of level or amount of training or experience, should be justified on the basis of the relationship between the content of the training or experience and the content of the job for which the training or experience is to be required or evaluated. The critical consideration is the resemblance between the specific behaviors, products, knowledges, skills, or abilities in the experience or training and the specific behaviors, products, knowledges, skills, or abilities required on the job, whether or not there is close resemblance between the experience or training as a whole and the job as a whole.

(7) *Content validity of training success.* Where a measure of success in a

training program is used as a selection procedure and the content of a training program is justified on the basis of content validity, the use should be justified on the relationship between the content of the training program and the content of the job.

(8) *Operational use.* A selection procedure which is supported on the basis of content validity may be used for a job if it represents a critical work behavior (i.e., a behavior which is necessary for performance of the job) or work behaviors which constitute most of the important parts of the job.

(9) *Ranking based on content validity studies.* If a user can show, by a job analysis or otherwise, that a higher score on a content valid selection procedure is likely to result in better job performance, the results may be used to rank persons who score above minimum levels. Where a selection procedure supported solely or primarily by content validity is used to rank job candidates, the selection procedure should measure those aspects of performance which differentiate among levels of job performance.

D. *Technical standards for construct validity studies—* (1) *Appropriateness of construct validity studies.* Construct validity is a more complex strategy than either criterion-related or content validity. Construct validation is a relatively new and developing procedure in the employment field, and there is at present a lack of substantial literature extending the concept to employment practices. The user should be aware that the effort to obtain sufficient empirical support for construct validity is both an extensive and arduous effort involving a series of research studies, which include criterion related validity studies and which may include content validity studies. Users choosing to justify use of a selection procedure by this strategy should therefore take particular care to assure that the validity study meets the standards set forth below.

(2) *Job analysis for construct validity studies.* There should be a job analysis. This job analysis should show the work behavior(s) required for successful performance of the job, or the groups of jobs being studied, the critical or important work behavior(s) in the job or group of jobs being studied, and an identification of the construct(s) believed to underlie successful performance of these critical or important work behaviors in the job or jobs in question. Each construct should be named and defined, so as to distinguish it from other constructs. If a group of jobs is being studied the jobs should have in common one or more critical or important work behaviors at a comparable level of complexity.

(3) *Relationship to the job.* A selection procedure should then be identified or developed which measures the construct identified in accord with subparagraph (2) above. The user should show by empirical evidence that the selection procedure is validly related to the construct and that the construct is validly related to the performance of critical or important work behavior(s). The relationship between the construct as measured by the selection procedure and the related work behavior(s) should be supported by empirical evidence from one or more criterion-related studies involving the job or jobs in question which satisfy the provisions of section 14B above.

(4) *Use of construct validity study without new criterion-related evidence—*(a) *Standards for use.* Until such time as professional literature provides more guidance on the use of construct validity in employment situations, the Federal agencies will accept a claim of construct validity without a criterion-related study which satisfies section 14B above only when the selection procedure has been used elsewhere in a situation in which a criterion-related study has been conducted and the use of a criterion-related validity study in this context meets the standards for transportability of criterion-related validity studies as set forth above in section 7. However, if a study pertains to a number of jobs having common critical or important work behaviors at a comparable level of complexity, and the evidence satisfies subparagraphs 14B (2) and (3) above for those jobs with criterion-related validity evidence for those jobs, the selection procedure may be used for all the jobs to which the study pertains. If construct validity is to be gen-

eralized to other jobs or groups of jobs not in the group studied, the Federal enforcement agencies will expect at a minimum additional empirical research evidence meeting the standards of subparagraphs section 14B (2) and (3) above for the additional jobs or groups of jobs.

(b) *Determination of common work behaviors.* In determining whether two or more jobs have one or more work behavior(s) in common, the user should compare the observed work behavior(s) in each of the jobs and should compare the observed work product(s) in each of the jobs. If neither the observed work behavior(s) in each of the jobs nor the observed work product(s) in each of the jobs are the same, the Federal enforcement agencies will presume that the work behavior(s) in each job are different. If the work behaviors are not observable, then evidence of similarity of work products and any other relevant research evidence will be considered in determining whether the work behavior(s) in the two jobs are the same.

DOCUMENTATION OF IMPACT AND
VALIDITY EVIDENCE

§ 1607.15 Documentation of impact and validity evidence.

A. *Required information.* Users of selection procedures other than those users complying with section 15A(1) below should maintain and have available for each job information on adverse impact of the selection process for that job and, where it is determined a selection process has an adverse impact, evidence of validity as set forth below.

(1) *Simplified recordkeeping for users with less than 100 employees.* In order to minimize recordkeeping burdens on employers who employ one hundred (100) or fewer employees, and other users not required to file EEO-1, et seq., reports, such users may satisfy the requirements of this section 15 if they maintain and have available records showing, for each year:

(a) The number of persons hired, promoted, and terminated for each job, by sex, and where appropriate by race and national origin;

(b) The number of applicants for hire and promotion by sex and where appropriate by race and national origin; and

(c) The selection procedures utilized (either standardized or not standardized).

These records should be maintained for each race or national origin group (see section 4 above) constituting more than two percent (2%) of the labor force in the relevant labor area. However, it is not necessary to maintain records by race and/or national origin (see § 4 above) if one race or national origin group in the relevant labor area constitutes more than ninety-eight percent (98%) of the labor force in the area. If the user has reason to believe that a selection procedure has an adverse impact, the user should maintain any available evidence of validity for that procedure (see sections 7A and 8).

(2) *Information on impact*—(a) *Collection of information on impact.* Users of selection procedures other than those complying with section 15A(1) above should maintain and have available for each job records or other information showing whether the total selection process for that job has an adverse impact on any of the groups for which records are called for by sections 4B above. Adverse impact determinations should be made at least annually for each such group which constitutes at least 2 percent of the labor force in the relevant labor area or 2 percent of the applicable workforce. Where a total selection process for a job has an adverse impact, the user should maintain and have available records or other information showing which components have an adverse impact. Where the total selection process for a job does not have an adverse impact, information need not be maintained for individual components except in circumstances set forth in subsection 15A(2)(b) below. If the determination of adverse impact is made using a procedure other than the "four-fifths rule," as defined in the first sentence of section 4D above, a justification, consistent with section 4D above, for the procedure used to determine adverse impact should be available.

(b) *When adverse impact has been eliminated in the total selection process.* Whenever the total selection process for a particular job has had an adverse impact, as defined in section 4 above, in any year, but no longer has an adverse impact, the user should maintain and have available the information on individual components of the selection process required in the preceding paragraph for the period in which there was adverse impact. In addition, the user should continue to collect such information for at least two (2) years after the adverse impact has been eliminated.

(c) *When data insufficient to determine impact.* Where there has been an insufficient number of selections to determine whether there is an adverse impact of the total selection process for a particular job, the user should continue to collect, maintain and have available the information on individual components of the selection process required in section 15(A)(2)(a) above until the information is sufficient to determine that the overall selection process does not have an adverse impact as defined in section 4 above, or until the job has changed substantially.

(3) *Documentation of validity evidence.—*(a) *Types of evidence.* Where a total selection process has an adverse impact (see section 4 above) the user should maintain and have available for each component of that process which has an adverse impact, one or more of the following types of documentation evidence:

(i) Documentation evidence showing criterion-related validity of the selection procedure (see section 15B, below).

(ii) Documentation evidence showing content validity of the selection procedure (see section 15C, below).

(iii) Documentation evidence showing construct validity of the selection procedure (see section 15D, below).

(iv) Documentation evidence from other studies showing validity of the selection procedure in the user's facility (see section 15E, below).

(v) Documentation evidence showing why a validity study cannot or need not be performed and why continued use of the procedure is consistent with Federal law.

(b) *Form of report.* This evidence should be compiled in a reasonably complete and organized manner to permit direct evaluation of the validity of the selection procedure. Previously written employer or consultant reports of validity, or reports describing validity studies completed before the issuance of these guidelines are acceptable if they are complete in regard to the documentation requirements contained in this section, or if they satisfied requirements of guidelines which were in effect when the validity study was completed. If they are not complete, the required additional documentation should be appended. If necessary information is not available the report of the validity study may still be used as documentation, but its adequacy will be evaluated in terms of compliance with the requirements of these guidelines.

(c) *Completeness.* In the event that evidence of validity is reviewed by an enforcement agency, the validation reports completed after the effective date of these guidelines are expected to contain the information set forth below. Evidence denoted by use of the word "(Essential)" is considered critical. If information denoted essential is not included, the report will be considered incomplete unless the user affirmatively demonstrates either its unavailability due to circumstances beyond the user's control or special circumstances of the user's study which make the information irrelevant. Evidence not so denoted is desirable but its absence will not be a basis for considering a report incomplete. The user should maintain and have available the information called for under the heading "Source Data" in sections 15B(11) and 15D(11). While it is a necessary part of the study, it need not be submitted with the report. All statistical results should be organized and presented in tabular or graphic form to the extent feasible.

B. *Criterion-related validity studies.* Reports of criterion-related validity for a selection procedure should include the following information:

(1) *User(s), location(s), and date(s) of study.* Dates and location(s) of the

job analysis or review of job information, the date(s) and location(s) of the administration of the selection procedures and collection of criterion data, and the time between collection of data on selection procedures and criterion measures should be provided (Essential). If the study was conducted at several locations, the address of each location, including city and State, should be shown.

(2) *Problem and setting.* An explicit definition of the purpose(s) of the study and the circumstances in which the study was conducted should be provided. A description of existing selection procedures and cutoff scores, if any, should be provided.

(3) *Job anlysis or review of job information.* A description of the procedure used to analyze the job or group of jobs, or to review the job information should be provided (Essential). Where a review of job information results in criteria which may be used without a full job analysis (see section 14B(3)), the basis for the selection of these criteria should be reported (Essential). Where a job analysis is required a complete description of the work behavior(s) or work outcome(s), and measures of their criticality or importance should be provided (Essential). The report should describe the basis on which the behavior(s) or outcome(s) were determined to be critical or important, such as the proportion of time spent on the respective behaviors, their level of difficulty, their frequency of performance, the consequences of error, or other appropriate factors (Essential). Where two or more jobs are grouped for a validity study, the information called for in this subsection should be provided for each of the jobs, and the justification for the grouping (see section 14B(1)) should be provided (Essential).

(4) *Job titles and codes.* It is desirable to provide the user's job title(s) for the job(s) in question and the corresponding job title(s) and code(s) from U.S. Employment Service's Dictionary of Occupational Titles.

(5) *Criterion measures.* The bases for the selection of the criterion measures should be provided, together with references to the evidence considered in making the selection of criterion measures (essential). A full description of all criteria on which data were collected and means by which they were observed, recorded, evaluated, and quantified, should be provided (essential). If rating techniques are used as criterion measures, the appraisal form(s) and instructions to the rater(s) should be included as part of the validation evidence, or should be explicitly described and available (essential). All steps taken to insure that criterion measures are free from factors which would unfairly alter the scores of members of any group should be described (essential).

(6) *Sample description.* A description of how the research sample was identified and selected should be included (essential). The race, sex, and ethnic composition of the sample, including those groups set forth in section 4A above, should be described (essential). This description should include the size of each subgroup (essential). A description of how the research sample compares with the relevant labor market or work force, the method by which the relevant labor market or work force was defined, and a discussion of the likely effects on validity of differences between the sample and the relevant labor market or work force, are also desirable. Descriptions of educational levels, length of service, and age are also desirable.

(7) *Description of selection procedures.* Any measure, combination of measures, or procedure studied should be completely and explicitly described or attached (essential). If commercially available selection procedures are studied, they should be described by title, form, and publisher (essential). Reports of reliability estimates and how they were established are desirable.

(8) *Techniques and results.* Methods used in analyzing data should be described (essential). Measures of central tendency (e.g., means) and measures of dispersion (e.g., standard deviations and ranges) for all selection procedures and all criteria should be reported for each race, sex, and ethnic group which constitutes a significant factor in the relevant labor market (essential). The magnitude and direction of all relationships between selection

procedures and criterion measures investigated should be reported for each relevant race, sex, and ethnic group and for the total group (essential). Where groups are too small to obtain reliable evidence of the magnitude of the relationship, need not be reported separately. Statements regarding the statistical significance of results should be made (essential). Any statistical adjustments, such as for less then perfect reliability or for restriction of score range in the selection procedure or criterion should be described and explained; and uncorrected correlation coefficients should also be shown (essential). Where the statistical technique categorizes continuous data, such as biserial correlation and the phi coefficient, the categories and the bases on which they were determined should be described and explained (essential). Studies of test fairness should be included where called for by the requirements of section 14B(8) (essential). These studies should include the rationale by which a selection procedure was determined to be fair to the group(s) in question. Where test fairness or unfairness has been demonstrated on the basis of other studies, a bibliography of the relevant studies should be included (essential). If the bibliography includes unpublished studies, copies of these studies, or adequate abstracts or summaries, should be attached (essential). Where revisions have been made in a selection procedure to assure compatability between successful job performance and the probability of being selected, the studies underlying such revisions should be included (essential). All statistical results should be organized and presented by relevant race, sex, and ethnic group (essential).

(9) *Alternative procedures investigated.* The selection procedures investigated and available evidence of their impact should be identified (essential). The scope, method, and findings of the investigation, and the conclusions reached in light of the findings, should be fully described (essential).

(10) *Uses and applications.* The methods considered for use of the selection procedure (e.g., as a screening device with a cutoff score, for grouping or ranking, or combined with other procedures in a battery) and available evidence of their impact should be described (essential). This description should include the rationale for choosing the method for operational use, and the evidence of the validity and utility of the procedure as it is to be used (essential). The purpose for which the procedure is to be used (e.g., hiring, transfer, promotion) should be described (essential). If weights are assigned to different parts of the selection procedure, these weights and the validity of the weighted composite should be reported (essential). If the selection procedure is used with a cutoff score, the user should describe the way in which normal expectations of proficiency within the work force were determined and the way in which the cutoff score was determined (essential).

(11) *Source data.* Each user should maintain records showing all pertinent information about individual sample members and raters where they are used, in studies involving the validation of selection procedures. These records should be made available upon request of a compliance agency. In the case of individual sample members these data should include scores on the selection procedure(s), scores on criterion measures, age, sex, race, or ethnic group status, and experience on the specific job on which the validation study was conducted, and may also include such things as education, training, and prior job experience, but should not include names and social security numbers. Records should be maintained which show the ratings given to each sample member by each rater.

(12) *Contact person.* The name, mailing address, and telephone number of the person who may be contacted for further information about the validity study should be provided (essential).

(13) *Accuracy and completeness.* The report should describe the steps taken to assure the accuracy and completeness of the collection, analysis, and report of data and results.

C. *Content validity studies.* Reports of content validity for a selection procedure should include the following information:

(1) *User(s), location(s) and date(s) of study.* Dates and location(s) of the job analysis should be shown (essential).

(2) *Problem and setting.* An explicit definition of the purpose(s) of the study and the circumstances in which the study was conducted should be provided. A description of existing selection procedures and cutoff scores, if any, should be provided.

(3) *Job analysis—Content of the job.* A description of the method used to analyze the job should be provided (essential). The work behavior(s), the associated tasks, and, if the behavior results in a work product, the work products should be completely described (essential). Measures of criticality and/or importance of the work behavior(s) and the method of determining these measures should be provided (essential). Where the job analysis also identified the knowledges, skills, and abilities used in work behavior(s), an operational definition for each knowledge in terms of a body of learned information and for each skill and ability in terms of observable behaviors and outcomes, and the relationship between each knowledge, skill, or ability and each work behavior, as well as the method used to determine this relationship, should be provided (essential). The work situation should be described, including the setting in which work behavior(s) are performed, and where appropriate, the manner in which knowledges, skills, or abilities are used, and the complexity and difficulty of the knowledge, skill, or ability as used in the work behavior(s).

(4) *Selection procedure and its content.* Selection procedures, including those constructed by or for the user, specific training requirements, composites of selection procedures, and any other procedure supported by content validity, should be completely described or attached (essential). If commercially available selection procedures are used, they should be described by title, form, and publisher (essential). The behaviors measured or sampled by the selection procedure should be explicitly described (essential). Where the selection procedure purports to measure a knowledge, skill, or ability, evidence that the se-

lection procedure measures and is a representative sample of the knowledge, skill, or ability should be provided (essential).

(5) *Relationship between the selection procedure and the job.* The evidence demonstrating that the selection procedure is a representative work sample, a representative sample of the work behavior(s), or a representative sample of a knowledge, skill, or ability as used as a part of a work behavior and necessary for that behavior should be provided (essential). The user should identify the work behavior(s) which each item or part of the selection procedure is intended to sample or measure (essential). Where the selection procedure purports to sample a work behavior or to provide a sample of a work product, a comparison should be provided of the manner, setting, and the level of complexity of the selection procedure with those of the work situation (essential). If any steps were taken to reduce adverse impact on a race, sex, or ethnic group in the content of the procedure or in its administration, these steps should be described. Establishment of time limits, if any, and how these limits are related to the speed with which duties must be performed on the job, should be explained. Measures of central tend- ency (e.g., means) and measures of dispersion (e.g., standard deviations) and estimates of reability should be reported for all selection procedures if available. Such reports should be made for relevant race, sex, and ethnic subgroups, at least on a statistically reliable sample basis.

(6) *Alternative procedures investigated.* The alternative selection procedures investigated and available evidence of their impact should be identified (essential). The scope, method, and findings of the investigation, and the conclusions reached in light of the findings, should be fully described (essential).

(7) *Uses and applications.* The methods considered for use of the selection procedure (e.g., as a screening device with a cutoff score, for grouping or ranking, or combined with other procedures in a battery) and available evidence of their impact should be described (essential). This description

should include the rationale for choosing the method for operational use, and the evidence of the validity and utility of the procedure as it is to be used (essential). The purpose for which the procedure is to be used (e.g., hiring, transfer, promotion) should be described (essential). If the selection procedure is used with a cutoff score, the user should describe the way in which normal expectations of proficiency within the work force were determined and the way in which the cutoff score was determined (essential). In addition, if the selection procedure is to be used for ranking, the user should specify the evidence showing that a higher score on the selection procedure is likely to result in better job performance.

(8) *Contact person.* The name, mailing address, and telephone number of the person who may be contacted for further information about the validity study should be provided (essential).

(9) *Accuracy and completeness.* The report should describe the steps taken to assure the accuracy and completeness of the collection, analysis, and report of data and results.

D. *Construct validity studies.* Reports of construct validity for a selection procedure should include the following information:

(1) *User(s), location(s), and date(s) of study.* Date(s) and location(s) of the job analysis and the gathering of other evidence called for by these guidelines should be provided (essential).

(2) *Problem and setting.* An explicit definition 'of the purpose(s) of the study and the circumstances in which the study was conducted should be provided. A description of existing selection procedures and cutoff scores, if any, should be provided.

(3) *Construct definition.* A clear definition of the construct(s) which are believed to underlie successful performance of the critical or important work behavior(s) should be provided (essential). This definition should include the levels of construct performance relevant to the job(s) for which the selection procedure is to be used (essential). There should be a summary of the position of the construct in the psychological literature, or in the

absence of such a position, a description of the way in which the definition and measurement of the construct was developed and the psychological theory underlying it (essential). Any quantitative data which identify or define the job constructs, such as factor analyses, should be provided (essential).

(4) *Job analysis.* A description of the method used to analyze the job should be provided (essential). A complete description of the work behavior(s) and, to the extent appropriate, work outcomes and measures of their criticality and/or importance should be provided (essential). The report should also describe the basis on which the behavior(s) or outcomes were determined to be important, such as their level of difficulty, their frequency of performance, the consequences of error or other appropriate factors (essential). Where jobs are grouped or compared for the purposes of generalizing validity evidence, the work behavior(s) and work product(s) for each of the jobs should be described, and conclusions concerning the similarity of the jobs in terms of observable work behaviors or work products should be made (essential).

(5) *Job titles and codes.* It is desirable to provide the selection procedure user's job title(s) for the job(s) in question and the corresponding job title(s) and code(s) from the United States Employment Service's dictionary of occupational titles.

(6) *Selection procedure.* The selection procedure used as a measure of the construct should be completely and explicitly described or attached (essential). If commercially available selection procedures are used, they should be identified by title, form and publisher (essential). The research evidence of the relationship between the selection procedure and the construct, such as factor structure, should be included (essential). Measures of central tendency, variability and reliability of the selection procedure should be provided (essential). Whenever feasible, these measures should be provided separately for each relevant race, sex and ethnic group.

(7) *Relationship to job performance.* The criterion-related study(ies) and

other empirical evidence of the relationship between the construct measured by the selection procedure and the related work behavior(s) for the job or jobs in question should be provided (essential). Documentation of the criterion-related study(ies) should satisfy the provisions of section 15B above or section 15E(1) below, except for studies conducted prior to the effective date of these guidelines (essential). Where a study pertains to a group of jobs, and, on the basis of the study, validity is asserted for a job in the group, the observed work behaviors and the observed work products for each of the jobs should be described (essential). Any other evidence used in determining whether the work behavior(s) in each of the jobs is the same should be fully described (essential).

(8) *Alternative procedures investigated.* The alternative selection procedures investigated and available evidence of their impact should be identified (essential). The scope, method, and findings of the investigation, and the conclusions reached in light of the findings should be fully described (essential).

(9) *Uses and applications.* The methods considered for use of the selection procedure (e.g., as a screening device with a cutoff score, for grouping or ranking, or combined with other procedures in a battery) and available evidence of their impact should be described (essential). This description should include the rationale for choosing the method for operational use, and the evidence of the validity and utility of the procedure as it is to be used (essential). The purpose for which the procedure is to be used (e.g., hiring, transfer, promotion) should be described (essential). If weights are assigned to different parts of the selection procedure, these weights and the validity of the weighted composite should be reported (essential). If the selection procedure is used with a cutoff score, the user should describe the way in which normal expectations of proficiency within the work force were determined and the way in which the cutoff score was determined (essential).

(10) *Accuracy and completeness.* The report should describe the steps taken to assure the accuracy and completeness of the collection, analysis, and report of data and results.

(11) *Source data.* Each user should maintain records showing all pertinent information relating to its study of construct validity.

(12) *Contact person.* The name, mailing address, and telephone number of the individual who may be contacted for further information about the validity study should be provided (essential).

E. *Evidence of validity from other studies.* When validity of a selection procedure is supported by studies not done by the user, the evidence from the original study or studies should be compiled in a manner similar to that required in the appropriate section of this section 15 above. In addition, the following evidence should be supplied:

(1) *Evidence from criterion-related validity studies.*—a. *Job information.* A description of the important job behavior(s) of the user's job and the basis on which the behaviors were determined to be important should be provided (essential). A full description of the basis for determining that these important work behaviors are the same as those of the job in the original study (or studies) should be provided (essential).

b. *Relevance of criteria.* A full description of the basis on which the criteria used in the original studies are determined to be relevant for the user should be provided (essential).

c. *Other variables.* The similarity of important applicant pool or sample characteristics reported in the original studies to those of the user should be described (essential). A description of the comparison between the race, sex and ethnic composition of the user's relevant labor market and the sample in the original validity studies should be provided (essential).

d. *Use of the selection procedure.* A full description should be provided showing that the use to be made of the selection procedure is consistent with the findings of the original validity studies (essential).

e. *Bibliography.* A bibliography of reports of validity of the selection procedure for the job or jobs in question should be provided (essential). Where any of the studies included an investigation of test fairness, the results of this investigation should be provided (essential). Copies of reports published in journals that are not commonly available should be described in detail or attached (essential). Where a user is relying upon unpublished studies, a reasonable effort should be made to obtain these studies. If these unpublished studies are the sole source of validity evidence they should be described in detail or attached (essential). If these studies are not available, the name and address of the source, an adequate abstract or summary of the validity study and data, and a contact person in the source organization should be provided (essential).

(2) *Evidence from content validity studies.* See section 14C(3) and section 15C above.

(3) *Evidence from construct validity studies.* See sections 14D(2) and 15D above.

F. *Evidence of validity from cooperative studies.* Where a selection procedure has been validated through a cooperative study, evidence that the study satisfies the requirements of sections 7, 8 and 15E should be provided (essential).

G. *Selection for higher level job.* If a selection procedure is used to evaluate candidates for jobs at a higher level than those for which they will initially be employed, the validity evidence should satisfy the documentation provisions of this section 15 for the higher level job or jobs, and in addition, the user should provide: (1) a description of the job progression structure, formal or informal; (2) the data showing how many employees progress to the higher level job and the length of time needed to make this progression; and (3) an identification of any anticipated changes in the higher level job. In addition, if the test measures a knowledge, skill or ability, the user should provide evidence that the knowledge, skill or ability is required for the higher level job and the basis for the conclusion that the knowledge, skill or ability is not expected to develop from the training or experience on the job.

H. *Interim use of selection procedures.* If a selection procedure is being used on an interim basis because the procedure is not fully supported by the required evidence of validity, the user should maintain and have available (1) substantial evidence of validity for the procedure, and (2) a report showing the date on which the study to gather the additional evidence commenced, the estimated completion date of the study, and a description of the data to be collected (essential).

(Approved by the Office of Management and Budget under control number 3046–0017)

(Pub. L. No. 96–511, 94 Stat. 2812 (44 U.S.C. 3501 et seq.))

[43 FR 38295, 38312, Aug. 25, 1978, as amended at 46 FR 63268, Dec. 31, 1981]

DEFINITIONS

§ 1607.16 Definitions.

The following definitions shall apply throughout these guidelines:

A. *Ability.* A present competence to perform an observable behavior or a behavior which results in an observable product.

B. *Adverse impact.* A substantially different rate of selection in hiring, promotion, or other employment decision which works to the disadvantage of members of a race, sex, or ethnic group. See section 4 of these guidelines.

C. *Compliance with these guidelines.* Use of a selection procedure is in compliance with these guidelines if such use has been validated in accord with these guidelines (as defined below), or if such use does not result in adverse impact on any race, sex, or ethnic group (see section 4, above), or, in unusual circumstances, if use of the procedure is otherwise justified in accord with Federal law. See section 6B, above.

D. *Content validity.* Demonstrated by data showing that the content of a selection procedure is representative of important aspects of performance on the job. See section 5B and section 14C.

E. *Construct validity.* Demonstrated by data showing that the selection procedure measures the degree to which candidates have identifiable characteristics which have been determined to be important for successful job performance. See section 5B and section 14D.

F. *Criterion-related validity.* Demonstrated by empirical data showing that the selection procedure is predictive of or significantly correlated with important elements of work behavior. See sections 5B and 14B.

G. *Employer.* Any employer subject to the provisions of the Civil Rights Act of 1964, as amended, including State or local governments and any Federal agency subject to the provisions of section 717 of the Civil Rights Act of 1964, as amended, and any Federal contractor or subcontractor or federally assisted construction contractor or subcontractor covered by Executive Order 11246, as amended.

H. *Employment agency.* Any employment agency subject to the provisions of the Civil Rights Act of 1964, as amended.

I. *Enforcement action.* For the purposes of section 4 a proceeding by a Federal enforcement agency such as a lawsuit or an administrative proceeding leading to debarment from or withholding, suspension, or termination of Federal Government contracts or the suspension or withholding of Federal Government funds; but not a finding of reasonable cause or a conciliation process or the issuance of right to sue letters under title VII or under Executive Order 11246 where such finding, conciliation, or issuance of notice of right to sue is based upon an individual complaint.

J. *Enforcement agency.* Any agency of the executive branch of the Federal Government which adopts these guidelines for purposes of the enforcement of the equal employment opportunity laws or which has responsibility for securing compliance with them.

K. *Job analysis.* A detailed statement of work behaviors and other information relevant to the job.

L. *Job description.* A general statement of job duties and responsibilities.

M. *Knowledge.* A body of information applied directly to the performance of a function.

N. *Labor organization.* Any labor organization subject to the provisions of the Civil Rights Act of 1964, as amended, and any committee subject thereto controlling apprenticeship or other training.

O. *Observable.* Able to be seen, heard, or otherwise perceived by a person other than the person performing the action.

P. *Race, sex, or ethnic group.* Any group of persons identifiable on the grounds of race, color, religion, sex, or national origin.

Q. *Selection procedure.* Any measure, combination of measures, or procedure used as a basis for any employment decision. Selection procedures include the full range of assessment techniques from traditional paper and pencil tests, performance tests, training programs, or probationary periods and physical, educational, and work experience requirements through informal or casual interviews and unscored application forms.

R. *Selection rate.* The proportion of applicants or candidates who are hired, promoted, or otherwise selected.

S. *Should.* The term "should" as used in these guidelines is intended to connote action which is necessary to achieve compliance with the guidelines, while recognizing that there are circumstances where alternative courses of action are open to users.

T. *Skill.* A present, observable competence to perform a learned psychomotor act.

U. *Technical feasibility.* The existence of conditions permitting the conduct of meaningful criterion-related validity studies. These conditions include: (1) An adequate sample of persons available for the study to achieve findings of statistical significance; (2) having or being able to obtain a sufficient range of scores on the selection procedure and job performance measures to produce validity results which can be expected to be representative of the results if the ranges normally expected were utilized; and (3) having or being able to devise unbiased, reliable and relevant measures of job performance or other criteria of employee adequacy. See section 14B(2). With respect to investigation of possible unfairness, the same considerations are applicable to each group for which the study is made. See section 14B(8).

V. *Unfairness of selection procedure.* A condition in which members of one race, sex, or ethnic group characteristically obtain lower scores on a selection procedure than members of another group, and the differences are not reflected in differences in measures of job performance. See section 14B(7).

W. *User.* Any employer, labor organization, employment agency, or licensing or certification board, to the extent it may be covered by Federal equal employment opportunity law, which uses a selection procedure as a basis for any employment decision. Whenever an employer, labor organization, or employment agency is required by law to restrict recruitment for any occupation to those applicants who have met licensing or certification requirements, the licensing or certifying authority to the extent it may be covered by Federal equal employment opportunity law will be considered the user with respect to those licensing or certification requirements. Whenever a State employment agency or service does no more than administer or monitor a procedure as permitted by Department of Labor regulations, and does so without making referrals or taking any other action on the basis of the results, the State employment agency will not be deemed to be a user.

X. *Validated in accord with these guidelines or properly validated.* A demonstration that one or more validity study or studies meeting the standards of these guidelines has been conducted, including investigation and, where appropriate, use of suitable alternative selection procedures as contemplated by section 3B, and has produced evidence of validity sufficient to warrant use of the procedure for the intended purpose under the standards of these guidelines.

Y. *Work behavior.* An activity performed to achieve the objectives of the job. Work behaviors involve observable (physical) components and unobservable (mental) components. A work behavior consists of the performance of one or more tasks. Knowledges, skills, and abilities are not behaviors, although they may be applied in work behaviors.

APPENDIX

§ 1607.17 Policy statement on affirmative action (see section 13B).

The Equal Employment Opportunity Coordinating Council was established by act of Congress in 1972, and charged with responsibility for developing and implementing agreements and policies designed, among other things, to eliminate conflict and inconsistency among the agencies of the Federal Government responsible for administering Federal law prohibiting discrimination on grounds of race, color, sex, religion, and national origin. This statement is issued as an initial response to the requests of a number of State and local officials for clarification of the Government's policies concerning the role of affirmative action in the overall equal employment opportunity program. While the Coordinating Council's adoption of this statement expresses only the views of the signatory agencies concerning this important subject, the principles set forth below should serve as policy guidance for other Federal agencies as well.

(1) Equal employment opportunity is the law of the land. In the public sector of our society this means that all persons, regardless of race, color, religion, sex, or national origin shall have equal access to positions in the public service limited only by their ability to do the job. There is ample evidence in all sectors of our society that such equal access frequently has been denied to members of certain groups because of their sex, racial, or ethnic characteristics. The remedy for such past and present discrimination is twofold.

On the one hand, vigorous enforcement of the laws against discrimination is essential. But equally, and perhaps even more important are affirmative, voluntary efforts on the part of public employers to assure that positions in the public service are genuinely and equally accessible to qualified persons, without regard to their sex, racial, or ethnic characteristics. Without such efforts equal employment opportunity is no more than a wish. The importance of voluntary affirmative action on the part of employers is underscored by title VII of the Civil Rights Act of 1964, Executive Order 11246, and related laws and regulations—all of which emphasize voluntary action to achieve equal employment opportunity.

As with most management objectives, a systematic plan based on sound organizational analysis and problem identification is crucial to the accomplishment of affirmative action objectives. For this reason, the Council urges all State and local governments to develop and implement results oriented affirmative action plans which deal with the problems so identified.

The following paragraphs are intended to assist State and local governments by illustrating the kinds of analyses and activities which may be appropriate for a public employer's voluntary affirmative action plan. This statement does not address remedies imposed after a finding of unlawful discrimination.

(2) Voluntary affirmative action to assure equal employment opportunity is appropriate at any stage of the employment process. The first step in the construction of any affirmative action plan should be an analysis of the employer's work force to determine whether precentages of sex, race, or ethnic groups in individual job classifications are substantially similar to the precentages of those groups available in the relevant job market who possess the basic job-related qualifications.

When substantial disparities are found through such analyses, each element of the overall selection process should be examined to determine which elements operate to exclude persons on the basis of sex, race, or ethnic group. Such elements include, but are not limited to, recruitment, testing, ranking certification, interview, recommendations for selection, hiring, promotion, etc. The examination of each element of the selection process should at a minimum include a determination of its validity in predicting job performance.

(3) When an employer has reason to believe that its selection procedures have the exclusionary effect described in paragraph 2 above, it should initiate affirmative steps to remedy the situation. Such steps, which in design and execution may be race, color, sex, or ethnic "conscious," include, but are not limited to, the following:

(a) The establishment of a long-term goal, and short-range, interim goals and timetables for the specific job classifications, all of which should take into account the availability of basically qualified persons in the relevant job market;

(b) A recruitment program designed to attract qualified members of the group in question;

(c) A systematic effort to organize work and redesign jobs in ways that provide opportunities for persons lacking "journeyman" level knowledge or skills to enter and, with appropriate training, to progress in a career field;

(d) Revamping selection instruments or procedures which have not yet been validated in order to reduce or eliminate exclusionary effects on particular groups in particular job classifications;

(e) The initiation of measures designed to assure that members of the affected group who are qualified to perform the job are included within the pool of persons from which the selecting official makes the selection;

(f) A systematic effort to provide career advancement training, both classroom and on-the-job, to employees locked into dead end jobs; and

(g) The establishment of a system for regularly monitoring the effectiveness of the particular affirmative action program, and procedures for making timely adjustments in this program where effectiveness is not demonstrated.

(4) The goal of any affirmative action plan should be achievement of genuine equal employment opportunity for all qualified persons. Selection under such plans should be based upon the ability of the applicant(s) to do the work. Such plans should not require the selection of the unqualified, or the unneeded, nor should they require the selection of persons on the basis of race, color, sex, religion, or national origin. Moreover, while the Council believes that this statement should serve to assist State and local employers, as well as Federal agencies, it recognizes that affirmative action cannot be viewed as a standardized

program which must be accomplished in the same way at all times in all places.

Accordingly, the Council has not attempted to set forth here either the minimum or maximum voluntary steps that employers may take to deal with their respective situations. Rather, the Council recognizes that under applicable authorities, State and local employers have flexibility to formulate affirmative action plans that are best suited to their particular situations. In this manner, the Council believes that affirmative action programs will best serve the goal of equal employment opportunity.

Respectfully submitted,

Harold R. Tyler, Jr.,
Deputy Attorney General and Chairman
of the Equal Employment Coordinating Council.
Michael H. Moskow,
Under Secretary of Labor.
Ethel Bent Walsh,
Acting Chairman, Equal Employment
Opportunity Commission.
Robert E. Hampton,
Chairman, Civil Service Commission.
Arthur E. Flemming,
Chairman, Commission on Civil Rights.

Because of its equal employment opportunity responsibilities under the State and Local Government Fiscal Assistance Act of 1972 (the revenue sharing act), the Department of Treasury was invited to participate in the formulation of this policy statement; and it concurs and joins in the adoption of this policy statement.

Done this 26th day of August 1976.

Richard Albrecht,
General Counsel,
Department of the Treasury.

§ 1607.18 Citations.

The official title of these guidelines is "Uniform Guidelines on Employee Selection Procedures (1978)". The Uniform Guidelines on Employee Selection Procedures (1978) are intended to establish a uniform Federal position in the area of prohibiting discrimination in employment practices on grounds of race, color, religion, sex, or national origin. These guidelines have been adopted by the Equal Employment Opportunity Commission, the Depart-

ment of Labor, the Department of Justice, and the Civil Service Commission.

The official citation is:

"Section ——, Uniform Guidelines on Employee Selection Procedure (1978); 43 FR —— (August 25, 1978)."

The short form citation is:

"Section ——, U.G.E.S.P. (1978); 43 FR —— (August 25, 1978)."

When the guidelines are cited in connection with the activities of one of the issuing agencies, a specific citation to the regulations of that agency can be added at the end of the above citation. The specific additional citations are as follows:

Equal Employment Opportunity Commission
29 CFR Part 1607
Department of Labor
Office of Federal Contract Compliance Programs
41 CFR Part 60-3
Department of Justice
28 CFR 50.14
Civil Service Commission
5 CFR 300.103(c)

Normally when citing these guidelines, the section number immediately preceding the title of the guidelines will be from these guidelines series 1-18. If a section number from the codification for an individual agency is needed it can also be added at the end of the agency citation. For example, section 6A of these guidelines could be cited for EEOC as follows: "Section 6A, Uniform Guidelines on Employee Selection Procedures (1978); 43 FR ——, (August 25, 1978); 29 CFR Part 1607, section 6A."

Appendix D
Title VII of the Civil Rights Act of 1964, as Amended

An Act

To enforce the constitutional right to vote, to confer jurisdiction upon the district courts of the United States to provide injunctive relief against discrimination in public accommodations, to authorize the Attorney General to institute suits to protect constitutional rights in public facilities and public education, to extend the Commission on Civil Rights, to prevent discrimination in federally assisted programs, to establish a Commission on Equal Employment Opportunity, and for other purposes.

Be it enacted by the Senate and House of Representatives of the United States of America in Congress assembled, That this Act may be cited as the "Civil Rights Act of 1964".

*   *   *   *   *

TITLE VII—EQUAL EMPLOYMENT OPPORTUNITY [1]

DEFINITIONS

SEC. 701. For the purposes of this title—

(a) The term "person" includes one or more individuals, *governments, governmental agencies, political subdivisions,* labor unions, partnerships, associations, corporations, legal representatives, mutual companies, joint-stock companies, trusts, unincorporated organizations, trustees, trustees in bankruptcy, or receivers.

(b) The term "employer" means a person engaged in an industry affecting commerce who has *fifteen* or more employees for each working day in each of twenty or more calendar weeks in the current or preceding calendar year, and any agent of such a person, but such term does not include (1) the United States, a corporation wholly owned by the Government of the United States, an Indian tribe, or *any department or agency of the District of Columbia subject by statute to procedures of the competitive service (as defined in section 2102 of title 5 of the United States Code), or* (2) a bona fide private membership club (other than a labor organization) which is exempt from taxation under section 501(c) of the Internal Revenue Code of 1954, *except that during the first year after the date of enactment of the Equal Employment Opportunity Act of 1972,* persons having fewer than *twenty-five* employees (and their agents) shall not be considered *employers.*

(c) The term "employment agency" means any person regularly undertaking with or without compensation to procure employees for an employer or to procure for employees opportunities to work for an employer and includes an agent of such a person.

[1] Includes 1972 amendments, made by P.L. 92-2., printed in Italic.

(d) The term "labor organization" means a labor organization engaged in an industry affecting commerce, and any agent of such an organization, and includes any organization of any kind, any agency, or employee representation committee, group, association, or plan so engaged in which employees participate and which exists for the purpose, in whole or in part, of dealing with employers concerning grievances, labor disputes, wages, rates of pay, hours, or other terms or conditions of employment, and any conference, general committee, joint or system board, or joint council so engaged which is subordinate to a national or international labor organization.

(e) A labor organization shall be deemed to be engaged in an industry affecting commerce if (1) it maintains or operates a hiring hall or hiring office which procures employees for an employer or procures for employees opportunities to work for an employer, or (2) the number of its members (or, where it is a labor organization composed of other labor organizations or their representatives, if the aggregate number of the members of such other labor organization) is (A) *twenty-five* or more during the first year after the *date of enactment of the Equal Employment Opportunity Act of 1972, or (B) fifteen* or more thereafter, and such labor organization—

(1) is the certified representative of employees under the provisions of the National Labor Relations Act, as amended, or the Railway Labor Act, as amended;

(2) although not certified, is a national or international labor organization or a local labor organization recognized or acting as the representative of employees of an employer or employers engaged in an industry affecting commerce; or

(3) has chartered a local labor organization or subsidiary body which is representing or actively seeking to represent employees of employers within the meaning of paragraph (1) or (2); or

(4) has been chartered by a labor organization representing or actively seeking to represent employees within the meaning of paragraph (1) or (2) as the local or subordinate body through which such employees may enjoy membership or become affiliated with such labor organization; or

(5) is a conference, general committee, joint or system board, or joint council subordinate to a national or international labor organization, which includes a labor organization engaged in an industry affecting commerce within the

meaning of any of the preceding paragraphs of this subsection.

(f) The term "employee" means an individual employed by an employer, *except that the term 'employee' shall not include any person elected to public office in any State or political subdivision of any State by the qualified voters thereof, or any person chosen by such officer to be on such officer's personal staff, or an appointee on the policymaking level or an immediate adviser with respect to the excercise of the constitutional or legal powers of the office. The exemption set forth in the preceding sentence shall not include employees subject to the civil service laws of a State government, governmental agency or political subdivision.*

(g) The term "commerce" means trade, traffic, commerce, transportation, transmission, or communication among the several States; or between a State and any place outside thereof; or within the District of Columbia, or a possession of the United States; or between points in the same State but through a point outside thereof.

(h) The term "industry affecting commerce" means any activity, business, or industry in commerce or in which a labor dispute would hinder or obstruct commerce or the free flow of commerce and includes any activity or industry "affecting commerce" within the meaning of the Labor-Management Reporting and Disclosure Act of 1959, *and further includes any governmental industry, business, or activity.*

(i) The term "State" includes a State of the United States, the District of Columbia, Puerto Rico, the Virgin Islands, American Samoa, Guam, Wake Island, the Canal Zone, and Outer Continental Shelf lands defined in the Outer Continental Shelf Lands Act.

(j) *The term "religion" includes all aspects of religious observance and practice, as well as belief, unless an employer demonstrates that he is unable to reasonably accommodate to an employee's or prospective employee's, religious observance or practice without undue hardship on the conduct of the employer's business.*

EXEMPTION

SEC. 702. This title shall not apply to an employer with respect to the employment of aliens outside any State, or to a religious corporation, association, *educational institution,* or society with respect to the employment of individuals of a particular religion to perform work connected with the carrying on by such corporation, association, *educational institution,* or society of its *activities.*

DISCRIMINATION BECAUSE OF RACE, COLOR, RELIGION, SEX, OR NATIONAL ORIGIN

SEC. 703. (a) It shall be an unlawful employment practice for an employer—

(1) to fail or refuse to hire or to discharge any individual, or otherwise to discriminate against any individual with respect to his compensation, terms, conditions, or privileges of employment, because of such individual's race, color, religion, sex, or national origin; or

(2) to limit, segregate, or classify his employees *or applicants for employment* in any way which would deprive or tend to deprive any individual of employment opportunities or otherwise adversely affect his status as an employee, because of such individual's race, color, religion, sex, or national origin.

(b) It shall be an unlawful employment practice for an employment agency to fail or refuse to refer for employment, or otherwise to discriminate against, any individual because of his race, color, religion, sex, or national origin, or to classify or refer for employment any individual on the basis of his race, color, religion, sex, or national origin.

(c) It shall be an unlawful employment practice for a labor organization—

(1) to exclude or to expel from its membership, or otherwise to discriminate against, any individual because of his race, color, religion, sex, or national origin;

(2) to limit, segregate, or classify its membership, *or applicants for membership* or to classify or fail or refuse to refer for employment any individual, in any way which would deprive or tend to deprive any individual of employment opportunities, or would limit such employment opportunities or otherwise adversely affect his status as an employee or as an applicant for employment, because of such individual's race, color, religion, sex, or national origin; or

(3) to cause or attempt to cause an employer to discriminate against an individual in violation of this section.

(d) It shall be an unlawful employment practice for any employer, labor organization, or joint labor-management committee controlling apprenticeship or other training or retraining, including on-the-job training programs to discriminate against any individual because of his race, color, religion, sex, or national origin in admission to, or employment in, any program established to provide apprenticeship or other training.

(e) Notwithstanding any other provision of this title, (1) it shall not be an unlawful employment practice for an employer to hire and employ employees, for an employment agency to classify, or refer for employment any individual, for a labor organization to classify its membership or to classify or refer for employment any individual, or for an employer, labor organization, or joint labor-management committee controlling apprenticeship or other training or retraining programs to admit or employ any individual in any such program, on the basis of his religion, sex, or national origin in those certain instances where religion, sex, or national origin is a bona fide occupational qualification reasonably necessary to the normal operation of that particular business or enterprise, and (2) it shall not be an unlawful employment practice for a school, college, university, or other education institution or institution of learning to hire and employ employees of a particular religion if such school, college, university, or other educational institution or institution of learning is, in whole or in substantial part, owned, supported, controlled, or managed by a particular religion or by a particular religious corporation, association, or society, or if the curriculum of such school, college, university, or other educational institution or institution of learning is directed toward the propagation of a particular religion.

(f) As used in this title, the phrase "unlawful employment practice" shall not be deemed to include any action or measure taken by an employer, labor organization, joint labor-management committee, or employment agency with respect to an individual who is a member of the Communist Party of the United States or of any other organization required to register as a Communist-action or Communist-front organization by final order of the Subversive Activities Control Board pursuant to the Subversive Activities Control Act of 1950.

(g) Notwithstanding any other provision of this title, it shall not be an unlawful employment practice for an employer to fail or refuse to hire and employ any individual for any position, for an employer to discharge any individual from any position, or for an employment agency to fail or refuse to refer any individual for employment in any position, or for a labor organization to fail or refuse to refer any individual for employment in any position, if—

(1) the occupancy of such position, or access to the premises in or upon which any part of the duties of such position is performed or is to be performed, is subject to any requirement im-posed in the interest of the national security of the United States under any security program in effect pursuant to or administered under any statute of the United States or any Executive order of the President; and

(2) such individual has not fulfilled or has ceased to fulfill that requirement.

(h) Notwithstanding any other provision of this title, it shall not be an unlawful employment practice for an employer to apply different standards of compensation, or different terms, conditions, or privileges of employment pursuant to a bona fide seniority or merit system, or a system which measures earnings by quantity or quality of production or to employees who work in different locations, provided that such differences are not the result of an intention to discriminate because of race, color, religion, sex, or national origin, or shall it be an unlawful employment practice for an employer to give and to act upon the results of any professionally developed ability test provided that such test, its administration or action upon the results is not designed, intended or used to discriminate because of race, color, religion, sex, or national origin. It shall not be an unlawful employment practice under this title for any employer to differentiate upon the basis of sex in determining the amount of the wages or compensation paid or to be paid to employees of such employer if such differentiation is authorized by the provisions of section 6(d) of the Fair Labor Standards Act of 1938, as amended (29 U.S.C. 206(d)).

(i) Nothing contained in this title shall apply to any business or enterprise on or near an Indian reservation with respect to any publicly announced employment practice of such business or enterprise under which a preferential treatment is given to any individual because he is an Indian living on or near a reservation.

(j) Nothing contained in this title shall be interpreted to require any employer, employment agency, labor organization, or joint labor-management committee subject to this title to grant preferential treatment to any individual or to any group because of the race, color, religion, sex, or national origin of such individual or group on account of an imbalance which may exist with respect to the total number or percentage of persons of any race, color, religion, sex, or national origin employed by any employer, referred or classified for employment by any employment agency or labor organization, admitted to membership or classified by any labor organization, or admitted to, or employed in, any apprenticeship or other training program, in comparison with the total number or percentage of persons of such race, color, religion, sex, or national origin in any community, State, section, or other area, or in the available work force in any community, State, section, or other area.

OTHER UNLAWFUL EMPLOYMENT PRACTICES

SEC. 704. (a) It shall be an unlawful employment practice for an employer to discriminate against any of his employees or applicants for employment, for an employment agency, *or joint labor-management committee controlling apprenticeship or other training or retraining, including on-the-job training programs,* to discriminate against any individual, or for a labor organization to discriminate against any member thereof or applicant for membership, because he has opposed any practice made an unlawful employment practice by this title, or because he has made a charge, testified, assisted, or participated in any manner in an investigation, proceeding, or hearing under this title.

(b) It shall be an unlawful employment practice for an employer, labor organization, employment *agency, or joint labor-management committee controlling apprenticeship or other training or retraining, including on-the-job training programs,* to print or publish or cause to be printed or published any notice or advertisement relating to employment by such an employer or membership in or any classification or referral for employment by such a labor organization, or relating to any classification or referral for employment by such an employment *agency, or relating to admission to, or employment in, any program established to provide apprenticeship or other training by such a joint labor-management committee* indicating any preference, limitation, specification, or discrimination, based on race, color, religion, sex, or national origin, except that such a notice or advertisement may indicate a preference, limitation, specification, or discrimination based on religion, sex, or national origin when religion, sex, or national origin is a bona fide occupational qualification for employment.

EQUAL EMPLOYMENT OPPORTUNITY COMMISSION

SEC. 705. (a) There is hereby created a Commission to be known as the Equal Employment Opportunity Commission, which shall be composed of five members, not more than three of whom shall be members of the same political party. *Members of the Commission* shall be appointed by the President by and with the advice and consent of the *Senate* for a term of five *years. Any individual chosen to fill a vacancy shall be appointed only for the unexpired term of the member whom he shall succeed, and all members of the Commission shall continue to serve until their successors are appointed and qualified, except that no such member of the Commission shall continue to serve (1) for more than sixty days when the Congress is in session unless a nomination to fill such vacancy shall have been submitted to the Senate, or (2) after the adjournment sine die of the session of the Senate in which such nomination was submitted.* The President shall designate one member to serve as Chairman of the Commission, and one member to serve as Vice Chairman. The Chairman shall be responsible on behalf of the Commission for the administrative operations of the Commission, and *except as provided in subsection (b),* shall appoint, in accordance with the *provisions of title 5, United States Code, governing appointments in the competitive service, such officers, agents, attorneys, hearing examiners, and employees as he deems necessary to assist it in the performance of its functions and to fix their compensation in accordance with the provisions of chapter 51 and subchapter III of chapter 53 of title 5, United States Code, relating to classification and General Schedule pay rates: Provided, That assignment, removal, and compensation of hearing examiners shall be in accordance with sections 3105, 3344, 5362, and 7521 of title 5, United States Code.*

(b)(1) There shall be a General Counsel of the Commission appointed by the President, by and with the advice and consent of the Senate, for a term of four years. The General Counsel shall have responsibility for the conduct of litigation as provided in sections 706 and 707 of this title. The General Counsel shall have such other duties as the Commission may prescribe or as may be provided by law and shall concur with the Chairman of the Commission on the appointment and supervision of regional attorneys. The General Counsel of the Commission on the effective date of this Act shall continue in such position and perform the functions specified in this subsection until a successor is appointed and qualified.

(2) Attorneys appointed under this section may, at the direction of the Commission, appear for and represent the Commission in any case in court, provided that the Attorney General shall conduct all litigation to which the Commission is a party in the Supreme Court pursuant to this title.

(c) A vacancy in the Commission shall not impair the right of the remaining members to exercise all the powers of the Commission and three members thereof shall constitute a quorum.

(d) The Commission shall have an official seal which shall be judicially noticed.

(e) The Commission shall at the close of each fiscal year report to the Congress and to the President concerning the action it has taken; the names, salaries, and duties of all individuals in its employ and the moneys it has disbursed; and shall make such further reports on the cause of and means of eliminating discrimination and such recommendations for further legislation as may appear desirable.

(f) The principal office of the Commission shall be in or near the District of Columbia, but it may meet or exercise any or all its powers at any other place. The Commission may establish such regional or State offices as it deems necessary to accomplish the purpose of this title.

(g) The Commission shall have power—

(1) to cooperate with and, with their consent, utilize regional State, local, and other agencies, both public and private, and individuals;

(2) to pay to witnesses whose depositions are taken or who are summoned before the Commission or any of its agents the same witness and mileage fees as are paid to witnesses in the courts of the United States;

(3) to furnish to persons subject to this title such technical assistance as they may request to further their compliance with this title or an order issued thereunder;

(4) upon the request of (i) any employer, whose employees or some of them, or (ii) any labor organization, whose members or some of them, refuse or threaten to refuse to cooperate in effectuating the provisions of this title, to assist in such effectuation by conciliation or such other remedial action as is provided by this title;

(5) to make such technical studies as are appropriate to effectuate the purposes and policies of this title and to make the results of such studies available to the public;

(6) to *intervene* in a civil action brought *under section 706* by an aggrieved party *against a respondent other than a government, governmental agency, or political subdivision.*

(h) The Commission shall, in any of its educational or promotional activities, cooperate with other departments and agencies in the performance of such educational and promotional activites.

(i) All officers, agents, attorneys, and employees of the Commission shall be subject to the provisions of

section 9 of the Act of August 2, 1939, as amended (the Hatch Act), notwithstanding any exemption contained in such section.

PREVENTION OF UNLAWFUL EMPLOYMENT PRACTICES

SEC. 706. (a) *The Commission is empowered, as hereinafter provided, to prevent any person from engaging in any unlawful employment practice as set forth in section 703 or 704 of this title.*

(b) Whenever *a charge is filed by or on behalf of a* person claiming to be aggrieved, or by a member of the Commission, *alleging* that an employer, employment agency, labor *organization, or joint labor-management committee controlling apprenticeship or other training or retraining, including on-the-job training programs,* has engaged in an unlawful employment practice, the Commission shall *serve a notice of the charge (including the date, place and circumstances of the alleged unlawful employment practice) on* such employer, employment agency, labor *organization, or joint labor-management committee* (hereinafter referred to as the "respondent") *within ten days, and shall make an investigation thereof. Charges shall be in writing under oath or affirmation and shall contain such information and be in such form as the Commission requires. Charges* shall not be made public by the Commission. If the Commission *determines* after such investigation that there is *not* reasonable cause to believe that the charge is true, *it shall dismiss the charge and promptly notify the person claiming to be aggrieved and the respondent of its action. In determining whether reasonable cause exists, the Commission shall accord substantial weight to final findings and orders made by State or local authorities in proceedings commenced under State or local law pursuant to the requirements of subsections (c) and (d). If the Commission determines after such investigation that there is reasonable cause to believe that the charge is true,* the Commission shall endeavor to eliminate any such alleged unlawful employment practice by informal methods of conference, conciliation, and persuasion. Nothing said or done during and as a part of such *informal* endeavors may be made public by the *Commission, its officers or employees, or used as evidence in a subsequent proceeding* without the written consent of the *persons concerned.* Any *person* who *makes* public information in violation of this subsection shall be fined not more than $1,000 or imprisoned *for* not more than one *year, or both. The Commission shall make its determination on reasonable cause as promptly as possible and, so far as* practicable, not later than one hundred and twenty days from the filing of the charge or, where applicable under subsection (c) or (d) from the date upon which the Commission is authorized to take action with respect to the charge.

(c) In the case of an alleged unlawful employment practice occurring in a State, or political subdivision of a State, which has a State or local law prohibiting the unlawful employment practice alleged and establishing or authorizing a State or local authority to grant or seek relief from such practice or to institute criminal proceedings with respect thereto upon receiving notice thereof, no charge may be filed under subsection (a) by the person aggrieved before the expiration of sixty days after proceedings have been commenced under the State or local law, unless such proceedings have been earlier terminated, provided that such sixty-day period shall be extended to one hundred and twenty days during the first year after the effective date of such State or local law. If any requirement for the commencement of such proceedings is imposed by a State or local authority other than a requirement of the filing of a written and signed statement of the facts upon which the proceeding is based, the proceeding shall be deemed to have been commenced for the purposes of this subsection at the time such statement is sent by registered mail to the appropriate State or local authority.

(d) In the case of any charge filed by a member of the Commission alleging an unlawful employment practice occurring in a State or political subdivision of a State which has a State or local law prohibiting the practice alleged and establishing or authorizing a State or local authority to grant or seek relief from such practice or to institute criminal proceedings with respect thereto upon receiving notice thereof, the Commission shall, before taking any action with respect to such charge, notify the appropriate State or local officials and, upon request, afford them a reasonable time, but not less than sixty days (provided that such sixty-day period shall be extended to one hundred and twenty days during the first year after the effective *date* of such State or local law), unless a shorter period is requested, to act under such State or local law to remedy the practice alleged.

(e) A charge under *this section* shall be filed within *one hundred and eighty* days after the alleged unlawful employment practice *occurred and notice of the charge (including the date, place and circumstances of the alleged unlawful employment practice) shall be* served upon the person against whom such charge is made within ten days thereafter, except that in a case of an unlawful employment practice with respect to which the person aggrieved has *initially instituted proceedings with a State or local agency with authority to grant or seek relief from such practice or to institute criminal proceedings with respect thereto upon receiving notice thereof,* such charge shall be filed by *or on behalf of* the person aggrieved within *three hundred* days after the alleged unlawful employment practice occurred, or within thirty days after receiving notice that the State or local agency has terminated the proceedings under the State or local law, whichever is earlier, and a copy of such charge shall be filed by the Commission with the State or local agency.

(f)(1) If within thirty days after a charge is filed with the Commission or within thirty days after expiration of any period of reference under subsection (c) or (d), the Commission has been unable to *secure from the respondent a conciliation agreement acceptable to the Commission,* the Commission *may bring a civil action against any respondent not a government, governmental agency, or political subdivision named in the charge. In the case of a respondent which is a government, governmental agency, or political subdivision, if the Commission has been unable to secure from the respondent a conciliation agreement acceptable to the Commission, the Commission shall take no further action and shall refer the case to the Attorney General who may bring a civil action against such respondent in the appropriate United States district court. The person or persons aggrieved shall have the right to intervene in a civil action brought by the Commission or the Attorney General in a case involving a government, governmental agency, or political subdivision. If a charge filed with the Commission pursuant to subsection (b) is dismissed by the Commission, or if within one hundred and eighty days from the filing of such charge or the expiration of any period of reference under subsection (c) or (d), whichever is later, the Commission has not filed a civil action under this section or the Attorney General has notified a civil action in a case involving a government, governmental agency, or political subdivision, or the Commission has not entered into a conciliation agreement to which the person aggrieved is a party, the Commission, or the Attorney General in a case involving a government, governmental agency, or political subdivision, shall so notify the person aggrieved and within ninety days after the giving of such notice a civil action may be brought*

against the respondent named in the charge (A) by the person claiming to be aggrieved, or (B) if such charge was filed by a member of the Commission, by any person whom the charge alleges was aggrieved by the alleged unlawful employment practice. Upon application by the complainant and in such circumstances as the court may deem just, the court may appoint an attorney for such complainant and may authorize the commencement of the action without the payment of fees, costs, or security. Upon timely application, the court may, in its discretion, permit the *Commission*, or the Attorney General in a case involving a government, governmental agency, or political subdivision, to intervene in such civil action *upon certification* that the case is of general public importance. Upon request, the court may, in its discretion, stay further proceedings for not more than sixty days pending the termination of State or local proceedings described in subsections (c) *or (d) of this section or further* efforts of the Commission to obtain voluntary compliance.

(2) Whenever a charge is filed with the Commission and the Commission concludes on the basis of a preliminary investigation that prompt judicial action is necessary to carry out the purposes of this Act, the Commission, or the Attorney General in a case involving a government, governmental agency, or political subdivision, may bring an action for appropriate temporary or preliminary relief pending final disposition of such charge. Any temporary restraining order or other order granting preliminary or temporary relief shall be issued in accordance with rule 65 of the Federal Rules of Civil Procedure. It shall be the duty of a court having jurisdiction over proceedings under this section to assign cases for hearing at the earliest practicable date and to cause such cases to be in every way expedited.

(3) Each United States district court and each United States court of a place subject to the jurisdiction of the United States shall have jurisdiction of actions brought under this title. Such an action may be brought in any judicial district in the State in which the unlawful employment practice is alleged to have been committed, in the judicial district in which the employment records relevant to such practice are maintained and administered, or in the judicial district in which the aggrieved person would have worked but for the alleged unlawful employment practice, but if the respondent is not found within any such district, such an action may be brought within the judicial district in which the respondent has his principal office. For purposes of sections 1404 and 1406 *of title 28 of the United States Code, the judicial district in which the respondent has his principal office shall in all cases be considered a district in which the action might have been brought.*

(4) It shall be the duty of the chief judge of the district (or in his absence, the acting chief judge) in which the case is pending immediately to designate a judge in such district to hear and determine the case. In the event that no judge in the district is available to hear and determine the case, the chief judge of the district, or the acting chief judge, as the case may be, shall certify this fact to the chief judge of the circuit (or in his absence, the acting chief judge) who shall then designate a district or circuit judge of the circuit to hear and determine the case.

(5) It shall be the duty of the judge designated pursuant to this subsection to assign the case for hearing at the earliest practicable date and to cause the case to be in every way expedited. If such judge has not scheduled the case for trial within one hundred and twenty days after issue has been joined, that judge may appoint a master pursuant to rule 53 of the Federal Rules of Civil Procedure.

(g) If the court finds that the respondent has intentionally engaged in or is intentionally engaging in an unlawful employment practice charged in the complaint, the court may enjoin the respondent from engaging in such unlawful employment practice, and order such affirmative action as may be appropriate, which may include, but is not limited to, reinstatement or hiring of employees, with or without back pay (payable by the employer, employment agency, or labor organization, as the case may be, responsible for the unlawful employment practice), or any other equitable relief as the court deems appropriate. Back pay liability shall not accrue from a date more than two years prior to the filing of a charge with the Commission. Interim earnings or amounts earnable with reasonable diligence by the person _ or persons discriminated against shall operate to reduce the back pay otherwise allowable. No order of the court shall require the admission or reinstatement of an individual as a member of a union, or the hiring, reinstatement, or promotion of an individual as an employee, or the payment to him of any back pay, if such individual was refused admission, suspended, or expelled, or was refused employment or advancement or was suspended or discharged for any reason other than discrimination on account of race, color, religion, sex, or national origin or in violation of section 704(a).

(h) The provisions of the Act entitled "An Act to

amend the Judicial Code and to define and limit the jurisdiction of courts sitting in equity, and for other purposes," approved March 23, 1932 (29 U.S.C. 101-115), shall not apply with respect to civil actions brought under this section.

(i) In any case in which an employer, employment agency, or labor organization fails to comply with an order of a court issued in a civil action brought under *this section*, the Commission may commence proceedings to compel compliance with such order.

(j) Any civil action brought under *this section* and any proceedings brought under subsection (i) shall be subject to appeal as provided in sections 1291 and 1292, title 28, United States Code.

(k) In any action or proceeding under this title the court, in its discretion, may allow the prevailing party, other than the Commission or the United States, a reasonable attorney's fee as part of the costs, and the Commission and the United States shall be liable for costs the same as a private person.

SEC. 707. (a) Whenever the Attorney General has reasonable cause to believe that any person or group of persons is engaged in a pattern or practice of resistance to the full enjoyment of any of the rights secured by this title, and that the pattern or practice is of such a nature and is intended to deny the full exercise of the rights herein described, the Attorney General may bring a civil action in the appropriate district court of the United States by filing with it a complaint (1) signed by him (or in his absence the Acting Attorney General), (2) setting forth facts pertaining to such pattern or practice, and (3) requesting such relief, including an application for a permanent or temporary injunction, restraining order or other order against the person or persons responsible for such pattern or practice, as he deems necessary to insure the full enjoyment of the rights herein described.

(b) The district courts of the United States shall have and shall exercise jurisdiction of proceedings instituted pursuant to this section, and in any such proceeding the Attorney General may file with the clerk of such court a request that a court of three judges be convened to hear and determine the case. Such request by the Attorney General shall be accompanied by a certificate that, in his opinion, the case is of general public importance. A copy of the certificate and request for a three-judge court shall be immediately furnished by such clerk to the chief judge of the circuit (or in his absence, the presiding circuit judge of the circuit) in which the case is pending. Upon receipt of such request it shall be the duty of the chief judge of the circuit or the presiding circuit judge, as the case may be, to designate immediately three judges in such circuit, of whom at least one shall be a circuit judge and another of whom shall be a district judge of the court in which the proceeding was instituted, to hear and determine such case, and it shall be the duty of the judges so designated to assign the case for hearing at the earliest practicable date, to participate in the hearing and determination thereof, and to cause the case to be in every way expedited. An appeal from the final judgment of such court will lie to the Supreme Court.

In the event the Attorney General fails to file such a request in any such proceeding, it shall be the duty of the chief judge of the district (or in his absence, the acting chief judge) in which the case is pending immediately to designate a judge in such district to hear and determine the case. In the event that no judge in the district is available to hear and determine the case, the chief judge of the district, or the acting chief judge, as the case may be, shall certify this fact to the chief judge of the circuit (or in his absence, the acting chief judge) who shall then designate a district or circuit judge of the circuit to hear and determine the case.

It shall be the duty of the judge designated pursuant to this section to assign the case for hearing at the earliest practicable date and to cause the case to be in every way expedited.

(c) Effective two years after the date of enactment of the Equal Employment Opportunity Act of 1972, the functions of the Attorney General under this section shall be transferred to the Commission, together with such personnel, property, records, and unexpended balances of appropriations, allocations, and other funds employed, used, held, available, or to be made available in connection with such functions unless the President submits, and neither House of Congress vetoes, a reorganization plan pursuant to chapter 9, of title 5, United States Code, inconsistent with the provisions of this subsection. The Commission shall carry out such functions in accordance with subsections (d) and (e) of this section.

(d) Upon the transfer of functions provided for in subsection (c) of this section, in all suits commenced pursuant to this section prior to the date of such transfer, proceedings shall continue without abatement, all court orders and decrees shall remain in effect, and the Commission shall be substituted as a party for the United States of America, the Attorney General, or the Acting Attorney General, as appropriate.

(e) *Subsequent to the date of enactment of the Equal Employment Opportunity Act of 1972, the Commission shall have authority to investigate and act on a charge of a pattern or practice of discrimination, whether filed by or on behalf of a person claiming to be aggrieved or by a member of the Commission. All such actions shall be conducted in accordance with the procedures set forth in section 706 of this Act.*

EFFECT ON STATE LAWS

SEC. 708. Nothing in this title shall be deemed to exempt or relieve any person from any liability, duty, penalty, or punishment provided by any present or future law of any State or political subdivision of a State, other than any such law which purports to require or permit the doing of any act which would be an unlawful employment practice under this title.

INVESTIGATIONS, INSPECTIONS, RECORDS, STATE AGENCIES

SEC. 709. (a) In connection with any investigation of a charge filed under section 706, the Commission or its designated representative shall at all reasonable times have access to, for the purposes of examination, and the right to copy any evidence of any person being investigated or proceeded against that relates to unlawful employment practices covered by this title and is relevant to the charge under investigation.

(b) The Commission may cooperate with State and local agencies charged with the administration of State fair employment practices laws and, with the consent of such agencies, may, for the purpose of carrying out its functions and duties under this title and within the limitation of funds appropriated specifically for such purpose, *engage in and contribute to the cost of research and other projects of mutual interest undertaken by such agencies,* and utilize the services of such agencies and their employees, and, notwithstanding any other provision of law, *pay by advance or reimbursement* such agencies and their employees for services rendered to assist the Commission in carrying out this title. In furtherance of such cooperative efforts, the Commission may enter into written agreements with such State or local agencies and such agreements may include provisons under which the Commission shall refrain from processing a charge in any cases or class of cases specified in such agreements or under which the Commission shall relieve any person or class of persons in such State or locality from requirements imposed under this section. The Commission shall rescind any such

agreement whenever it determines that the agreement no longer serves the interest of effective enforcement of this title.

(c) *Every* employer, employment agency, and labor organization subject to this title shall (1) make and keep such records relevant to the determinations of whether unlawful employment practices have been or are being committed, (2) preserve such records for such periods, and (3) make such reports therefrom, as the Commission shall prescribe by regulation or order, after public hearing, as reasonable, necessary, or appropriate for the enforcement of this title or the regulations or orders thereunder. The Commission shall, by regulation, require each employer, labor organization, and joint labor-management committee subject to this title which controls an apprenticeship or other training program to maintain such records as are reasonably necessary to carry out the purpose of this title, including, but not limited to, a list of applicants who wish to participate in such program, including the chronological order in which applications were received, and *to* furnish to the Commission upon request, a detailed description of the manner in which persons are selected to participate in the apprenticeship or other training program. Any employer, employment agency, labor organization, or joint labor-management committee which believes that the application to it of any regulation or order issued under this section would result in undue hardship may apply to the Commission for an exemption from the application of such regulation or order, *and, if such application for an exemption is denied,* bring a civil action in the United States district court for the district where such records are kept. If the Commission or the court, as the case may be, finds that the application of the regulation or order to the employer, employment agency, or labor organization in question would impose an undue hardship, the Commission or the court, as the case may be, may grant appropriate relief. *If any person required to comply with the provisions of this subsection fails or refuses to do so, the United States district court for the district in which such person is found, resides, or transacts business, shall, upon application of the Commission, or the Attorney General in a case involving a government, governmental agency or political subdivision, have jurisdiction to issue to such person an order requiring him to comply.*

(d) *In prescribing requirements pursuant to subsection (c) of this section, the Commission shall consult with other interested State and Federal agencies and shall endeavor to coordinate its requirements with those adopted by such agencies. The Commission shall furnish upon request and without cost to any State or local agency, charged with the administration of a fair employment practice law information obtained pursuant to subsection (c) of this section from any employer, employment agency, labor organization, or joint labor-management committee subject to the jurisdiction of such agency. Such information shall be furnished on condition that it not be made public by the recipient agency prior to the institution of a proceeding under State or local law involving such information. If this condition is violated by a recipient agency, the Commission may decline to honor subsequent requests pursuant to this subsection.*

(e) It shall be unlawful for any officer or employee of the Commission to make public in any manner whatever any information obtained by the Commission pursuant to its authority under this section prior to the institution of any proceeding under this title involving such information. Any officer or employee of the Commission who shall make public in any manner whatever any information in violation of this subsection shall be guilty of a misdemeanor and upon conviction thereof, shall be fined not more than $1,000, or imprisoned not more than one year.

INVESTIGATORY POWERS

Sec. 710. For the purpose of all hearings and investigations conducted by the Commission or its duly authorized agents or agencies, section 11 of the National Labor Relations Act (49 Stat. 455; 29 U.S.C. 161) shall apply.

NOTICES TO BE POSTED

Sec. 711. (a) Every employer, employment agency, and labor organization, as the case may be, shall post and keep posted in conspicuous places upon its premises where notices to employees, applicants for employment, and members are customarily posted a notice to be prepared or approved by the Commission setting forth excerpts from, or summaries of, the pertinent provisions of this title and information pertinent to the filing of a complaint.

(b) A willful violation of this section shall be punishable by a fine of not more than $100 for each separate offense.

VETERANS' PREFERENCE

Sec. 712. Nothing contained in this title shall be construed to repeal or modify any Federal, State, territorial, or local law creating special rights or preference for veterans.

RULES AND REGULATIONS

Sec. 713. (a) The Commission shall have authority from time to time to issue, amend, or rescind suitable procedural regulations to carry out the provisions of this title. Regulations issued under the section shall be in conformity with the standards and limitations of the Administrative Procedure Act.

(b) In any action or proceeding based on any alleged unlawful employment practice, no person shall be subject to any liability or punishment for or on account of (1) the commission by such person of an unlawful employment practice if he pleads and proves that the act or omission complained of was in good faith, in conformity with, and in reliance on any written interpretation or opinion of the Commission, or (2) the failure of such person to publish and file any information required by any provision of this title if he pleads and proves that he failed to publish and file such information in good faith, in conformity with the instructions of the Commission issued under this title regarding the filing of such information. Such a defense, if established, shall be a bar to the action or proceeding, notwithstanding that (A) after such act or omission, such interpretation or opinion is modified or rescinded or is determined by judicial authority to be invalid or of no legal effect, or (B) after publishing or filing the description and annual reports, such publication or filing is determined by judicial authority not to be in conformity with the requirements of this title.

FORCIBLY RESISTING THE COMMISSION OR ITS REPRESENTATIVES

Sec. 714. The provisions of *sections 111 and 1114* title 18, United States Code, shall apply to officers, agents, and employees of the Commission in the performance of their official duties. *Notwithstanding the provisions of sections 111 and 1114 of title 18, United States Code, whoever in violation of the provisions of section 1114 of such title kills a person while engaged in or on account of the performance of his official functions under this Act shall be punished by imprisonment for any term of years or for life.*

EQUAL EMPLOYMENT OPPORTUNITY COORDINATING COUNCIL

Sec. 715. There shall be established an Equal Employment Opportunity Coordinating Council (hereinafter referred to in this section as the Council) composed of the Secretary of Labor, the Chairman of the Equal Employment Opportunity Commission, the Attorney General, the Chairman of the United States Civil Service Commission, and the Chairman of the United States Civil Rights Commission, or their respective delegates. The Council shall have the responsibility for developing and implementing agreements, policies and practices designed to maximize effort, promote efficiency, and eliminate conflict, competition, duplication and inconsistency among the operations, functions and jurisdictions of the various departments, agencies and branches of the Federal government responsible for the implementation and enforcement of equal employment opportunity legislation, orders, and policies. On or before July 1 of each year, the Council shall transmit to the President and to the Congress a report of its activities, together with such recommendations for legislative or administrative changes as it concludes are desirable to further promote the purposes of this section.

EFFECTIVE DATE

SEC. 716. (a) This title shall become effective one year after the date of its enactment.

(b) Notwithstanding subsection (a), sections of this title other than sections 703, 704, 706, and 707 shall become effective immediately.

(c) The President shall, as soon as feasible after the enactment of this title, convene one or more conferences for the purpose of enabling the leaders of groups whose members will be affected by this title to become familiar with the rights afforded and obligations imposed by its provisions, and for the purpose of making plans which will result in the fair and effective administration of this title when all of its provisions become effective. The President shall invite the participation in such conference or conferences of (1) the members of the President's Committee on Equal Employment Opportunity, (2) the members of the Commission on Civil Rights, (3) representatives of State and local agencies engaged in furthering equal employment opportunity, (4) representatives of private agencies engaged in furthering equal employment opportunity, and (5) representatives of employers, labor organizations, and employment agencies who will be subject to this title.

NONDISCRIMINATION IN FEDERAL GOVERNMENT EMPLOYMENT

SEC. 717. (a) All personnel actions affecting employees or applicants for employment (except with regard

to aliens employed outside the limits of the United States) in military departments as defined in section 102 of title 5, United States Code, in executive agencies (other than the General Accounting Office) as defined in section 105 of title 5, United States Code (including employees and applicants for employment who are paid from nonappropriated funds), in the United States Postal Service and the Postal Rate Commission, in those units of the Government of the District of Columbia having positions in the competitive service, and in those units of the legislative and judicial branches of the Federal Government having positions in the competitive service, and in the Library of Congress shall be made free from any discrimination based on race, color, religion, sex, or national origin.

(b) Except as otherwise provided in this subsection, the Civil Service Commission shall have authority to enforce the provisions of subsection (a) through appropriate remedies, including reinstatement or hiring of employees with or without back pay, as will effectuate the policies of this section, and shall issue such rules, regulations, orders, and instructions as it deems necessary and appropriate to carry out its responsibilities under this section. The Civil Service Commission shall—

(1) be responsible for the annual review and approval of a national and regional equal employment opportunity plan which each department and agency and each appropriate unit referred to in subsection (a) of this section shall submit in order to maintain an affirmative program of equal employment opportunity for all such employees and applicants for employment;

(2) be responsible for the review and evaluation of the operation of all agency equal employment opportunity programs, periodically obtaining and publishing (on at least a semiannual basis) progress reports from each such department, agency, or unit; and

(3) consult with and solicit the recommendations of interested individuals, groups, and organizations relating to equal employment opportunity.

The head of each such department, agency, or unit shall comply with such rules, regulations, orders, and instructions which shall include a provision that an employee or applicant for employment shall be notified of any final action taken on any complaint of discrimination filed by him thereunder. The plan submitted by each department, agency, and unit shall include, but not be limited to—

(1) provision for the establishment of training and education programs designed to provide a maximum opportunity for employees to advance so as to perform at their highest potential; and

(2) a description of the qualifications in terms of training and experience relating to equal employment opportunity for the principal and operating officials of each such department, agency, or unit responsible for carrying out the equal employment opportunity program and of the allocation of personnel and resources proposed by such department, agency, or unit to carry out its equal employment opportunity program.

With respect to employment in the Library of Congress, authorities granted in this subsection to the Civil Service Commission shall be exercised by the Librarian of Congress.

(c) Within thirty days of receipt of notice of final action taken by a department, agency, or unit referred to in subsection 717(a), or by the Civil Service Commission upon an appeal from a decision or order of such department, agency, or unit on a complaint of discrimination based on race, color, religion, sex, or national origin, brought pursuant to subsection (a) of this section, Executive Order 11478 or any succeeding Executive orders, or after one hundred and eighty days from the filing of the initial charge with the department, agency, or unit or with the Civil Service Commission on appeal from a decision or order of such department, agency, or unit until such time as final action may be taken by a department, agency, or unit, an employee or applicant for employment, if aggrieved by the final disposition of his complaint, or by the failure to take final action on his complaint, may file a civil action as provided in section 706, in which civil action the head of the department, agency, or unit, as appropriate, shall be the defendant.

(d) The provisions of section 706(f) through (k), as applicable, shall govern civil actions brought hereunder.

(e) Nothing contained in this Act shall relieve any Government agency or official of its or his primary responsibility to assure nondiscrimination in employment as required by the Constitution and statutes or of its or his responsibilities under Executive Order 11478 relating to equal employment opportunity in the Federal Government.

SPECIAL PROVISIONS WITH RESPECT TO DENIAL, TERMINATION, AND SUSPENSION OF GOVERNMENT CONTRACTS

SEC. 718. No Government contract, or portion thereof, with any employer, shall be denied, withheld, terminated, or suspended, by any agency or officer of the United States under any equal employment opportunity law or order, where such employer has an affirmative action plan which has previously been accepted by the Government for the same facility within the past twelve months without first according such employer full hearing and adjudication under the provisions of title 5, United States Code, section 554, and the following pertinent sections: Provided, That if such employer has deviated substantially from such previously agreed to affirmative action plan, this section shall not apply: Provided further, That for the purposes of this section an affirmative action plan shall be deemed to have been accepted by the Government at the time the appropriate compliance agency has accepted such plan unless within forty-five days thereafter the Office of Federal Contract Compliance has disapproved such plan.

PROVISIONS OF EQUAL EMPLOYMENT OPPORTUNITY ACT OF 1972 WHICH RELATE TO BUT DO NOT AMEND THE CIVIL RIGHTS ACT OF 1964

SEC. 9. (a) Section 5314 of title 5 of the United States Code is amended by adding at the end thereof the following new clause:

"(58) Chairman, Equal Employment Opportunity Commission."

(b) Clause (72) of section 5315 of such title is amended to read as follows:

"(72) Members, Equal Employment Opportunity Commission (4)."

(c) Clause (111) of section 5316 of such title is repealed.

(d) Section 5316 of such title is amended by adding at the end thereof the following new clause:

"(131) General Counsel of the Equal Employment Opportunity Commission."

SEC. 12. Section 5108(c) of title 5, United States Code, is amended by—

(1) striking out the word "and" at the end of paragraph (9);

(2) striking out the period at the end of paragraph (10) and inserting in lieu thereof a semicolon and the word "and"; and

(3) by adding immediately after paragraph (10) the last time it appears therein in the following new paragraph:

"(11) the Chairman of the Equal Employment Opportunity Commission, subject to the standards and procedures prescribed by this chapter, may place an additional ten positions in the Equal Employment Opportunity Commission in GS–16, GS–17, and GS–18 for the purposes of carrying out title VII of the Civil Rights Act of 1964."

SEC. 14. The amendments made by this Act to section 706 of the Civil Rights Act of 1964 shall be applicable with respect to charges pending with the Commission on the date of enactment of this Act and all charges filed thereafter.

[¶ 300]

[¶ 301]   [Enacting Provision]

Be it enacted by the Senate and House of Representatives of the United States of America in Congress assembled.

[¶ 302]   [Ban on Pregnancy Discrimination]

Section 1. That Section 701 of the Civil Rights Act of 1964 is amended by adding at the end thereof the following new subsection:

"(k) The terms, 'because of sex' or 'on the basis of sex' include, but are not limited to, because of or on the basis of pregnancy, childbirth or related medical conditions; and women affected by pregnancy, childbirth, or related medical conditions shall be treated the same for all employment-related purposes, including receipt of benefits under fringe benefit programs, as other persons not so affected but similar in their ability or inability to work, and nothing in section 703(h) of this title shall be interpreted to permit otherwise. This subsection shall not require an employer to pay for health insurance benefits for abortion, except where the life of the mother would be endangered if the fetus were carried to term, or except where medical complications have arisen from an abortion: Provided, That nothing herein shall preclude an employer from providing abortion benefits or otherwise affect bargaining agreements in regard to abortion.".

[¶ 303]   [Effective Dates]

Sec. 2. (a) Except as provided in subsection (b), the amendment made by this Act shall be effective on the date of enactment.

(b) The provisions of the amendment made by the first section of this Act shall not apply to any fringe benefit program or fund, or insurance program which is in effect on the date of enactment on the date of enactment of this Act until 180 days after enactment of this Act.

[¶ 304]   [Adjustments in Benefit Plans]

Sec. 3. Until the expiration of a period of one year from the date of enactment of this Act or, if there is an applicable collective-bargaining agreement in effect on the date of enactment of this Act, until the termination of that agreement, no person who, on the date of enactment of this Act is providing either by direct payment or by making contributions to a fringe benefit fund or insurance program benefits in violation with this Act shall, in order to come into compliance with this Act, reduce the benefits or the compensation provided any employee on the date of enactment of this Act, either directly or by failing to provide sufficient contributions to a fringe benefit fund or insurance program: Provided, That where the costs of such benefits on the date of enactment of this Act are apportioned between employers and employees, the payments or contributions required to comply with this Act may be made by employers and employees in the same proportion: And provided further, That nothing in this section shall prevent the readjustment of benefits or compensation for reasons unrelated to compliance with this Act.

Appendix E
The Age Discrimination in Employment Act of 1967, as Amended

An Act

To prohibit age discrimination in employment

Be it enacted by the Senate and House of Representatives of the United States of American in Congress assembled, that this Act may be cited as the "Age Discrimination in Employment Act of 1967".

STATEMENT OF FINDINGS AND PURPOSE

SEC. 2. (a) The Congress hereby finds and declares that—

(1) in the face of rising productivity and affluence, older workers find themselves disadvantaged in their efforts to retain employment, and especially to regain employment when displaced from jobs;

(2) the setting of arbitrary age limits regardless of potential for job performance has become a common practice, and certain otherwise desirable practices may work to the disadvantage of older persons;

(3) the incidence of unemployment, especially longterm unemployment with resultant deterioration of skill, morale, and employer acceptability is, relative to the younger ages, high among older workers; their numbers are great and growing; and their employment problems grave;

(4) the existence in industries affecting commerce, of arbitrary discrimination in employment because of age, burdens commerce and the free flow of goods in commerce.

(b) It is therefore the purpose of this Act to promote employment of older persons based on their ability rather than age; to prohibit arbitrary age discrimination in the employment; to help employers and workers find ways of meeting problems arising from the impact of age on employment.

EDUCATION AND RESEARCH PROGRAM

SEC. 3. (a) The Secretary of Labor shall undertake studies and provide information to labor unions, management, and the general public concerning the needs and abilities of older workers, and their potentials for continued employment and contribution to the economy. In order to achieve the purposes of this Act, the Secretary of Labor shall carry on a continuing program of education and information, under which he may, among other measures—

(1) undertake research, and promote research, with a view to reducing barriers to the employment of older persons, and the promotion of measures for utilizing their skills;

(2) publish and otherwise make available to employers, professional societies, the various media of communication, and other interested persons the findings of studies and other materials for the promotion of employment;

(3) foster through the public employment service system and through cooperative effort the development of facilities of public and private agencies for expanding the opportunities and potentials of older persons;

(4) sponsor and assist State and community informational and educational programs.

(b) Not later than six months after the effective date of this Act, the Secretary shall recommend to the Congress any measures he may deem desirable to change the lower or upper age limits set forth in section 12.

PROHIBITION OF AGE DISCRIMINATION

SEC. 4. (a) It shall be unlawful for an employer—

(1) to fail or refuse to hire or to discharge any individual or otherwise discriminate against any individual with respect to his compensation, terms, conditions, or privileges of employment, because of such individual's age;

(2) to limit, segregate, or classify his employees in any way which would deprive or tend to deprive any individual of employment opportunities or otherwise adversely affect his status as an employee, because of such individual's age; or

(3) to reduce the wage rate of any employee in order to comply with this Act.

(b) It shall be unlawful for an employment agency to fail or refuse to refer for employment, or otherwise to discriminate against, any individual because of such individual's age, or to classify or refer for employment any individual on the basis of such individual's age.

---

*The original text of the Age Discrimination in Employment Act of 1967 is set in the "Century" typeface. Added or amended language as enacted by subsequent amendments is represented by other typefaces as indicated below.

Amendments	Typeface Used	Public Law	Date Enacted	Statute Citation
Original	Century	90–202	12/15/67	81 Stat. 602
1974	Century Boldface	93–259	4/8/74	88 Stat. 55
1978	Century Italics	95–256	4/6/78	92 Stat. 189

(c) it shall be unlawful for a labor organization—

(1) to exclude or to expel from its membership, or otherwise to discriminate against, any individual because of his age,

(2) to limit, segregate, or classify its membership, or to classify or fail or refuse to refer for employment any individual, in any way which would deprive or tend to deprive any individual of employment opportunities, or would limit such employment opportunities or otherwise adversely affect his status as an employee or as an applicant for employment, because of such individual's age;

(3) to cause or attempt to cause an employee to discriminate against an individual in violation of this section.

(d) It shall be unlawful for an employer to discriminate against any of his employees or applicants for employment, for an employment agency to discriminate against any individual, or for a labor organization to discriminate against any member thereof or applicant for membership because such individual, member or applicant for membership has opposed any practice made unlawful by this section, or because such individual, member or applicant for membership has made a charge, testified, assisted, or participated in any manner in an investigation, proceeding, or litigation under this Act.

(e) It shall be unlawful for an employer, labor organization, or employment agency to print or publish, or cause to be printed or published, any notice or advertisement relating to employment by such an employer or membership in or any classification or referral for employment by such a labor organization, or relating to any classification or referral for employment by such an employment agency, indicating any preference, limitation, specification, or discrimination, based on age.

(f) It shall not be unlawful for an employer, employment agency, or labor organization—

(1) to take any action otherwise prohibited under subsections (a), (b), (c), or (e) of this section where age is a bona fide occupational qualification reasonably necessary to the normal operation of the particular business, or where the differentiation is based on reasonable factors other than age;

(2) to observe the terms of a bona fide seniority system or any bona fide employee benefit plan such as a retirement, pension, or insurance plan, which is not a subterfuge to evade the purposes of this Act, except that no such employee benefit plan shall excuse the failure to hire any individual, *and no such seniority system or employee benefit plan shall require or permit the involuntary retirement of any individual specified by section 12(a) of this Act because of the age of such individual;* [1] or

(3) to discharge or otherwise discipline an individual for good cause.

STUDY BY SECRETARY OF LABOR

SEC. 5. *(a)(1)* The Secretary of Labor is directed to undertake an appropriate study of institutional and other arrangements giving rise to involuntary retirement, and report his findings and any appropriate legislative recommendations to the President and to the Congress. *Such study shall include—*

(A) an examination of the effect of the amendment made by section 3(a) of the Age Discrimination in Employment Act Amendments of 1978 in raising the upper age limitation established by section 12(a) of this Act to 70 years of age;

(B) a determination of the feasibility of eliminating such limitations;

(C) a determination of the feasibility of raising such limitation above 70 years of age; and

(D) an examination of the effect of the exemption contained in section 12(c), relating to certain executive employees, and the exemption contained in section 12(d), relating to tenured teaching personnel.

(2) The Secretary may undertake the study required by paragraph (1) of this subsection directly or by contract or other arrangement.

(b) The report required by subsection (a) of this section shall be transmitted to the President and the Congress as an interim report not later than January 1, 1981, and in final form not later than January 1, 1982.

ADMINISTRATION

SEC. 6. The Secretary shall have the power—

(a) to make delegations, to appoint such agents and employees, and to pay for technical assistance on a fee for service basis, as he deems

---

[1] As amended by section 2(a) of the Age Discrimination in Employment Act Amendments of 1978. The effective date of this amendment is set forth in section 2(b) of the 1978 amendments: "*The amendment made by subsection (a) of this section shall take effect on the date of enactment of this Act, except that, in the case of employees covered by a collective bargaining agreement which is in effect on September 1, 1977, which was entered into by a labor organization (as defined by section 6(d)(4) of the Fair Labor Standards Act of 1938), and which would otherwise be prohibited by the amendment made by section 3(a) of this Act, the amendment made by subsection (a) of this section shall take effect upon the termination of such agreement or on January 1, 1980, whichever occurs first.*" The revision of section 12 of the ADEA is the "amendment made by section 3(a) of this Act" referred to in the previous sentence.

necessary to assist him in the performance of his functions under this Act;

(b) to cooperate with regional, State, local, and other agencies, and to cooperate with and furnish technical assistance to employers, labor organizations, and employment agencies to aid in effectuating the purposes of this Act.

RECORDKEEPING, INVESTIGATION, AND ENFORCEMENT

SEC. 7. (a) The Secretary shall have the power to make investigations and require the keeping of records necessary or appropriate for the administration of this Act in accordance with the powers and procedures provided in sections 9 and 11 of the Fair Labor Standards Act of 1938, as amended (29 U.S.C. 209 and 211).

(b) The provisions of this Act shall be enforced in accordance with the powers, remedies, and procedures provided in sections 11(b), 16 (except for subsection (a) thereof), and 17 of the Fair Labor Standards Act of 1938, as amended (29 U.S.C. 211(b), 216, 217), and subsection (c) of this section. Any act prohibited under section 4 of this Act shall be deemed to be a prohibited act under section 15 of the Fair Labor Standards Act of 1938, as amended (29 U.S.C. 215). Amounts owing to a person as a result of a violation of this Act shall be deemed to be unpaid minimum wages or unpaid overtime compensation for purposes of sections 16 and 17 of the Fair Labor Standards Act of 1938, as amended (29 U.S.C. 216, 217): *Provided,* That liquidated damages shall be payable only in cases of willful violations of this Act. In any action brought to enforce this Act the court shall have jurisdiction to grant such legal or equitable relief as may be appropriate to effectuate the purposes of this Act, including without limitation judgments compelling employment, reinstatement or promotion, or enforcing the liability for amounts deemed to be unpaid minimum wages or unpaid overtime compensation under this section. Before instituting any action under this section, the Secretary shall attempt to eliminate the discriminatory practice or practices alleged, and to effect voluntary compliance with requirements of this Act through informal methods of conciliation, conference, and persuasion.

(c)(*1*) Any person aggrieved may bring a civil action in any court of competent jurisdiction for such legal or equitable relief as will effectuate the purposes of this Act: *Provided,* That the right of any person to bring such action shall terminate upon the commencement of an action by the Secretary to enforce the right of such employee under this Act.

(2) In an action brought under paragraph (1), a person shall be entitled to a trial by jury of any issue of fact in any such action for recovery of amounts owing as a result of a violation of this Act, regardless of whether equitable relief is sought by any party in such action. [2]

(d) No civil action may be commenced by an individual under this section until 60 days after a charge alleging unlawful discrimination has been filed with the Secretary. Such a charge shall be filed—

    (1) within 180 days after the alleged unlawful practice occurred; or

    (2) in a case to which section 14(b) applies, within 300 days after the alleged unlawful practice occurred, or within 30 days after receipt by the individual of notice of termination of proceedings under State law, whichever is earlier.

Upon receiving such a charge, the Secretary shall promptly notify all persons named in such charge as prospective defendants in the action and shall promptly seek to eliminate any alleged unlawful practice by informal methods of conciliation, conference, and persuasion. [3]

(e)(1) Sections 6 and 10 of the Portal-to-Portal Act of 1947 shall apply to actions under this Act.

(2) For the period during which the Secretary is attempting to effect voluntary compliance with requirements of this Act through informal methods of conciliation, conference, and persuasion pursuant to subsection (b), the statute of limitations as provided in section 6 of the Portal-to-Portal Act of 1947 shall be tolled, but in no event for a period in excess of one year. [4]

NOTICE TO BE POSTED

SEC. 8. Every employer, employment agency, and labor organization shall post and keep posted in conspicuous places upon its premises a notice to be prepared or approved by the Secretary setting forth information as the Secretary deems appropriate to effectuate the purposes of this Act.

RULES AND REGULATIONS

SEC. 9. In accordance with the provisions of subchapter II of chapter 5 of title 5, United States Code, the Secretary of Labor may issue such rules and regulations as he may consider necessary or appropriate for carrying out this Act, and may establish

---

[1] Effective with respect to civil actions brought after April 6, 1978.

[2] Effective with respect to civil actions brought after April 6, 1978. Prior to the Age Discrimination in Employment Act Amendments of 1978, section 7(d) read as it does now, except that it required a "notice of intent to sue" rather than a "charge alleging unlawful discrimination."

[3] Effective with respect to conciliations commenced by the Secretary of Labor after April 6, 1978.

such reasonable exemptions to and from any or all provisions of this Act as he may find necessary and proper in the public interest.

CRIMINAL PENALTIES

SEC. 10. Whoever shall forcibly resist, oppose, impede, intimidate or interfere with a duly authorized representative of the Secretary while he is engaged in the performance of duties under this Act shall be punished by a fine of not more than $500 or by imprisonment for not more than one year, or both: *Provided, however,* That no person shall be imprisoned under this section except when there has been a prior conviction hereunder.

DEFINITIONS

SEC. 11. for the purposes of this Act—

(a) The term "person" means one or more individuals, partnerships, associations, labor organizations, corporations, business trusts, legal representatives, or any organized groups of persons.

(b) The term "employer" means a person engaged in an industry affecting commerce who has **twenty** [5] or more employees for each working day in each of twenty or more calendar weeks in the current or preceding calendar year: *Provided,* That prior to June 30, 1968, employers having fewer than fifty employees shall not be considered employers. **The term also means (1) any agent of such a person, and (2) a State or political subdivision of a State and any agency or instrumentality of a State or a political subdivision of a State, and any interstate agency, but such term does not include the United States, or a corporation wholly owned by the Government of the United States.**

(c) The term "employment agency" means any person regularly undertaking with or without compensation to procure employees for an employer and includes an agent of such a person; but shall not include an agency of the United States.[6]

(d) The term "labor organization" means a labor organization engaged in an industry affecting commerce, and any agent of such an organization, and includes any organization of any kind, any agency, or employee representation committee, group, association, or plan so engaged in which employees participate and which exists for the purpose, in whole or in

part, of dealing with employers concerning grievances, labor disputes, wages, rates of pay, hours, or other terms or conditions of employment, and any conference, general committee, joint or system board, or joint council so engaged which is subordinate to a national or international labor organization.

(e) A labor organization shall be deemed to be engaged in an industry affecting commerce if (1) it maintains or operates a hiring hall or hiring office which procures employees for an employer or procures for employees opportunities to work for an employer, or (2) the number of its members (or, where it is a labor organization composed of other labor organizations or their representatives, if the aggregate number of the members of such other labor organization) is fifty or more prior to July 1, 1968, or twenty-five or more on or after July 1, 1968, and such labor organization—

(1) is the certified representative of employees under the provisions of the National Labor Relations Act, as amended, or the Railway Labor Act, as amended; or

(2) although not certified, is a national or international labor organization or a local labor organization recognized or acting as the representative or employees of an employer or employers engaged in an industry affecting commerce; or

(3) has chartered a local labor organization or subsidiary body which is representing or actively seeking to represent employees of employers within the meaning of paragraph (1) or (2); or

(4) has been chartered by a labor organization representing or actively seeking to represent employees within the meaning of paragraph (1) or (2) as the local or subordinate body through which such employees may enjoy membership or become affiliated with such labor organization; or

(5) is a conference, general committee, joint or system board, or joint council subordinate to a national or international labor organization, which includes a labor organization engaged in an industry affecting commerce within the meaning of any of the preceding paragraphs of this subsection.

(f) The term "employee" means an individual employed by any employer **except that the term "employee" shall not include any person elected to public office in any State or political subdivision of any State by the qualified voters thereof, or any person chosen by such officer to be on such officer's**

---

[5] Section 28(a)(1) of the Fair Labor Standards Amendments of 1974 substituted "twenty" for "twenty-five," effective May 1, 1974.

[6] Prior to the Fair Labor Standards Amendments of 1974 the Act's definition of an "employment agency" excluded "an agency of a State or political subdivision of a State, except that such term shall include the United States Employment Service and the system of State and local employment services receiving Federal assistance."

personal staff, or an appointee on the policymaking level or an immediate adviser with respect to the exercise of the constitutional or legal powers of the office. The exemption set forth in the preceding sentence shall not include employees subject to the civil service laws of a State government, governmental agency, or political subdivision.

(g) The term "commerce" means trade, traffic, commerce, transportation, transmission, or communication among the several States; or between a State and any place outside thereof; or within the District of Columbia, or a possession of the United States; or between points in the same State but through a point outside thereof.

(h) The term "industry affecting commerce" means any activity, business, or industry in commerce or in which a labor dispute would hinder or obstruct commerce or the free flow of commerce and includes any activity or industry "affecting commerce" within the meaning of the Labor-Management Reporting and Disclosure Act of 1959.

(i) The term "State" includes a State of the United States, the District of Columbia, Puerto Rico, the Virgin Islands, American Samoa, Guam, Wake Island, the Canal Zone, and Outer Continental Shelf lands defined in the Outer Continental Shelf Lands Act.

AGE LIMITATION

SEC. 12. (a)[7] *The prohibitions in this Act shall be limited to individuals who are at least 40 years of age but less than 70 years of age.*

(b)[8] *In the case of any personnel action affecting employees or applicants for employment which is subject to the provisions of section 15 of this Act, the prohibitions established in section 15 of this Act shall be limited to individuals who are at least 40 years of age.*

(c)[9] *(1) Nothing in this Act shall be construed to prohibit compulsory retirement of any employee who has attained 65 years of age but not 70 years of age, and who, for the 2-year period immediately before retirement, is employed in a bona fide executive or a high policymaking position, if such employee is entitled to an immediate nonforfeitable annual retirement benefit from a pension, profit-sharing, savings,*

or deferred compensation plan, or any combination of such plans, of the employer of such employee, which equals, in the aggregate, at least $27,000.

(2) In applying the retirement benefit test of paragraph (1) of this subsection, if any such retirement benefit is in a form other than a straight life annuity (with no ancillary benefits), or if employees contribute to any such plan or make rollover contributions, such benefit shall be adjusted in accordance with regulations prescribed by the Secretary, after consultation with the Secretary of the Treasury, so that the benefit is the equivalent of a straight life annuity (with no ancillary benefits) under a plan to which employees do not contribute and under which no rollover contributions are made.

(d)[10] Nothing in this Act shall be construed to prohibit compulsory retirement of any employee who has attained 65 years of age but not 70 years of age, and who is serving under a contract of unlimited tenure (or similar arrangement providing for unlimited tenure) at an institution of higher education (as defined by section 1201(a) of the Higher Education Act of 1965).

ANNUAL REPORT

SEC. 13. The Secretary shall submit annually in January a report to the Congress covering his activities for the preceding year and including such information, data, and recommendations for further legislation in connection with the matters covered by this act as he may find advisable. Such report shall contain an evaluation and appraisal by the Secretary of the effect of the minimum and maximum ages established by this Act, together with his recommendations to the Congress. In making such evaluation and appraisal, the Secretary shall take into consideration any changes which may have occurred in the general age level of the population, the effect of the Act upon workers not covered by its provisions, and such other factors as he may deem pertinent.

FEDERAL-STATE RELATIONSHIP

SEC. 14. (a) Nothing in this Act shall affect the jurisdiction of any agency of any State performing like functions with regard to discriminatory employment practices on account of age except that upon commencement of action under this Act such action shall supersede any State action.

(b) In the case of an alleged unlawful practice occuring in a State which has a law prohibiting

---

[7] Subsection 12(a) takes effect on January 1, 1979. Prior to the Age Discrimination in employment Act Amendments of 1978, section 12 provided in its entirety: "The prohibitions in this Act shall be limited to individuals who are at least forty years of age but less than sixty-five years of age."
[8] Subsection 12(b), which was added by the 1978 Amendments, takes effect on September 30, 1978.
[9] Subsection 12(c), which was added by the 1978 Amendment', takes effect on January 1, 1979.

[10] Subsection 12(d), which was added by the 1978 Amendments, takes effect on January 1, 1979. It is repealed on July 1, 1982.

discrimination in employment because of age and establishing or authorizing a State authority to grant or seek relief from such discriminatory practice, no suit may be brought under section 7 of this Act before the expiration of sixty days after proceedings have been commenced under the State law, unless such proceedings have been earlier terminated: *Provided,* That such sixty-day period shall be extended to one hundred and twenty days during the first year after the effective date of such State law. If any requirement for the commencement of such proceedings is imposed by a State authority other than a requirement of the filing of a written and signed statement of the facts upon which the proceeding is based, the proceeding shall be deemed to have been commenced for the purposes of this subsection at the time such statement is sent by registered mail to the appropriate State authority.

NONDISCRIMINATION ON ACCOUNT OF AGE IN FEDERAL GOVERNMENT EMPLOYMENT

Sec. 15. (a) All personnel actions affecting employees or applicants for employment *who are at least 40 years of age* (except *personnel actions* with regard to aliens employed outside the limits of the United States) in military departments as defined in section 102 of title 5, United States Code, in executive agencies as defined in section 105 of title 5, United States Code (including employees and applicants for employment who are paid from nonappropriated funds), in the United States Postal Service and the Postal Rate Commission, in those units in the government of the District of Columbia having positions in the competitive service, and in those units of the legislative and judicial branches of the Federal Government having positions in the competitive service, and in the Library of Congress shall be made free from any discrimination based on age.

(b) Except as otherwise provided in this subsection, the Civil Service Commission is authorized to enforce the provisions of subsection (a) through appropriate remedies, including reinstatement or hiring of employees with or without backpay, as will effectuate the policies of this section. The Civil Service Commission shall issue such rules, regulations, orders and instructions as it deems necessary and appropriate to carry out its responsibilities under this section. The Civil Service Commission shall—

(1) be responsible for the review and evaluation of the operation of all agency programs designed to carry out the policy of this section, periodically obtaining and publishing (on at least a semiannual basis) progress reports from each department, agency, or unit referred to in subsection (a);

(2) consult with and solicit the recommendations of interested individuals, groups, and organizations relating to nondiscrimination in employment on account of age; and

(3) provide for the acceptance and processing of complaints of discrimination in Federal employment on account of age.

The head of each such department, agency, or unit shall comply with such rules, regulations, orders, and instructions of the Civil Service Commission which shall include a provision that an employee or applicant for employment shall be notified of any final action taken on any complaint of discrimination filed by him thereunder. Reasonable exemptions to the provisions of this section may be established by the Commission but only when the Commission has established a maximum age requirement on the basis of a determination that age is a bona fide occupational qualification necessary to the performance of the duties of the position. With respect to employment in the Library of Congress, authorities granted in this subsection to the Civil Service Commission shall be exercised by the Librarian of Congress.

(c) Any person aggrieved may bring a civil action in any Federal district court of competent jurisdiction for such legal or equitable relief as will effectuate the purposes of this Act.

(d) When the individual has not filed a complaint concerning age discrimination with the Commission, no civil action may be commenced by an individual under this section until the individual has given the Commission not less that thirty days' notice of an intent to file such action. Such notice shall be filed within one hundred and eighty days after the alleged unlawful practice occurred. Upon receiving a notice of intent to sue, the Commission shall promptly notify all persons named therein as prospective defendants in the action and take any appropriate action to assure the elimination of any unlawful practice.

(e) Nothing contained in this section shall relieve any Government agency or official of the responsibility to assure nondiscrimination on account of age in employment as required under any provision of Federal law.

(f)[11] *Any personnel action of any department, agen-*

---

[11] Effective September 30, 1978.

cy, or other entity referred to in subsection (a) of this section shall not be subject to or affected by, any provision of this Act, other than the provisions of section 12(b) of this Act and the provisions of this section.

(g)[12] *(1) The Civil Service Commission shall undertake a study relating to the effects of the amendments made to this section by the Age Discrimination in Employment Act Amendments of 1978, and the effects of section 12(b) of this Act, as added by the Age Discrimination in Employment Act Amendments of 1978.*

(2) The Civil Service Commission shall transmit a report to the President and to the Congress containing the findings of the Commission resulting from the study of the Commission under paragraph (1) of this subsection. Such report shall be transmitted no later than January 1, 1980.

EFFECTIVE DATE [13]

SEC. 16. This Act shall become effective one hundred and eighty days after enactment, except (a) that the Secretary of Labor may extend the delay in effective date of any provision of this Act up to an additional ninety days thereafter if he finds that such time is necessary in permitting adjustments to the provisions hereof, and (b) that on or after the date of enactment the Secretary of Labor is authorized to issue such rules and regulations as may be necessary to carry out its provisions.

APPROPRIATIONS

SEC. 17. There are hereby authorized to be appropriated such sums as may be necessary to carry out this Act.[14]

Approved December 15, 1967.

---

[12] Effective April 6, 1978.

[13] The effective date of the provisions added by the Fair Labor Standards Amendments of 1974, which are shown in bold face type, was May 1, 1974. See section 29(a) of the Fair Labor Standards Amendments of 1974. The effective dates of the provisions added by the Age Discrimination in Employment Act Amendments of 1978, which are shown in italic type, are indicated in footnotes to each provision.

[14] Section 7 of the Age Discrimination in Employment Act Amendments of 1978 amended this section by eliminating the $5 million authorization ceiling on appropriations.

[PUBLIC LAW 95-256]

[95TH CONGRESS, 2D SESSION]

An Act

To amend the Age Discrimination in Employment Act of 1967 to extend the age group of employees who are protected by the provisions of such Act, and for other purposes.

Be it enacted by the Senate and House of Representatives of the United States of America in Congress assembled, That this Act may be cited as the "Age Discrimination in Employment Act Amendments of 1978".

[Sections 2 through 4, 5(a), 6 and 7 of the Age Discrimination in Employment Act Amendments of 1978 amend the Age Discrimination in Employment Act of 1967, and are incorporated in their proper place in the Act. Where the effective dates of these amendments are not part of the Act proper, they are noted in footnotes. Section 5(b), (c) and (d) of the 1978 Amendments amend title 5 of the United States Code, and are set forth below.]

FEDERAL GOVERNMENT EMPLOYMENT

SEC. 5.[15] * * *

(b)(1) Section 3322 of title 5, United States Code, relating to temporary appointments after age 70, is repealed.

(2) The analysis for chapter 33 of title 5, United States Code, is amended by striking out the item relating to section 3322.

---

[15] The amendments in Section 5(b), (c) and (d) take effect on September 30, 1978.

(c) Section 8335 of title 5, United States Code, relating to mandatory separation, is amended—

(1) by striking out subsections (a), (b), (c), (d), and (e) thereof;

(2) by redesignating subsections (f) and (g) as subsections (a) and (b), respectively; and

(3) by adding after subsection (b), as so redesignated, the following new subsections:

"(c) An employee of the Alaska Railroad in Alaska and an employee who is a citizen of the United States employed on the Isthmus of Panama by the Panama Canal Company or the Canal Zone Government, who becomes 62 years of age and completes 15 years of service in Alaska or on the Isthmus of Panama shall be automatically separated from the service. The separation is effective on the last day of the month in which the employee becomes age 62 or completes 15 years of service in Alaska or on the Isthmus of Panama if then over that age. The employing office shall notify the employee in writing of the date of separation at least 60 days in advance thereof. Action to separate the employee is not effective, without the consent of the employee, until the last day of the month in which the 60-day notice expires.

"(d) The President, by Executive order, may exempt an employee from automatic separation under this section when he determines the public interest so requires".

(d) Section 8339(d) of title 5, United States Code, relating to computation of annuity, is amended by striking out "section 8335(g)" and inserting in lieu thereof "section 8335(b)".

Appendix F
Equal Employment Opportunity Commission's *Guidelines on Discrimination Because of Sex*

PART 1604—GUIDELINES ON DISCRIMINATION BECAUSE OF SEX

AUTHORITY: Sec. 713(b), 78 Stat. 265, 42 U.S.C. 2000e-12.

SOURCE: 37 FR 6836, April 5, 1972, unless otherwise noted.

§ 1604.1 General principles.

(a) References to "employer" or "employers" in this Part 1604 state principles that are applicable not only to employers but also to labor organizations and to employment agencies insofar as their action or inaction may adversely affect employment opportunities.

(b) To the extent that the views expressed in prior Commission pronouncements are inconsistent with the views expressed herein, such prior views are hereby overruled.

(c) The Commission will continue to consider particular problems relating to sex discrimination on a case-by-case basis.

§ 1604.2 Sex as a bona fide occupational qualification.

(a) The commission believes that the bona fide occupational qualification exception as to sex should be interpreted narrowly. Label—"Men's jobs" and "Women's jobs"—tend to deny employment opportunities unnecessarily to one sex or the other.

(1) The Commission will find that the following situations do not warrant the application of the bona fide occupational qualification exception:

(i) The refusal to hire a woman because of her sex based on assumptions of the comparative employment characteristics of women in general. For example, the assumption that the turnover rate among women is higher than among men.

(ii) The refusal to hire an individual based on stereotyped characterizations of the sexes. Such stereotypes include, for example, that men are less capable of assembling intricate equipment: that women are less capable of aggressive salesmanship. The principle of nondiscrimination requires that individuals be considered on the basis of individual capacities and not on the basis of any characteristics generally attributed to the group.

(iii) The refusal to hire an individual because of the preferences of coworkers, the employer, clients or customers except as covered specifically in paragraph (a)(2) of this section.

(2) Where it is necessary for the purpose of authenticity or genuineness, the Commission will consider sex to be a bona fide occupational qualification, e.g., an actor or actress.

(b) Effect of sex-oriented State employment legislation.

(1) Many States have enacted laws or promulgated administrative regulations with respect to the employment of females. Among these laws are those which prohibit or limit the employment of females, e.g., the employment of females in certain occupations, in jobs requiring the lifting or carrying of weights exceeding certain prescribed limits, during certain hours of the night, for more than a specified number of hours per day or per week, and for certain periods of time before and after childbirth. The Commission has found that such laws and regulations do not take into account the capacities, preferences, and abilities of individual females and, therefore, discriminate on the basis of sex. The Commission has concluded that such laws and regulations conflict with and are superseded by title VII of the Civil Rights Act of 1964. Accordingly, such laws will not be considered a defense to an otherwise established unlawful employment practice or as a basis for the application of the bona fide occupational qualification exception.

(2) The Commission has concluded that State laws and regulations which discriminate on the basis of sex with regard to the employment of minors are in conflict with and are superseded by title VII to the extent that such laws are more restrictive for one sex. Accordingly, restrictions on the employment of minors of one sex over and above those imposed on minors of the other sex will not be considered a defense to an otherwise established unlawful employment practice or as a basis for the application of the bona fide occupational qualification exception.

(3) A number of States require that minimum wage and premium pay for overtime be provided for female employees. An employer will be deemed to have engaged in an unlawful employment practice if:

(i) It refuses to hire or otherwise adversely affects the employment opportunities of female applicants or employees in order to avoid the payment of minimum wages or overtime pay required by State law; or

(ii) It does not provide the same benefits for male employees.

(4) As to other kinds of sex-oriented State employment laws, such as those requiring special rest and meal periods or physical facilities for women, provision of these benefits to one sex only will be a violation of title VII. An employer will be deemed to have engaged in an unlawful employment practice if:

(i) It refuses to hire or otherwise adversely affects the employment opportunities of female applicants or employees in order to avoid the provision of such benefits; or

(ii) It does not provide the same benefits for male employees. If the employer can prove that business necessity precludes providing these benefits to both men and women, then the State law is in conflict with and superseded by title VII as to this employer. In this situation, the employer shall not provide such benefits to members of either sex.

(5) Some States require that separate restrooms be provided for employees of each sex. An employer will be deemed to have engaged in an unlawful employment practice if it refuses to hire or otherwise adversely affects the employment opportunities of applicants or employees in order to avoid the provision of such restrooms for persons of that sex.

§ 1604.3 Separate lines of progression and seniority systems.

(a) It is an unlawful employment practice to classify a job as "male" or "female" or to maintain separate lines of progression or separate seniority lists based on sex where this would adversely affect any employee unless sex is a bona fide occupational qualification for that job. Accordingly, employment practices are unlawful which arbitrarily classify jobs so that:

(1) A female is prohibited from applying for a job labeled "male," or for a job in a "male" line of progression; and vice versa.

(2) A male scheduled for layoff is prohibited from displacing a less senior female on a "female" seniority list; and vice versa.

(b) A Seniority system or line of progression which distinguishes between "light" and "heavy" jobs constitutes an unlawful employment practice if it operates as a disguised form of classification by sex, or creates unreasonable obstacles to the advancement by members of either sex into jobs which members of that sex would reasonably be expected to perform.

§ 1604.4 Discrimination against married women.

(a) The Commission has determined that an employer's rule which forbids or restricts the employment of married women and which is not applicable to married men is a discrimination based on sex prohibited by title VII of the Civil Rights Act. It does not seem to us relevant that the rule is not directed against all females, but only against married females, for so long as sex is a factor in the application of the rule, such application involves a discrimination based on sex.

(b) It may be that under certain circumstances, such a rule could be justified within the meaning of section 703(e)(1) of title VII. We express no opinion on this question at this time except to point out that sex as a bona fide occupational qualification must be justified in terms of the peculiar requirements of the particular job and not on the basis of a general principle such as the desirability of spreading work.

§ 1604.5 Job opportunities advertising.

It is a violation of title VII for a help-wanted advertisement to indicate a preference, limitation, specification, or discrimination based on sex unless sex is a bona fide occupational qualification for the particular job involved. The placement of an advertisement in columns classified by publishers on the basis of sex, such as columns headed "Male" or "Female," will be considered an expression of a preference, limitation, specification, or discrimination based on sex.

§ 1604.6 Employment agencies.

(a) Section 703(b) of the Civil Rights Act specifically states that it shall be unlawful for an employment agency to discriminate against any individual because of sex. The Commission has determined that private employment agencies which deal exclusively with one sex are engaged in an unlawful employment practice, except to the extent that such agencies limit their services to furnishing employees for particular jobs for which sex is a bona fide occupational qualification.

(b) An employment agency that receives a job order containing an unlawful sex specification will share responsibility with the employer placing the job order if the agency fills the order knowing that the sex specification is not based upon a bona fide occupational qualification. However, an employment agency will not be deemed to be in violation of the law, regardless of the determination as to the employer, if the agency does not have reason to believe that the employer's claim of bona fide occupations qualification is without substance and the agency makes and maintains a written record available to the Commission of each such job order. Such record shall include the name of the employer, the description of the job and the basis for the employer's claim of bona fide occupational qualification.

(c) It is the responsibility of employment agencies to keep informed of opinions and decisions of the Commission on sex discrimination.

§ 1604.7 Pre-employment inquiries as to sex.

A pre-employment inquiry may ask "Male........., Female........."; or "Mr. Mrs. Miss," provided that the inquiry is made in good faith for a nondiscriminatory purpose. Any pre-employment inquiry in connection with prospective employment which expresses directly or indirectly any limitation, specification, or discrimination as to sex shall be unlawful unless based upon a bona fide occupational qualification.

§ 1604.8 Relationship of title VII to the Equal Pay Act.

(a) The employee coverage of the prohibitions against discrimination based on sex contained in title VII is coextensive with that of the other prohibitions contained in title VII and is not limited by section 703(h) to those employees covered by the Fair Labor Standards Act.

(b) By virtue of section 703(h), a defense based on the Equal Pay Act may be raised in a proceeding under title VII.

(c) Where such a defense is raised the Commission will give appropriate consideration to the interpretations of the Administrator, Wage and Hour Division, Department of Labor, but will not be bound thereby.

§ 1604.9 Fringe benefits.

(a) "Fringe benefits," as used herein, includes medical, hospital, accident, life insurance and retirement benefits; profit-sharing and bonus plans; leave; and other terms, conditions, and privileges of employment.

(b) It shall be an unlawful employment practice for an employer to discriminate between men and women with regard to fringe benefits.

(c) Where an employer conditions benefits available to employees and their spouses and families on whether the employee is the "head of the household" or "principal wage earner" in the family unit, the benefits tend to be available only to male employees and their families. Due to the fact that such conditioning discriminatorily affects the rights of women employees, and that "head of household" or "principal wage earner" status bears no relationship to job performance, benefits which are so conditioned will be found a prima facie violation of the prohibitions against sex discrimination contained in the act.

(d) It shall be an unlawful employment practice for an employer to make available benefits for the wives and families of male employees where the same benefits are not made available for the husbands and families of female employees; or to make available benefits for the wives of male employees which are not made available for female employees; or to make available benefits to the husbands of female employees which are not made available for male employees. An example of such an unlawful employment practice is a situation in which wives of male employees receive maternity benefits while female employees receive no such benefits.

(e) It shall not be a defense under title VIII to a charge of sex discrimination in benefits that the cost of such benefits is greater with respect to one sex than the other.

(f) It shall be an unlawful employment practice for an employer to have a pension or retirement plan which establishes different optional or compulsory retirement ages based on sex, or which differentiates in benefits on the basis of sex. A statement of the General Counsel of September 13, 1968, providing for a phasing out of differentials with regard to optional retirement age for certain incumbent employees is hereby withdrawn.

§ 1604.10 Employment policies relating to pregnancy and childbirth.

(a) A written or unwritten employment policy or practice which excludes from employment applicants or employees because of pregnancy, childbirth or related medical conditions is in prima facie violation of Title VII.

(b) Disabilities caused or contributed to by pregnancy, childbirth, or related medical conditions, for all job-related purposes, shall be treated the same as disabilities caused or contributed to by other medical conditions, under any health or disability insurance or sick leave plan available in connection with employment. Written or unwritten employment policies and practices involving matters such as the commencement and duration of leave, the availability of extensions, the accrual of seniority and other benefits and privileges, reinstatement, and payment under any health or disability insurance or sick leave plan, formal or informal, shall be applied to disability due to pregnancy, childbirth or related medical conditions on the same terms and conditions as they are applied to other disabilities. Health insurance benefits for abortion, except where the life of the mother would be endangered if the fetus were carried to term or where medical complications have arisen from an abortion, are not required to be paid by an employer; nothing herein, however, precludes an employer from providing abortion benefits or otherwise affects bargaining agreements in regard to abortion.

(c) Where the termination of an employee who is temporarily disabled is caused by an employment policy under which insufficient or no leave is available, such a termination violates the Act if it has a disparate impact on employees of one sex and is not justified by business necessity.

(d)(1) Any fringe benefit program, or fund, or insurance program which is in effect on October 31, 1978, which does not treat women affected by pregnancy, childbirth, or related medical conditions the same as other persons not so affected but similar in their ability or inability to work, must be in compliance with the provisions of § 1604.10(b) by April 29, 1979. In order to come into compliance with the provisions of 1604.10(b), there can be no reduction of benefits or compensation which were in effect on October 31, 1978, before October 31, 1979 or the expiration of a collective bargaining agreement in effect on October 31, 1978, whichever is later.

(2) Any fringe benefit program implemented after October 31, 1978, must comply with the provisions of § 1604.10(b) upon implementation.

[44 FR 23805, Apr. 20, 1979]

§ 1604.11 Sexual harassment.

(a) Harassment on the basis of sex is a violation of Sec. 703 of Title VII.[1] Unwelcome sexual advances, requests for sexual favors, and other verbal or physical conduct of a sexual nature constitute sexual harassment when (1) submission to such conduct is made either explicitly or implicitly a term or condition of an individual's employment, (2) submission to or rejection of such conduct by an individual is used as the basis for employment decisions affecting such individual, or (3) such conduct has the purpose or effect of unreasonably interfering with an individual's work performance or creating an intimidating, hostile, or offensive working environment.

(b) In determining whether alleged conduct constitutes sexual harassment, the Commission will look at the record as a whole and at the totality of the circumstances, such as the nature of the sexual advances and the context in which the alleged incidents occurred. The determination of the legality of a particular action will be made from the facts, on a case by case basis.

(c) Applying general Title VII principles, an employer, employment agency, joint apprenticeship committee or labor organization (hereinafter collectively referred to as "employer") is responsible for its acts and those of its agents and supervisory employees with respect to sexual harassment regardless of whether the specific acts complained of were authorized or even forbidden by the employer and regardless of whether the employer knew or should have known of their occurrence. The Commission will examine the circumstances of the particular employment relationship and the job junctions performed by the individual in determining whether an individual acts in either a supervisory or agency capacity.

(d) With respect to conduct between fellow employees, an employer is responsible for acts of sexual harassment in the workplace where the employer (or its agents or supervisory employees) knows or should have known of the conduct, unless it can show that it took immediate and appropriate corrective action.

(e) An employer may also be responsible for the acts of non-employees, with respect to sexual harassment of employees in the workplace, where the employer (or its agents or supervisory employees) knows or should have known of the conduct and fails to take immediate and appropriate corrective action. In reviewing these cases the Commission will consider the extent of the employer's control and any other legal responsibility which the employer may have with respect to the conduct of such non-employees.

(f) Prevention is the best tool for the elimination of sexual harassment. An employer should take all steps necessary to prevent sexual harassment from occurring, such as affirmatively raising the subject, expressing strong disapproval, developing appropriate sanctions, informing employees of their right to raise and how to raise the issue of harassment under Title VII, and developing methods to sensitize all concerned.

(g) Other related practices: Where employment opportunities or benefits are granted because of an individual's submission to the employer's sexual advances or requests for sexual favors, the employer may be held liable for unlawful sex discrimination against other persons who were qualified for but denied that employment opportunity or benefit.

(Title VII, Pub. L. 88–352, 78 Stat. 253 (42 U.S.C. 2000e et seq.))

[45 FR 74677, Nov. 10, 1980]

Pt. 1604, App.

APPENDIX—QUESTIONS AND ANSWERS ON THE PREGNANCY DISCRIMINATION ACT, PUB. L. 95–555, 92 STAT. 2076 (1978)

INTRODUCTION

On October 31, 1978, President Carter signed into law the *Pregnancy Discrimination Act* (Pub. L. 95–955). The Act is an amendment to Title VII of the Civil Rights Act of 1964 which prohibits, among other things, discrimination in employment on the basis of sex. The *Pregnancy Discrimination Act* makes it clear that "because of sex"

---

[1]The principles involved here continue to apply to race, color, religion or national origin.

or "on the basis of sex", as used in Title VII, includes "because of or on the basis of pregnancy, childbirth or related medical conditions." Therefore, Title VII prohibits discrimination in employment against women affected by pregnancy or related conditions.

The basic principle of the Act is that women affected by pregnancy and related conditions must be treated the same as other applicants and employees on the basis of their ability or inability to work. A woman is therefore protected against such practices as being fired, or refused a job or promotion, merely because she is pregnant or has had an abortion. She usually cannot be forced to go on leave as long as she can still work. If other employees who take disability leave are entitled to get their jobs back when they are able to work again, so are women who have been unable to work because of pregnancy.

In the area of fringe benefits, such as disability benefits, sick leave and health insurance, the same principle applies. A woman unable to work for pregnancy-related reasons is entitled to disability benefits or sick leave on the same basis as employees unable to work for other medical reasons. Also, any health insurance provided must cover expenses for pregnancy-related conditions on the same basis as expenses for other medical conditions. However, health insurance for expenses arising from abortion is not required except where the life of the mother would be endangered if the fetus were carried to term, or where medical complications have arisen from an abortion.

Some questions and answers about the *Pregnancy Discrimination Act* follow. Although the questions and answers often use only the term "employer," the Act—and these questions and answers—apply also to unions and other entities covered by Title VII.

1. **Q.** What is the effective date of the Pregnancy Discrimination Act?

A. The Act became effective on October 31, 1978, except that with respect to fringe benefit programs in effect on that date, the Act will take effect 180 days thereafter, that is, April 29, 1979.

To the extent that Title VII already required employers to treat persons affected by pregnancy-related conditions the same as persons affected by other medical conditions, the Act does not change employee rights arising prior to October 31, 1978, or April 29, 1979. Most employment practices relating to pregnancy, childbirth and related conditions—whether concerning fringe benefits or other practices—were already controlled by Title VII prior to this Act. For example, Title VII has always prohibited an employer from firing, or refusing to hire or promote, a woman because of pregnancy or related conditions, and from failing to accord a woman on pregnancy-related leave

the same seniority retention and accrual accorded those on other disability leaves.

2. **Q.** If an employer had a sick leave policy in effect on October 31, 1978, by what date must the employer bring its policy into compliance with the Act?

A. With respect to payment of benefits, an employer has until April 29, 1979, to bring into compliance any fringe benefit or insurance program, including a sick leave policy, which was in effect on October 31, 1978. However, any such policy or program created after October 31, 1978, must be in compliance when created.

With respect to all aspects of sick leave policy other than payment of benefits, such as the terms governing retention and accrual of seniority, credit for vacation, and resumption of former job on return from sick leave, equality of treatment was required by Title VII without the Amendment.

3. **Q.** Must an employer provide benefits for pregnancy-related conditions to an employee whose pregnancy begins prior to April 29, 1979, and continues beyond that date?

A. As of April 29, 1979, the effective date of the Act's requirements, an employer must provide the same benefits for pregnancy-related conditions as it provides for other conditions, regardless of when the pregnancy began. Thus, disability benefits must be paid for all absences on or after April 29, 1979, resulting from pregnancy-related temporary disabilities to the same extent as they are paid for absences resulting from other temporary disabilities. For example, if an employee gives birth before April 29, 1979, but is still unable to work on or after that date, she is entitled to the same disability benefits available to other employees. Similarly, medical insurance benefits must be paid for pregnancy-related expenses incurred on or after April 29, 1979.

If an employer requires an employee to be employed for a predetermined period prior to being eligible for insurance coverage, the period prior to April 29, 1979, during which a pregnant employee has been employed must be credited toward the eligibility waiting period on the same basis as for any other employee.

As to any programs instituted for the first time after October 31, 1978, coverage for pregnancy-related conditions must be provided in the same manner as for other medical conditions.

4. **Q.** Would the answer to the preceding question be the same if the employee became pregnant prior to October 31, 1978?

A. Yes.

5. **Q.** If, for pregnancy-related reasons, an employee is unable to perform the functions of her job, does the employer have to provide her an alternative job?

A. An employer is required to treat an employee temporarily unable to perform the functions of her job because of her pregnancy-related condition in the same manner as it treats other temporarily disabled employees, whether by providing modified tasks, alternative assignments, disability leaves, leaves without pay, etc. For example, a woman's primary job function may be the operation of a machine, and, incidental to that function, she may carry materials to and from the machine. If other employees temporarily unable to lift are relieved of these functions, pregnant employees also unable to lift must be temporarily relieved of the function.

6. Q. What procedures may an employer use to determine whether to place on leave as unable to work a pregnant employee who claims she is able to work or deny leave to a pregnant employee who claims that she is disabled from work?

A. An employer may not single out pregnancy-related conditions for special procedures for determining an employee's ability to work. However, an employer may use any procedure used to determine the ability of all employees to work. For example, if an employer requires its employees to submit a doctor's statement concerning their inability to work before granting leave or paying sick benefits, the employer may require employees affected by pregnancy-related conditions to submit such statement. Similarly, if an employer allows its employees to obtain doctor's statements from their personal physicians for absences due to other disabilities or return dates from other disabilities, it must accept doctor's statements from personal physicians for absences and return dates connected with pregnancy-related disabilities.

7. Q. Can an employer have a rule which prohibits an employee from returning to work for a predetermined length of time after childbirth?

A. No.

8. Q. If an employee has been absent from work as a result of a pregnancy-related condition and recovers, may her employer require her to remain on leave until after her baby is born?

A. No. An employee must be permitted to work at all times during pregnancy when she is able to perform her job.

9. Q. Must an employer hold open the job of an employee who is absent on leave because she is temporarily disabled by pregnancy-related conditions?

A. Unless the employee on leave has informed the employer that she does not intend to return to work, her job must be held open for her return on the same basis as jobs are held open for employees on sick or disability leave for other reasons.

10. Q. May an employer's policy concerning the accrual and crediting of seniority during absences for medical conditions be different for employees affected by pregnancy-related conditions than for other employees?

A. No. An employer's seniority policy must be the same for employees absent for pregnancy-related reasons as for those absent for other medical reasons.

11. Q. For purposes of calculating such matters as vacations and pay increases, may an employer credit time spent on leave for pregnancy-related reasons differently than time spent on leave for other reasons?

A. No. An employer's policy with respect to crediting time for the purpose of calculating such matters as vacations and pay increases cannot treat employees on leave for pregnancy-related reasons less favorably than employees on leave for other reasons. For example, if employees on leave for medical reasons are credited with the time spent on leave when computing entitlement to vacation or pay raises, an employee on leave for pregnancy-related disability is entitled to the same kind of time credit.

12. Q. Must an employer hire a woman who is medically unable, because of a pregnancy-related condition, to perform a necessary function of a job?

A. An employer cannot refuse to hire a women because of her pregnancy-related condition so long as she is able to perform the major functions necessary to the job. Nor can an employer refuse to hire her because of its preferences against pregnant workers or the preferences of co-workers, clients, or customers.

13. Q. May an employer limit disability benefits for pregnancy-related conditions to married employees?

A. No.

14. Q. If an employer has an all female workforce or job classification, must benefits be provided for pregnancy-related conditions?

A. Yes. If benefits are provided for other conditions, they must also be provided for pregnancy-related conditions.

15. Q. For what length of time must an employer who provides income maintenance benefits for temporary disabilities provide such benefits for pregnancy-related disabilities?

A. Benefits should be provided for as long as the employee is unable to work for medical reasons unless some other limitation is set for all other temporary disabilities, in which case pregnancy-related disabilities should be treated the same as other temporary disabilities.

16. Q. Must an employer who provides benefits for long-term or permanent disabilities provide such benefits for pregnancy-related conditions?

A. Yes. Benefits for long-term or permanent disabilities resulting from pregnancy-

Chapter XIV—Equal Employment Opportunity Comm.   **Pt. 1604, App.**

related conditions must be provided to the same extent that such benefits are provided for other conditions which result in long-term or permanent disability.

17. Q. If an employer provides benefits to employees on leave, such as installment purchase disability insurance, payment of premiums for health, life or other insurance, continued payments into pension, saving or profit sharing plans, must the same benefits be provided for those on leave for pregnancy-related conditions?

A. Yes, the employer must provide the same benefits for those on leave for pregnancy-related conditions as for those on leave for other reasons.

18. Q. Can an employee who is absent due to a pregnancy-related disability be required to exhaust vacation benefits before receiving sick leave pay or disability benefits?

A. No. If employees who are absent because of other disabling causes receive sick leave pay or disability benefits without any requirement that they first exhaust vacation benefits, the employer cannot impose this requirement on an employee absent for a pregnancy-related cause.

18(A). Q. Must an employer grant leave to a female employee for childcare purposes after she is medically able to return to work following leave necessitated by pregnancy, childbirth or related medical conditions?

A. While leave for childcare purposes is not covered by the Pregnancy Discrimination Act, ordinary Title VII principles would require that leave for childcare purposes be granted on the same basis as leave which is granted to employees for other non-medical reasons. For example, if an employer allows its employees to take leave without pay or accrued annual leave for travel or education which is not job related, the same type of leave must be granted to those who wish to remain on leave for infant care, even though they are medically able to return to work.

19. Q. If state law requires an employer to provide disability insurance for a specified period before and after childbirth, does compliance with the state law fulfill the employer's obligation under the Pregnancy Discrimination Act?

A. Not necessarily. It is an employer's obligation to treat employees temporarily disabled by pregnancy in the same manner as employees affected by other temporary disabilities. Therefore, any restrictions imposed by state law on benefits for pregnancy-related disabilities, but not for other disabilities, do not excuse the employer from treating the individuals in both groups of employees the same. If, for example, a state law requires an employer to pay a maximum of 26 weeks benefits for disabilities other than pregnancy-related ones but only six weeks for pregnancy-related disabilities, the employer must provide benefits for the ad-

ditional weeks to an employee disabled by pregnancy-related conditions, up to the maximum provided other disabled employees.

20. Q. If a State or local government provides its own employees income maintenance benefits for disabilities, may it provide different benefits for disabilities arising from pregnancy-related conditions than for disabilities arising from other conditions?

A. No. State and local governments, as employers, are subject to the Pregnancy Discrimination Act in the same way as private employers and must bring their employment practices and programs into compliance with the Act, including disability and health insurance programs.

21. Q. Must an employer provide health insurance coverage for the medical expenses of pregnancy-related conditions of the spouses of male employees? Of the dependents of all employees?

A. Where an employer provides no coverage for dependents, the employer is not required to institute such coverage. However, if an employer's insurance program covers the medical expenses of spouses of female employees, then it must equally cover the medical expenses of spouses of male employees, including those arising from pregnancy-related conditions.

But the insurance does not have to cover the pregnancy-related conditions of other dependents as long as it excludes the pregnancy-related conditions of the dependents of male and female employees equally.

22. Q. Must an employer provide the same level of health insurance coverage for the pregnancy-related medical conditions of the spouses of male employees as it provides for its female employees?

A. No. It is not necessary to provide the same level of coverage for the pregnancy-related medical conditions of spouses of male employees as for female employees. However, where the employer provides coverage for the medical conditions of the spouses of its employees, then the level of coverage for pregnancy-related medical conditions of the spouses of male employees must be the same as the level of coverage for all other medical conditions of the spouses of female employees. For example, if the employer covers employees for 100 percent of reasonable and customary expenses sustained for a medical condition, but only covers dependent spouses for 50 percent of reasonable and customary expenses for their medical conditions, the pregnancy-related expenses of the male employee's spouse must be covered at the 50 percent level.

23. Q. May an employer offer optional dependent coverage which excludes pregnancy-related medical conditions or offers less coverage for pregnancy-related medical con-

ditions where the total premium for the optional coverage is paid by the employee?

A. No. Pregnancy-related medical conditions must be treated the same as other medical conditions under any health or disability insurance or sick leave plan *available in connection with employment*, regardless of who pays the premiums.

24. Q. Where an employer provides its employees a choice among several health insurance plans, must coverage for pregnancy-related conditions be offered in all of the plans?

A. Yes. Each of the plans must cover pregnancy-related conditions. For example, an employee with a single coverage policy cannot be forced to purchase a more expensive family coverage policy in order to receive coverage for her own pregnancy-related condition.

25. Q. On what basis should an employee be reimbursed for medical expenses arising from pregnancy, childbirth or related conditions?

A. Pregnancy-related expenses should be reimbursed in the same manner as are expenses incurred for other medical conditions. Therefore, whether a plan reimburses the employees on a fixed basis, or a percentage of reasonable and customary charge basis, the same basis should be used for reimbursement of expenses incurred for pregnancy-related conditions. Furthermore, if medical costs for pregnancy-related conditions increase, reevaluation of the reimbursement level should be conducted in the same manner as are cost reevaluations of increases for other medical conditions.

Coverage provided by a health insurance program for other conditions must be provided for pregnancy-related conditions. For example, if a plan provides major medical coverage, pregnancy-related conditions must be so covered. Similarly, if a plan covers the cost of a private room for other conditions, the plan must cover the cost of a private room for pregnancy-related conditions. Finally, where a health insurance plan covers office visits to physicians, pre-natal and post-natal visits must be included in such coverage.

26. Q. May an employer limit payment of costs for pregnancy-related medical conditions to a specified dollar amount set forth in an insurance policy, collective bargaining agreement or other statement of benefits to which an employee is entitled?

A. The amounts payable for the costs incurred for pregnancy-related conditions can be limited only to the same extent as are costs for other conditions. Maximum recoverable dollar amounts may be specified for pregnancy-related conditions if such amounts are similarly specified for other conditions, and so long as the specified amounts in all instances cover the same proportion of actual costs. If, in addition to the

scheduled amount for other procedures, additional costs are paid for, either directly or indirectly, by the employer, such additional payments must also be paid for pregnancy-relate procedures.

27. Q. May an employer impose a different deductible for payment of costs for pregnancy-related medical conditions than for costs of other medical conditions?

A. No. Neither an additional deductible, an increase in the usual deductible, nor a larger deductible can be imposed for coverage for pregnancy-related medical costs, whether as a condition for inclusion of pregnancy-related costs in the policy or for payment of the costs when incurred. Thus, if pregnancy-related costs are the first incurred under the policy, the employee is required to pay only the same deductible as would otherwise be required had other medical costs been the first incurred. Once this deductible has been paid, no additional deductible can be required for other medical procedures. If the usual deductible has already been paid for other medical procedures, no additional deductible can be required when pregnancy-related costs are later incurred.

28. Q. If a health insurance plan excludes the payment of benefits for any conditions existing at the time the insured's coverage becomes effective (pre-existing condition clause), can benefits be denied for medical costs arising from a pregnancy existing at the time the coverage became effective?

A. Yes. However, such benefits cannot be denied unless the pre-existing condition clause also excludes benefits for other pre-existing conditions in the same way.

29. Q. If an employer's insurance plan provides benefits after the insured's employment has ended (i.e. extended benefits) for costs connected with pregnancy and delivery where conception occurred while the insured was working for the employer, but not for the costs of any other medical condition which began prior to termination of employment, may an employer (a) continue to pay these extended benefits for pregnancy-related medical conditions but not for other medical conditions, or (b) terminate these benefits for pregnancy-related conditions?

A. Where a health insurance plan currently provides extended benefits for other medical conditions on a less favorable basis than for pregnancy-related medical conditions, extended benefits must be provided for other medical conditions on the same basis as for pregnancy-related medical conditions. Therefore, an employer can neither continue to provide less benefits for other medical conditions nor reduce benefits currently paid for pregnancy-related medical conditions.

30. Q. Where an employer's health insurance plan currently requires total disability

as a prerequisite for payment of extended benefits for other medical conditions but not for pregnancy-related costs, may the employer now require total disability for payment of benefits for pregnancy-related medical conditions as well?

A. Since extended benefits cannot be reduced in order to come into compliance with the Act, a more stringent prerequisite for payment of extended benefits for pregnancy-related medical conditions, such as a requirement for total disability, cannot be imposed. Thus, in this instance, in order to comply with the Act, the employer must treat other medical conditions as pregnancy-related conditions are treated.

31. Q. Can the added cost of bringing benefit plans into compliance with the Act be apportioned between the employer and employee?

A. The added cost, if any, can be apportioned between the employer and employee in the same proportion that the cost of the fringe benefit plan was apportioned on October 31, 1978, if that apportionment was nondiscriminatory. If the costs were not apportioned on October 31, 1978, they may not be apportioned in order to come into compliance with the Act. However, in no circumstance may male or female employees be required to pay unequal apportionments on the basis of sex or pregnancy.

32. Q. In order to come into compliance with the Act, may an employer reduce benefits or compensation?

A. In order to come into compliance with the Act, benefits or compensation which an employer was paying on October 31, 1978 cannot be reduced before October 31, 1979 or before the expiration of a collective bargaining agreement in effect on October 31, 1978, whichever is later.

Where an employer has not been in compliance with the Act by the times specified in the Act, and attempts to reduce benefits, or compensation, the employer may be required to remedy its practices in accord with ordinary Title VII remedial principles.

33. Q. Can an employer self-insure benefits for pregnancy-related conditions if it does not self-insure benefits for other medical conditions?

A. Yes, so long as the benefits are the same. In measuring whether benefits are the same, factors other than the dollar coverage paid should be considered. Such factors include the range of choice of physicians and hospitals, and the processing and promptness of payment of claims.

34. Q. Can an employer discharge, refuse to hire or otherwise discriminate against a woman because she has had an abortion?

A. No. An employer cannot discriminate in its employment practices against a woman who has had an abortion.

35. Q. Is an employer required to provide fringe benefits for abortions if fringe benefits are provided for other medical conditions?

A. All fringe benefits other than health insurance, such as sick leave, which are provided for other medical conditions, must be provided for abortions. Health insurance, however, need be provided for abortions only where the life of the woman would be endangered if the fetus were carried to term or where medical complications arise from an abortion.

36. Q. If complications arise during the course of an abortion, as for instance excessive hemorrhaging, must an employer's health insurance plan cover the additional cost due to the complications of the abortion?

A. Yes. The plan is required to pay those additional costs attributable to the complications of the abortion. However, the employer is not required to pay for the abortion itself, except where the life of the mother would be endangered if the fetus were carried to term.

37. Q. May an employer elect to provide insurance coverage for abortions?

A. Yes. The Act specifically provides that an employer is not precluded from providing benefits for abortions whether directly or through a collective bargaining agreement, but if an employer decides to cover the costs of abortion, the employer must do so in the same manner and to the same degree as it covers other medical conditions.

[44 FR 23805, Apr. 20, 1979]

Index

About the Author

Cliff Roberson received his Ph.D. in human behavior from U.S. International University, his LL.M from George Washington University, his J.D. from American University, and his B.A. in political science from the University of Missouri.

Dr. Roberson joined the Marine Corps in 1955. After retiring from the service in 1979, he taught at St. Edward's University in Austin, Texas, for four years, then became director of programs for the National College of District Attorneys at the University of Houston Law Center. He is presently a professor and director of the Justice Center at California State University, Fresno.

The author is admitted to practice before the U.S. Supreme Court and the Supreme Courts of Texas and California. He has written numerous articles on various legal subjects and is active in the American Bar Association.